Real World
SALES
STRATEGIES
That
WORK

Insight Publishing Company
Sevierville, Tennessee

Real World
SALES
STRATEGIES
That
WORK

Published by,
Insight Publishing Company
PO Box 4189
Sevierville, TN 37862

Printed in the United States of America

ISBN 1-885640-99-4

Table Of Contents

A Message From The Publisher

Some of my most rewarding experiences in business—or in my personal life, for that matter—have been at meetings, conventions or gatherings after the formal events have concluded. Inevitably, small groups of ten to fifteen men and women gather together to rehash the happenings of the day and to exchange war stories, recently heard jokes or the latest gossip from their industry. It is in these informal gatherings where some of the best lessons can be learned.

Usually, in informal groups of professionals, there are those who clearly have lived through more battles and learned more lessons than others. These are the men and women who are really getting the job done, and everyone around the room knows it. When they comment on the topic of the moment, they don't just spout the latest hot theory or trend, and they don't ramble on and on without a relevant point. These battle-scarred warriors have lessons to share that everyone senses are just a little more real, more relevant and therefore, worthy of more attention.

These are the kind of people we have recruited for the Power Learning series of books. Each title offers contributions from men and women who are making a significant impact on their culture, in their field, and on their colleagues and clients. This edition offers a variety of themes in the area of Sales Strategies. It is ripe with "the good stuff," as an old friend of mine used to always say. Inside these pages you'll find ideas, insights, strategies and philosophies that are working with real people, in real companies and under real circumstances.

It is our hope that you keep this book with you until you've dog-eared every chapter and made so many notes in the margins that you have trouble seeing the original words on the pages. There is treasure here. Enjoy digging!

Chapter 1

Welcome to the New World of Selling

Thomas A. Pall

We're doing business in a reshaped world.

We're doing business in a reshaped world where the fusion of technology, computing, and communications is transforming society, altering the way we work and play, and shaping the economy in new ways. The power to navigate the world at the push of a button, the sound of your voice, or the click of a mouse is the force transforming business like none before. Consumers can connect and get information to shop anytime, anyplace, and anywhere. The wireless revolution has arrived as more of us are using cell phones to connect to the Internet. The Internet has become just another business tool, like the cell phone or the laptop. The new age of business requires new ways of making sales. American companies and their sales forces have embraced the idea of 24/7 access and the convenience of operating in real time. The reality of the New World we live in is that sales transactions take place 24 hours a day, seven days a week. It's not surprising that this new connectivity and quick access to competitors make it more difficult for salespeople to get more than paper-thin customer loyalty these days. There have never been so many ways to lose a customer.

Sales Efficiency Tools Give Way to Effectiveness

That's why I've found that giving your salespeople more of a say and asking them for input is more critical today. The faster and more frequent your business stays in touch with what customers and the marketplace are thinking, the better off you'll be in this interactive age. Instant connectivity, making distance matter less, is in the process of revolutionizing sales territories and go-to-market sales channel planning. I unchained my sales reps from their desks and provided over 2,000 field and telemarketing sales reps with online sales force automation that enhanced our pre-sale, transaction, and post-sale capability. I'm convinced that being well equipped and prepared to serve customers better and faster helped us achieve industry leading revenue growth for our business. Likewise, we freed up more productive and precious sales time for selling instead of doing paperwork and other non-sales tasks. The next step is to make customer relationship management software work for you to enhance the overall customer experience, understand your customers better, and improve transaction efficiencies. To optimize CRM initiatives, you want to move into customer lifecycle management capabilities that fully immerse salespeople and the customer.

The burden is on the sales forces of American business to find new ways to operate and compete since customers determine the fate of every enterprise. Customer loyalty is key to maximizing profitability and market share. In fact, research tells us that companies can boost profits by almost 100% just by retaining 5% more of their customers. The key step to retaining those customers is gaining a better understanding of them and emphasizing service. The success of your business depends on your ability to attract, keep, and grow the right customers.

Relationship Selling is Evolving

Is personal selling still important in this new era? Do companies and people still buy based on personal relationships? They do when the relationship is based on value and not on a free dinner or baseball tickets. Today you can't just sell one way; you must integrate the tangibles like product, price, and delivery with the intangibles of service, reputation, and speed. The trick is keeping customers loyal in a rapidly changing business environment. We generated 88% of our revenues from repeat customers at SBC Directory operations. Strengthening customer relationships during turbulent times is the secret of success. You're gaining a competitive edge while others are hunkering down and drastically cutting their sales and marketing investment. My philosophy is to maximize the value I receive from customers by optimizing the value I deliver to them. How do we identify and create lasting relationships with the customers who will be of greatest value to the business?

Selling can be a lonely world, and maintaining a positive mindset is vital when you're faced with weakened buyer confidence, a rise in price-based competition, and an unpredictable economy. Furthermore, you have to deal with the effect of war, the hazard of terrorism, corporate scandals, and a volatile stock market. Unlike sports, there are no time outs in the sales game, and it's up to you to make the best of the situation. Remember, attitude drives behavior, and you have to succeed in any environment, regardless how tough, in order to survive. Like it or not, radical change is beating down the door, and in selling it's not what happens that affects your performance; it's how you respond to situations that makes the difference. I once sent out bumper stickers to all salespeople that read, "We refuse to participate in a recession." This helped the sales force mindset outsell the industry by over 300%.

Break Through the Clutter in a Noisy Business Environment

In the New World of selling, the proliferation of email messages, paging, voicemail, faxes, and Web sites can accelerate communications. In simpler times, salespeople were able to get by with less preparation and still survive. The challenges we face in selling today make paying attention to what's crucial a critical element for success.

Here's what you're faced with in the New World of selling: more complex sales situations, more knowledgeable buyers, fierce competition, shrinking product lifecycles, multiple decision- makers, and less customer loyalty. In addition, when you deal with larger accounts you have multilevel selling situations, and it takes longer to close a sale. It has become harder to delineate product differentiation in a sea of new and copycat products that you must contend with in the marketplace. On top of that, customers no longer accept generic solutions to their problems; they want and deserve customized solutions specifically tailored for their needs. Many industries are finding out that price increases are more difficult to achieve without making any product enhancements.

The world is changing faster than ever before, with more random events like war and terrorism, mergers, and acquisitions; economic swings and technological shifts are affecting buying decisions. If that's not enough to deal with, there is more overall clutter, information, advertising, and communications that muddy the water.

With the advent of e-commerce and new mobile technologies, the salesperson's role is undoubtedly changing. It's difficult to expect salespeople to shift from product-oriented creatures to customer-centric trusted advisors on their own. For those of us leading a sales organization, this requires overhauling the sales process to break through the clutter to engage the buyer. To sell anything, you must get on the customer's radar screen. The purpose of your sales message is to get people to do what you want them to do...and that's ultimately to buy from you. Your goal is to become the preferred choice, and that takes persuasion, creativity, guts, and hard work. Yet, you don't have a choice...you have to stand out and get the business, or you're left out in the cold. In selling, second place is not a viable option. Here's how to hold your prospect's attention in a noisy business environment and move toward making a sale.

Get on the customer's agenda and radar screen:

1. Get customer-engaged and break through the clutter
2. Know the customer and personalize the experience
3. Become a trusted business advisor and listen intently
4. Use smart questions to identify and frame the problems and goals
5. Constantly upgrade your selling skills

Give Compelling Reasons to Buy From You

More than ever, you have to provide compelling reasons for customers to buy from you rather than your competitors. Understand the customer's goals so that you can align your sales proposal with the customer's agenda. Be prepared to ask open-ended questions, and do some research to increase your knowledge base. Introduce new information that's relevant to the customer's buying decision. Demonstrate how your recommendation will add value. Keep in mind that most customers don't buy things; they buy solutions to their problems. In business-to-business selling, clients want salespeople who are genuinely interested in them, their problems, and their business goals. What are compelling reasons that your customers should buy from you? Review these 12 reasons with your own list: product performance, ROI, service and intangibles, greater customer value, less risk, timely delivery, proven results, unique offer, brand strength, product quality, creative solutions, and price.

Clarify the sales agenda based on the value you deliver:

1. Clarify your value proposition
2. Develop unique points of differentiation
3. Demonstrate strong reasons to buy from you
4. Create a sense of urgency for action
5. Follow up after the sale

Become the Preferred Choice

To become the preferred choice in any competitive selling situation, you first establish the buying relationship on trust and value. You need to fully understand the buyer's expectations. Then you work on becoming a partner and a valuable resource, not just another vendor looking for business. You want and need an edge. You may have to customize or personalize your product and service to link more closely with your customer's expectations. Understanding the customer and their needs is how you sharpen your focus on what's important to the purchasing decision. When you zero in on exactly what the buyer is looking for in the purchase, you're halfway home to the sale. The rest is putting your sales arsenal to work to support how to meet and exceed the customer's expectations. By using a laser beam focus on the customer's desired outcome, it also becomes your desired outcome...a sale! What you end up doing is delivering a custom solution tailored to the goals of the buyer. To become the preferred choice, you simply transform sales calls into problem solving meetings where you have the best answer. This requires six steps: preparing for customer engagements, listening to what customers are saying, determining the real needs of the customer, solving customers' problems, providing customers with value added solutions, and aligning your recommendation with the customers' goals. Build the customer relationship around these key sales elements, and you can earn the preferred choice status.

Achieving the edge:

1. Provide the best customer solution
2. Stay focused on the customer's goals
3. Build the customer relationship on knowledge, value, and trust
4. Use emotion and logic to solve customer problems

Stand Out or Be Left Out!

Excelling at the point of contact is the ultimate business advantage. There's a wafer-thin difference between success and failure. You have to find ways to stand out from the rest of the crowd. There are 15 million salespeople in America today; why should somebody buy from you? It's a battle for the buyer. Every company, marketer, advertiser, salesperson, and brand is fighting for the business. You have to be unique to win. Uniqueness is the edge you want and the advantage you need, and is what separates you from the pack. You want to optimize the effect you have on the buyer.

The Customer's Objective is Value

The customer's number one objective when making a purchase is value. Customer value creation is the focus of great companies. Use *value links* as the path to the sale. Identify your business's *value links*. What are your company's unique strengths that competitors can't easily match? For example, one of Anheuser-Busch's beer *value links* is their product born-on-date that communicates freshness to customers. Another unique *value link* to the customer is the Select Comfort Mattress use of an individual sleep number designed to enable you to adjust your side of the bed to the exact firmness you want. They don't sell mattresses; they sell us a perfect night's sleep. When you create more unique value for customers, you'll sell more stuff. Capitalize on every capability you have, both tangible and intangible, to boost the customer value you deliver. Then sell and build the customer relationship on that value. Value links are pathways to the sale, and they provide elements for you to build on during each customer contact.

Master the Customer Connection

Nothing is more important to a salesperson or a business than mastering the customer connection. Excelling at the point of contact is the ultimate business advantage and the ultimate sales competitive edge. Therefore, you want extraordinary sales execution every time. To build a sustainable customer relationship, you want to define which element is most critical in achieving a competitive advantage based on the buyer's objective. Design your sales strategy with these two objectives in mind. Align your sales presentation with *the goals of the customer* and *your unique capabilities* to achieve those goals. Your effectiveness as a salesperson hinges on the sales process you use to connect with customers. Here's how to get the edge to write more business and win more customers.

Build competitive sales advantage

1. Find ways to stand out
2. Use value links as a path to the sale
3. Excel at the point of contact
4. Align your strengths with customers objectives
5. Exploit the intangibles you offer

The New World of Selling: 4-Stage Selling System

Stage 1:
The Foundation...is your preparation prior to the sale.

For the Salesperson

Know the buyer better and how customers think. In this New World of selling, what you do to prepare yourself to sell determines how successful you will be. The reality is that customers change suppliers at the drop of a hat, more competitors are chasing the same customers, and the pace of change is accelerating and affecting all transactions. Customer, product, and sales knowledge is the competitive edge and the cement that holds the foundation together. The more you know prior to the sales call and the more you learn during the sales call, the more you can sell! This new sales readiness process recognizes that the customer has more knowledge and more choices than ever before. Arm yourself with as much information as possible regarding anything that can influence the outcome of the sale. Find and use new information that keeps you on the cutting edge with your customer. Use the Internet and all other valuable sources of information to build your knowledge base. Then determine how to optimize the information you've gathered. Convert information into sales ideas that add value to your sales message. I call this TIPs or "The Idea Process sells!" The new sales readiness combines knowledge and ideas to build the selling relationship around these three things: *knowledge*, *trust*, and *value*. The idea, like a seed, must be planted, nurtured, and cultivated to grow. Use the power of ideas to sell more stuff!

Plan the sales process based on the customer's needs to get the desired outcome. New sales preparation must help to identify specific customer objectives, to clarify the ideas that will be used to augment those objectives, and to customize each sales presentation for each customer.

For the Company

Your company is faced with enormous competitive pressures from every conceivable angle, so make sure that you are providing the sales force with the technology, skills, information, and strategies that they need to win the business. Sales and marketing managers have to spend ample time in the field with customers and salespeople to keep sales collateral meaningful. Sales training and education to build skills is essential at every level of your sales organization. In an era of fewer product advantages, higher skills will produce higher levels of customer satisfaction and higher levels of sales performance.

Stage 2:
The Discovery...is using the right questions to increase your sales.

For the Salesperson

The discovery phase in the New World of selling is where the buyer and seller engage. Your first objective is to sell yourself and not the product. This phase is where the understanding between the decision-makers and the seller takes place. You have to build rapport by making a good impression in the first couple of minutes in order to get the time you'll need to make the sale. The customer must trust you and feel at ease in dealing with you before you can move on. You always want to have a good appearance, a confident image, a smile on your face, and eye contact with the buyer. Smart salespeople want to get on the same wavelength with customers by establishing ways to help them achieve their goals. Focus on the customer needs and expectations. This is where you do fact-finding to learn more about the customer's needs, problems, and desires. Use open—ended questions and listen carefully to the customer responses so that you understand specifically where the buyer is headed. Guide the conversation and store the pertinent information until later while continuing to focus on what the customer is interested in discussing. Put the customer first. Ask questions first, and make your sales proposal later. Open-ended questions that begin with who, what, where, why, and how are powerful tools that I've seen work to close more sales because they help expose the buyer's hot button. When you identify what excites the buyer, you can use that emotion to connect to your selling points.

For the Company

Put the customer in the center of your entire operation. This is the new customer focus for businesses...a sincere interest in serving the customer. Understanding is how you build a customer relationship that grows. Understanding each customer is the new secret weapon in the buying relationship.

Companies that combine technology with customer service in new ways will be the winners in the 21st century. United Parcel Service and their brown delivery trucks and uniformed drivers are on a mission to convince customers that they can do much more for their needs than deliver packages. UPS advertising asks, "What can Brown do for you?" Likewise Wal-Mart understands the importance of customers and local appeal as it works to tailor each store to its local area. This is a huge step for a company that averages 100 million customers a week. Discover new value added ways to serve customers, and you'll find new sources of revenue and profit for your company.

Stage 3:
The Solution...is your answer to solving the customer's problem.

For the Salesperson

For individual salespeople to win the battle for the buyer, they have to clarify customer's needs and prepare to offer the best solutions to fulfill these needs. This continues the process of looking at selling from the buyer's point of view. Customers don't buy things; they buy solutions to their problems. Sales calls are transforming into unique problem solving sessions. Harness technology to sell more effectively. Here are 10 power selling tips that, when you put them to work, will help you provide better customer solutions that will ultimately lead to greater sales:

- Optimize your effective sales time.
- Plan for success.
- Sharpen your sales message.
- Demonstrate trust.
- Create new value.
- Provide new information.
- Communicate frequently
- Be a knowledgeable resource.
- Align with customer's goals.
- Think beyond the single sale.

For the Company

Retailers are being asked more and more to help solve customer problems. In business-to-business selling, salespeople are becoming business problem solvers. IBM's new business strategy is built around serving customers in new ways, and now services have grown to over 50% of IBM's business revenue. Big Blue has shifted from a hardware vender to a solutions provider. Whatever you're selling, when you become a trusted business advisor, you become a more valuable resource to that business. When you dramatically help clients achieve their goals, you'll achieve your goals. It's investing in a long-term relationship versus a short-term focus. When you improve the customer's condition or make them better off than they were before dealing with you, you too will be better off. This solution or problem-solving phase of selling works because it focuses in the customer interests. When you do that, you are building a relationship based on value, and you increase the effect of every sales call.

Why is this intense customer focus important? Because in today's highly competitive sales environment, those who are most connected to what customers value will win. Those who provide the customer experience that is professional and meaningful will have the edge. In this New World of selling, you have to go way beyond satisfying customers. Just because you have satisfied customers does not mean you have loyal customers. You get loyal customers by building sales excellence, by executing a high level of customer service, and by consistently meeting and exceeding customer expectations.

Stage 4:
The Desired Outcome…is the commitment of the customer to buy from you.

For the Salesperson

When you determine and deliver the best message content in every sales opportunity, you position yourself to win the business. When you align your sales message with customer interests, you become more relevant in their mind. You must work every day at being worthy of a customer's patronage and never take the business for granted. Find every opportunity to customize and personalize the customer relationship so that you can bond with customers on a closer level. Make sure that you reach all of the decision-makers who can influence the outcome of the sale. Deal with sales objections along the way by anticipating them and addressing customer concerns as they come up rather than having them surface at the sales close. You want the sales transaction to be a positive logical conclusion that's free of any uncertainty.

When you move toward customer loyalty thinking, more sales will become automatic. After all, you are not in this for the single one-time sale are you? What most of you are after is repeat business. The first sale is just the beginning of a business relationship; what happens after that is up to you. The relationship after the initial sale is crucial to your customer retention capability. The harsh reality is that many of your customers are on the verge of defecting to the competition. All it takes is a better offer, a newer product, or a convincing sales presentation, and before you even know it…they're gone! The new era of selling is brutal, making it imperative that you constantly upgrade the customer value you deliver. By continually enhancing the perceived value you deliver, you will build an emotional bond with your customers that sticks. Making your product relevance greater in the customer's mind is the market edge that positions you to win in the 21st century. In this tough new business arena, you have to wage a sales war to win customer loyalty and keep it for life. The rules of engagement have shifted: every company is under attack, every product is challenged, and every brand is tested.

For the Company

Clearly identify your competitive advantages and build value around those advantages. For you to be the logical conclusion for the buyer, you have to clear the path, remove the obstacles, and stay focused on customer value creation. Customer value is delivered in many ways; both tangible and intangible elements create the customer experience. Know your customers better than the competition. Customers don't buy what your company sells; they buy what your products and services do for them. Creatively enhance the customer's perception of the value you deliver, and you'll dramatically increase your company's sales performance.

Use all potential sales channels effectively to optimize market penetration and customer growth. Do an opportunity assessment of customer potential, both with existing and new customers. Use telemarketing, direct mail, email, and the Internet to handle smaller accounts. This frees up the field sales force to focus on the highest potential customers. Sales costs are rising every year, and sales forces are spending only a third of their time with customers. Spend time aligning your sales capability and sales strategy with the right customers, and you will reap the benefits of customer growth, revenue growth, and bottom line growth. The broader your product line is, the more complex the ideal sales model becomes. Refine your sales structure until you achieve the product and market growth you expect. The sales resource is one of the most powerful assets you can leverage in your business. Focus on market opportunity, not market share, when you deploy resources; identify the customer potential, align the sales capability with customer needs, and train and educate salespeople to execute your sales plan effectively and provide the service that customers expect. Learning never ends in a successful sales organization.

The Ultimate Sales Cycle

The ultimate sales cycle is what every company aspires to achieve. That's the cycle you want to be on...the purchase, the repurchase, and the next purchase. Why is higher customer retention a pipe dream for most companies? Why is customer service deteriorating when businesses are investing large sums in customer relationship management software? The problem is that customers leave even when they appear to be satisfied. Some just want to change and try a competitor, or they feel that they are getting a better deal elsewhere. Others quit doing business with a company because they are dissatisfied with the product or service. Most customers defect because they don't feel that their business is appreciated, and the quality of service is less than satisfactory. How can you avoid making these same mistakes? Don't take your existing customer base for granted. This grave error is a costly one to your bottom line when it costs five times more to gain a new customer and ten times more to recover lost customers.

The Rule of Five

The Rule of Five is a sales process designed to leverage your customer asset. I used this unique system to build a base of more than 1 million customers that generated over $4 billion in revenue. In our business, like many, 80% of the sales revenue comes from only 20 to 30 percent of the customers who do business with us. These five methods provide a course of action that will lead to higher revenue performance, customer growth, and greater profits. The five methods are:

1. Identify and attract new customers
2. Retain more of your existing customers
3. Increase the average buy
4. Increase transaction frequency
5. Enhance customer lifecycle spending

Attract New Customers

Before your company can attract and influence the thinking of buyers, it has to know that your company and products exist. About 30% of the most companies' revenues are derived from new customers. You need a steady flow of new customers to augment the existing customers that you lose if you are going to grow your business. How can you create a pipeline of new customers in your business? Begin by developing a "new customer strategic business plan" that is entirely focused on the generation of new customers. Unless you have a focused plan dedicated to new business growth, chances are you won't carve out the proper time, resources, and investment to develop new business. What you're after is customer growth, product sales growth, and market share growth from new customers. Convert cold calls into warm calls with better knowledge of buying potential and by selecting the appropriate sales channel that matches customer needs.

It's essential that you target, reach, and influence your best prospects. Advertising is the most powerful way to do that. Advertise to reach more customers in less time and to influence how people think about what you sell. This advertising influences not only how they think but also what they buy. You have to communicate with your desired audience to create product awareness and ultimately preference for your product. That's why, in the United States, the media spends over $1,800 per person to communicate messages to each individual. Your prospects receive information about your products and services in two ways. They hear it or they read it! It doesn't matter what you are selling; you need to provide customers with reasons to buy.

To capture more new customers, strengthen your sales arsenal at each customer access point. Everything you do communicates with customers: advertising, public relations, marketing, personal selling, brand identity, product packaging, Web site, and store environment. Each of these elements influences the buying experience in different ways. Strengthen these elements and you will enhance your selling effort.

Retain More Customers

The facts are that 65% of most companies' sales revenues come from existing customers but over 85% of the profits. The strongest part of customer retention is profits. Even a small percentage increase in retention rate can have a dramatic effect on your bottom line. American businesses lose 50% of their customers over a five-year period. To change that trend for your business, you have to have another strategic plan to build customer loyalty. The focus on customer retention is totally different from the focus on getting new customers. Customer loyalty is built on service first, and customers, whether they're walking in the aisles or clicking a mouse, want their expectations to be met. Heading the list of customer expectations in the New World of selling beyond service are convenience, reliability, appreciation, selection, and value. What else do customers want when they are shopping? These items can all have an effect on the customer experience and purchase: readily available information, less hassle, friendly sales associates, best price or value, customization, control, and time savings.

Simply having customer loyalty programs or customer relationship management software is no longer sufficient to stem the tide of customer erosion. Your entire enterprise has to focus on the customer and not just on programs and technology. Every touch point to your business has an effect on the customer experience, and you have to make technology and customer loyalty work together.

Increase the Average Buy

The third way to leverage your customer asset is to use specific order building techniques at the point of purchase to boost transaction amounts. One example is the direct marketer Harry and David that sells fruit, flowers, and gift items mainly through catalogs. It excels at reminding you when to buy, reminding you of past purchases, and always suggesting special offers and ancillary purchases. With this information, you tend to buy more from them. The power of suggestion works at consumer electronic stores where they make it a habit to suggest the extended service warranty with the purchase of electronic equipment.

Another creative way to boost the transaction amounts of each customer is how you package and bundle your products and services to position the purchase size. Fast food restaurants have mastered the art of bundling various choices of meals to make it easy to buy and to make the purchase larger. They even super-size the meal for us for a little more cost! Car washes are also masters at providing us with options that extend the buy. We can spend anywhere from $4.99 to $39.99 to have our vehicle washed, cleaned, and polished. Likewise, fancier treatments are available like hand waxing and detailing that go for well over $100.

When you understand human behavior, you realize that we're creators of habit and simplicity. We buy a dozen eggs, not eight, and a six-pack of our favorite soft drink, not five, because that's the way they are sold. Find ways to increase each transaction amount in your business by using creative packaging, bundling, cross-selling, and up-selling strategies. These options are even stronger when you position them as value added benefits for the customer.

Increase Transaction Frequency

Create more reasons for customers to do business with you more often. The more opportunities you have to engage the customer with your business, the more potential you have to sell. Certainly one method to increase store traffic is invitation. Use direct mail or other advertising to invite people to do business with you. Give them a compelling reason to shop with you. For example, special holiday sales, private select customer sales, merchandise demonstrations, fashion shows, and entertainment are examples of ways to get the couch potatoes off of the sofa and into your store. Coupon offers by mail or on your Web site with a limited time offer are other ways to create a sense of urgency to shop. Retailers are finding out that they have to create an atmosphere of fun and excitement to pull more customers into their place of business. Shopping malls are becoming entertainment centers where shopping takes place.

One of the reasons that supermarkets have everything from video rental to lottery tickets is to bring you in more often. And, guess what, you buy more. You come in to rent a movie, and you buy ice cream or popcorn to go with it. Have you ever gone into a supermarket to buy one or two items and left with a huge bag full of stuff? Use your imagination to create more reasons for customers to come into your business or to visit your Web site, and you'll see an increase in sales revenues

Enhance Customer Lifecycle Spend

Building a customer-centric culture is a mindset that your business can instill in all employees, that customers are an investment and an asset and not just a one-time sale. You have to spend the time to train and educate everyone in the organization to think more insightfully about what customers are worth and how to treat them. You must instill the thinking throughout the company that the value of a customer goes beyond what they spend today. The true measure of customer value is their relationship with your business and the potential value of that relationship. This includes the value of purchases over time and the potential for them to purchase new products and services in the future. Likewise, loyal customers will influence on average five other people to do business with you based on their positive experience.

One illustration of customer lifetime value to a business can be demonstrated by using a local dry cleaning business. For example, when one week's family dry cleaning bill averages $39, their business spend with you over a five-year period is over $10,000. Build an employee mindset that a $10,000 bill is glued to every customer's forehead when they walk in your place of business. How you value a customer's worth to your business will have a direct effect on how you and your employees treat that customer and ultimately how much business they do with you. You want to leverage the customer asset and increase the amount of business you do with a customer at every stage of the lifecycle. The challenge is to use soft-listening skills, problem-solving skills, and multiple sales channels to create the best possible customer buying experience. The payoff is that you keep your most discerning customers coming back for more, and you let them access the company whenever and wherever they choose. Customers are in the driver's seat!

Winning the Battle for the Buyer

The business war of the 21st century is the battle for the buyer. One lesson we can learn from Wal-Mart's triumph over K-Mart is that you either have enough profitable customers who do business with you or you're toast! Wal-Mart took K-Mart to the mat because K-Mart's blue-light specials couldn't compete with Wal-Mart's everyday low prices. Nothing is more perishable than success. With more intense competition and customers in the driver's seat, you have to re-invent your business constantly to keep up. Running a business on cruise control is a dangerous thing when customers, products, and markets are changing faster than ever before. The success of your business depends on your ability to attract and engage the right customers to buy from you. The job of getting and keeping customers is tougher today, and every business has to be better than it was last year to keep pace. There is an abundance of choice for buyers regardless of the industry or category.

Today in the typical supermarket there are over 40,000 items for us to choose from. We are bombarded with choices and product-line extensions as food marketers fight over inches of eye-level shelf space to attract our attention. Business is out there, but you have to be more creative and focus on what buyers want in order to get your share. In the New World of selling, to convince customers to open up their wallets, you have to open your mind to new ways of connecting with them in this era of choice.

Leading American Companies Show Us the Way to Greater Sales

We can learn valuable lessons about selling and winning customers from some of America's leading companies. What sales concepts can we adopt to improve our own performance?

The Innovators

Heinz has turned its 57 varieties it began with at the turn of the last century into more than 5,700 products it offers today. The bold move that Heinz made was to introduce and sell its new EZ Squirt funky ketchup to appeal to kids. Now families are buying the EZ Squirt bottles of Funky Purple Ketchup and other new flavors to go along with the traditional red ketchup. This brilliant move is what marketers dream of as market share soars and millions of bottles of the new ketchup go flying off of the supermarket shelves.

Gillette thrives from bold product introduction that cannibalizes their existing products before the competitors bury them. Gillette introduces a product like Mach 3 while their old razor Sensor Excel still owns huge market share. Gillette is a master at designing superior products that command a premium price. Gillette sells five times more blades than anyone else does and owns 70% of the worldwide market for blades and razors. Gillette took its innovation beyond men's shaving products to the other half of the population and created the Venus shaving system for women.

The Rule Changers

Southwest Airlines changed the rules of flying to become the only profitable airline among the top eight. Southwest goes against the grain and has no seat assignments, no meals served onboard, no bulky drink carts, and no movies. Southwest is the only major short-haul, low fare, high frequency point-to-point carrier. They built a lower cost structure by flying only one kind of aircraft, the Boeing 737, that reduced maintenance costs and turn-around time.

Enterprise Rent-A-Car became the nation's largest car rental company by changing the industry standard and revolutionizing how people rent cars. The run on 4 magic words—we pick you up—and shattered the rules of the car rental business. Enterprise takes convenience to a whole new level with business locations within 15 miles of 90% of the U.S. population.

The Visionaries

Coke, the world's largest beverage company, redefined the word vision when they redefined their market several years ago from soft drinks to the 64 ounces of liquids consumed by humans on the planet each day. Since that decision Coke now has over 75% of its operating income outside of the United States. Coke now sells soft drinks, orange juice, bottled water, and more. Line extensions like Vanilla Coke are designed to attract new customers for Coca-Cola.

Starbucks had the vision to romance the bean of an old commodity like coffee into a phenomenal customer experience and an extraordinary business success story. Starbucks brews over 30 distinct creative drinks like Frappucccino, espresso, and café latte that command premium prices. Starbucks sells us more than coffee; is sells ice cream, board games, CDs and tea, and you can pay for it all with your Starbucks card. Over 4 million people have bought the Starbucks card already to speed up their purchases.

The Repositioners

Subway reinvented its business around new fresh ingredients and healthier sandwiches. Subway rode the Jared television popularity into a new business model built around the *"eat fresh"* mantra and the *"7 subs with 6 grams of fat or less"* message that resonated with customers. Subway's now experiencing double-digit sales growth since jumping on the "low-fat" concept.

IBM has reinvented the way its sales force does business to accommodate a shift from mainframes and personal computers to services and on-demand computing. Today, Big Blue sells more smarts than parts to win business as they transform their once complacent company into an e-business powerhouse. IBM's 35,000-member sales organization is now geared to serve all levels of customers better and has built more consistency into its sales methods.

The Experience Creators

Disney knows how to create a fabulous customer experience. Disney theme parks provide a wonderful experience with unmatched entertainment and pleasant surroundings. We're filled with creative surprises and technological wizardry from the moment we enter the Magic Kingdom. We know that everything from spotless sidewalks to superb service has been taken care of for our family's enjoyment.

Harley-Davidson is an American icon with a large loyal fan base that keeps churning out sleek power machines that fetch premium prices. Harley motorcycle lovers spend money like crazy on the Harley brand, and it shows up on the bottom line. GM has to sell 6 cars to make as much money as Harley does selling one motorcycle. When you have customers that tattoo who logo on their body, you know that they are loyal, and that's exactly what some Harley riders do. Some 650,000 Harley owners are members of the Harley Owners Group (H.O.G.) that has rides, rallies, and other special events.

The Dominators

UPS is a magnificent company that delivers over 14 million packages a day in over 200 countries. They have over 150,000 ways to deliver goods! They use trucks, tractor-trailers, planes, boats, vans, golf carts, bicycles, motor scooters, motorcycles, horses, mules, and sleds. That's how far they go to serve the customer. UPS used to be a trucking company with technology, and today they are a technology company with trucks. They have moved their business out of the $55 billion trucking industry to the $1 trillion logistics industry. Big Brown now handles everything from warehousing and financing to helping customers manage their supply chains.

Wal-Mart has the second largest computer system in the U.S. after the Pentagon. Using that computer power and their purchasing power has made Wal-Mart the largest seller of groceries in the United States. The world's largest retailer plans to go from 3,400 stores to 5,000 stores over the next five years. They had $1 billion dollars in sales in 1979, and today they sell that much in a day. Wal-Mart understands how important value, convenience, and customer knowledge have been to their phenomenal business success.

Lessons learned from these extraordinary companies are that business growth and competitive advantage can be extracted from hidden assets, core capabilities, product innovation, and aggressive customer portfolio management.

10 ways to increase your company's sales revenues:

1. Find the purple ketchup in your business. (Heinz)
2. Command a premium price through superior products. (Gillette)
3. Shatter the old rules in your industry and go against the grain. (Southwest)
4. Take customer convenience to a new level. (Enterprise)
5. Create a bold vision and pursue it. (Coke)
6. Turn the mundane into something special for customers. (Starbucks)
7. Reposition what you sell to create more customer value. (Subway)
8. Redefine what you sell and how you sell. (IBM)
9. Master the customer connection and sensationalize the experience. (Harley-Davidson)
10. Harness technology to add value to your business. (UPS)

All salespeople want the competitive advantage and a unique selling proposition. These companies teach us is that, *for greater effect, you can reestablish your value equation by exploiting hidden assets.* Get creative on your next sales call and put a new twist in your sales presentation that separates you from other sellers. Stand out by doing great things in new ways that appeal to buyers. That's exactly what Frank Perdue did when he took a commodity like chicken and branded it as special. You can do the same thing with some creative thinking on how you position what you sell. It's not just outselling the competition; it's out-thinking them. It's not about treating all customers alike; it's about treating them as unique individuals. In the New World of selling...*sales is not just about selling; it's about creating market superiority.*

The Future of Selling

Get ready for the electronic future. America's a mobile society that runs on digital connections found in everything from our phones to our cars. The American landscape has accelerated as the pace of life quickens on Main Street and Wall Street. Technology increases the velocity of everything in an exponential way. What this means to us in the selling profession is that business cycles we once measured in years, months, and weeks now are measured in days, hours, and minutes. All hours become business hours in our 24/7 society. Home and work blur as we live a life without boundaries. We get global news in real time and experience business shifts that seem to happen at the blink of an eye.

The pulse of the future beats on the day-to-day sales made by millions of salespeople across America. The sales profession can alter the course of a business, an industry, and the American economy. *Nothing happens until somebody sells something* has never been more meaningful than now at the dawn of the 21st century. American commerce is the circulatory system of our society where consumers spend $4 trillion a year, representing two-thirds of all economic activity.

American ingenuity continues to refine our way of life as new products come on the market faster, requiring salespeople to change with the times. Wireless applications, interactive television, network grids, ubiquitous computers, and robotics each contribute to the future sales environment. Are you ready to serve the next generation of customers?

Charting a New Course

By now I should have convinced you that to succeed in the next generation of selling you are going to have to break away from traditional selling methods and embrace change. Don't just solve problems; use ideas to seek new opportunities. Stir up emotion for what you are selling and back it up with logic. When you're passionate about what you are selling, the customer will respond to that enthusiasm. *Wake-up* and *shake-up* your sales presentations with more energy to support making your product relevance greater in the customer's mind. Build your sales message on the power of ideas.

I...Innovate
D...Differentiate
E...Execute
A...Act
S...Sensationalize

Blend the use of ideas with the four stages of selling designed to augment the way you sell in this new era. Then use the rule of five to maximize and leverage each customer asset. **Welcome to the New World of selling.** It's exciting and extremely rewarding when you're prepared to win the battle for the buyer.

About The Author

Thomas A. Pall

Tom Pall is recognized as one of America's leading authorities on sales. Tom, fresh from the corporate world where as Senior Vice President of Sales he grew revenues to over $4 billion and built a customer base of over 1 million clients across the United States. Tom was an Officer and Executive for SBC Communications Inc. a telecommunications giant and one of America's largest corporations. Tom's a proven business leader who consults, speaks and writes about specific techniques to win more customers and write more business. He is sought after by corporate America to share his vast business experience and expertise at conferences of all types and sizes. As a keynote speaker at national meetings and conventions Tom shares how to win the battle for the buyer in today's highly competitive marketplace. Tom's been recognized as a media expert and has appeared on the "Good Morning America" television show and was featured on the nationally syndicated radio program "The Achievement Challenge". Tom is a professional member of the National Speakers Association and serves clients across a vast number of industries throughout corporate America.

Thomas A. (Tom) Pall
Positioning Your Business to Win
17290 Courtyard Mill Lane
Chesterfield, MO 63005
Tel: 636-728-1616
Fax: 636-728-1131
Email: tompall1@swbell.net
www.tompall.com

Chapter 2

Prospecting...and Landing The Best Customers

Jack Daly

"What perception of value are you creating in your marketplace such that people will go out of their way and/or pay a premium to do business with you?" So many companies and salespeople spend their time emphasizing the real value of their product/service, yet overlook that sales (particularly first sales) occur more often based on perception. One big reason many salespeople don't do better is because they are promoting the wrong thing. Instead of selling themselves as professional value differentiators, they rely on their products, price, and company. As selling professionals, we need to differentiate our companies and ourselves from the competition. Here we will explore how.

"Who is your prospect, your customer?" This is such a simple question and concept, yet so often overlooked or taken for granted! When we ask this question in our workshops, we're greeted consistently with facial expressions and remarks that suggest "how simple." Yet, too many salespeople waste valuable time calling on people "undeserving" of such time and attention. FOCUS PRECEDES SUCCESS. Too many salespeople are lacking in focus. One of the basic tenets of leveraging one's selling efforts is targeting fewer prospects and clients. We endorse the idea of "getting many from few," as opposed to "getting a few from many." In that way we also have the time needed to foster a quality relationship. The underlying mission here is to generate more business with less work.

"How much is a customer worth?" Better yet, what is the lifetime value of your customers? The key to increased selling success is to spend more time with the "right people." There is a non-negotiable level of service that all customers should receive. From there, however, companies and salespeople should spend more time and money on accounts that can deliver more results. Bluntly, we say, "All customers should not be treated equally."

In this chapter we will identify special ideas on how to create a perceived value or approach campaign, thereby differentiating ourselves from the competition. We will explore a simplified method to determine lifetime value of our customers. We'll learn how to identify and categorize prospects, customers, and clients, and how others are "touching" their databases with uniqueness and effectiveness.

At its very core, selling is the transfer of trust. People do business with those whom they trust. They trust the people they get to know. If you call on too many prospects, you dilute yourself in your market and remain an "unknown." We must learn then to call regularly on the right people and gain their trust, which will ultimately help us to gain their business.

Before plunging head-first into the "how-to's" of effective prospecting, let's establish a solid base of understanding of professional selling.

A Review of the Basics

Our career growth depends upon our ability to build strong, continuing relationships with top-producing sources of business. Besides building these relationships, a sales professional is someone who:

1. Gets business from a prospect who is already committed to someone else.
2. Helps his or her business source to reach their full potential.
3. Constantly upgrades his or her clientele.

Therein lies a problem. How do you gain the attention of these attractive prospects? How do you overcome their commitment to another supplier? How do you combat their indifference to wanting to see you?

Professional selling is two people wanting to work together, and the details not standing in their way. Another key idea is that success with a client comes by giving "value added" service. You accomplish this by delivering more than your client expected when he or she decided to buy your service.

"Golden handcuffs" tie business sources to you. Your image, knowledge, sensitivity, attitude, and success create those bonds.

You become someone's business partner because they discover it is in their best interest to work with you. Another way to say this is that a sales professional helps his or her clients to be more successful.

Our clients and customers are changing as they gain access to more information about competing products. Many are becoming more sophisticated and demanding within the sales process.

Selling will continue to become more information intensive, requiring the salesperson to be more of an expert consultant and problem solver. Today, a sales professional's position description is—"to help my customers make more money."

Building a relationship starts with overcoming their indifference toward you even before your first meeting. You shouldn't call on a probable prospect unless you have "pre-marketed" yourself.

A good approach campaign, in which you pre-market yourself, changes the acceptance rating considerably. Create a positive image in your prospect's minds by sending them helpful ideas and general market information. The greater the positive image you build, the greater your success will be.

Path to Success

Sales success begins at the bottom of the Critical Path Pyramid in Figure 1.

Figure 1

Our first objective is to define the highest value needs of the prospect. To do this, we must conduct a meaningful interview in a favorable environment.

When calling prospects for an appointment, or just before reconfirming the time and place, ask if they would reserve their conference room for your meeting. Tell your prospect that you will have some things to demonstrate and that the conference room would be helpful.

The real purpose is getting the prospect away from his or her telephone during the interview. At that time you will want to determine four primary things:

1. Highest value needs (HVNs) held by the prospect.
2. Social style of the person.
3. Current relationships with competitors.
4. Objections to be resolved.

Professionals never recommend an action until hopefully they have determined the problem, opportunity, or need in the relationship. How would you feel toward a physician who prescribed a medicine prior to conducting a thorough physical? You might sue for malpractice a lawyer who suggested language for your will without determining your wishes.

Interview for Results

When you call on someone, do you "show up and throw up?" Do you dump product information on them? We all know that traditional salespeople talk too much. Sales professionals listen—and listen—and listen! A salesperson who shows up and throws up also should be sued for malpractice.

Traditional salespeople spend most of their time on pitching and selling features. But, professional selling focuses on finding customer needs and problems and offering solutions to meet those needs. Less emphasis and time is devoted to aggressive selling and more to building relationships and providing value to the customer.

It is suggested that we spend the same amount of time in an interview as we are doing now—but that we spend it differently. Our emphasis should be on information gathering and "needs analysis" rather than pitching features.

When you are in front of a prospect, how much time do you talk and how much time do you listen? It is important to remember that the listener controls the interview.

We don't sell our products or services to someone unless they perceive it is in their personal interest to have us do so. Therefore, we must determine their interests and highest value needs.

Once we know those needs, we know that we will do business with him or her. We just don't know how long it will take to do so.

Fulfilling Unmet Needs

Moving up the Critical Path, we next determine our prospect's social style. We need to be sensitive to a prospect's style so that we can prepare an appealing presentation for him or her.

When asking about a prospect's current business sources, find out the strength of those relationships. You should be aware of any unmet needs already. While interviewing someone, you will be able to determine what their objections are going to be when you ask for their business. If someone surprises you with an objection, it is because you didn't ask enough questions or you didn't listen during the interview phase of the selling process.

If we know our prospects' needs, social styles, and objections, we are in a position to offer solutions that they will find not only acceptable but also desirable. Thus we can "motivate" prospects to move in our direction.

It's amazing how many experienced salespeople "wing it" here. Sales professionals should have identified and documented reasons a prospect should work with them and with their company.

Our solution should suggest an action that will move us into, or toward, a business relationship. If we are not successful initially, we position ourselves to call on our targeted prospects continually. Our goal is more to move our relationship along than it is to concentrate on a single transaction.

Prospects tend to react negatively when a salesperson pleads, "Just give me a try, and I'll show you what I can do," because the statement has become trite. It's far better to suggest some action that will directly benefit the prospect.

We are not suggesting avoiding asking for the business, but don't be in a hurry. We want all this top prospect's business—not just a single order.

When you feel the time is right to ask for your prospect's business, we suggest an open-ended question: "Considering what we have been discussing, do we have a basis for doing business together?" The answer will determine your progress and where the relationship is headed.

If you have demonstrated your knowledge, sensitivity, and constructive help, the answer will often be "yes" with some qualifications. Meet these conditions, and then we're on our way to building a business partnership.

Make Fewer Sales Calls

We start building strong business relationships by targeting a select number of prospects. A successful career as a sales professional is built upon maintaining a limited number of highly productive clients and not on seeing how many calls can be made in any week. "Focus precedes success" is a core concept of Professional Selling, which is shown in Figure 2.

APPROACH

```
                    ┌─────────────────┐
              ┌────►│   Interview     │────┐
              │     │   Discover      │    │
              │     │   (HVN)*        │    ▼
              │     └─────────────────┘
┌─────────────────┐                   ┌─────────────────┐
│    Ask For      │                   │    Present      │
│  The Business   │                   │    Solve        │
│                 │                   │    (HVN)*       │
└─────────────────┘                   └─────────────────┘
         ▲           ┌─────────────────┐        │
         │           │    Discuss      │        │
         └───────────│ Manage Objections│◄──────┘
                     └─────────────────┘
```

* Highest Value Need   Figure 2

Every sales professional should have a written list—by name—of those whom they have targeted as future business partners. Determine in advance—through your intelligence sources—prospects with whom you would like to be doing business in the immediate future.

It is essential that we continually upgrade our clientele in order to increase our production. Since we can work with a limited number of clients only, they must be the best available sources of the kind of business we want.

Prospects are open to a new salesperson who will help them to be more successful. Despite this fact, most prospects are reluctant to change, and the more successful they are, the more this is true.

Our goal is to have a pre-determined number of clients as business partners. We must select them carefully because it is going to take some time to win them over to us. Additionally, we must get to know our target's managers, since often they either assist us—or stand in our way. It is not cavalier to say, "Find out what someone wants and then deliver." Doing so is far more effective than pitching your products and service in the hope that your prospect will respond. Top prospects are too sophisticated for this outdated selling style.

Preparing for Action

Once we have defined our prospect's HVNs, we must decide whether it's best to ask for a subsequent appointment in order to present our solution, or if we need to suggest some immediate action.

We are influenced in this decision by how well we have determined needs, the prospect's social style, his or her present relationships, and what the objections will be. If you are in doubt on these issues, continue your interview. Or, if you're pressed for time, suggest making another appointment.

Tell your prospect that you would like to gather some information and ideas to take on your next visit. Make sure to schedule your following appointment before leaving!

You can see that it doesn't matter how many sales calls you make. What's important is how effective each one is. See fewer people if you want to do more business, and be sure that they are the right business sources for you.

The Approach Campaign

We opened this chapter with a key prospecting question: "What perception of value are you creating in your marketplace such that people will go out of their way and/or pay a premium to do business with you?" Let's take a look.

Determining whom to call on and then initiating an approach are the most difficult parts of the sales process for most salespeople, no matter what industry they're in.

How often do we hide behind our desks doing unproductive work because we don't have a targeted list of prospects and a comfortable system for approaching them in order to initiate a business relationship? Once we have an interested prospect, generally we can proceed with confidence.

Call reluctance usually rises or falls in intensity depending on our current circumstances and recent results. But, remember this: Salespeople are paid more for their time than any other professionals are because salespeople do what others are not comfortable doing. We can say that we are in the rejection business because so many of our approaches have that result.

Our major problem, then, is not the economy or our product line. It is our self-esteem.

Call reluctance thresholds are related directly to our self-esteem levels. A person with a healthy sense of self-worth is more willing to accept criticism, rejection, or even failure when pursuing a business relationship. While no one enjoys rejection, individuals with high self-esteem are able to overcome it and then move on to other opportunities.

High achievers count only their wins, and ignore their losses. Outstanding success results most often after high levels of initial failure. The road to success is full of potholes.

What to Avoid

Too often salespeople make frequent sales calls in an effort simply to be visible, hoping to find easy business by being "in the right place at the right time." Being product pushers, such salespeople are big on price and products, and thus tend to be "show up and throw up."

When meeting with a prospect, they do an "information dump" of product features. Is it any wonder that some people place Pit Bulls at their front door when they see salespeople driving up?

This obsolete sales method perpetuates itself, since some success can be found when using it. Yet it is a prime cause of burnout also, which occurs when we don't establish career building professional relationships.

Some salespeople have been in this business five years—while others have repeated the first year five times. If we aren't constantly developing new referral relationships and adding value to old ones, we will be forced to keep prospecting like a rookie.

A second career trap occurs once we've achieved an initial level of success. At times successful salespeople slack off on new business development and "live off their own fat." When we fail to upgrade our clientele continuously, we risk a falloff of income if any of our clients quit using us.

Becoming a professional salesperson isn't that difficult. Experience shows that there are techniques that can enable us to earn more while actually working less. We then tend to be excited about making sales calls, and ultimately enjoy our career more than we previously had.

We start with several assumptions:

1. We want to do business with highly productive sources.
2. We want to get most of our business from fewer referral sources.
3. By constantly upgrading the quality of our sources, we will earn more with less effort.
4. We need to create a positive environment in which prospects are receptive to our approach.

STEP 1

Regardless of our current success level or the amount of time we've been in the business, we should write down a list of persons with whom we want to do business.

Pre-selecting those with whom we want to do business because of their reputation, social style, and quality production is the foundation of our career. Too often salespeople make calls in a territory and then work with whomever will give them a deal. Using this shotgun approach causes call reluctance, and often is disappointing.

Every salesperson should create and then carry with them a specific—by name—list of those who have been targeted as future business sources. Focus precedes success. Salespeople should develop their target list with the assistance of:

- Your manager
- Your support staff
- Industry trade papers
- Your centers of influence
- Attendance at industry conferences/meetings
- Your own observations

Consider your business niche when making your list. You want to identify those for whom you can bring the highest value. What strengths can you emphasize? Who generally are the best business sources for your company? High achievers then ask their current, satisfied clients for referrals to those whom they have targeted.

STEP 2

With your target list organized, you are ready to set up an approach campaign. The key to approach success lies in creating a favorable image before calling for an appointment. Today's prospects are too sophisticated to respond to cold calls. We want to build an image, which will cause the prospect to be willing—if not eager—to see us.

A good approach campaign, by which you pre-market yourself, changes the acceptance ratio considerably. The greater the positive image, the greater the success. Our experience shows that different marketing activities results in appointments the following percent of the time:

- Cold call (no pre-marketing)—10%
- Pre-approach letter—20%
- Marketing Campaign—40%
- Referred lead plus campaign—60%

Personal Marketing

A well-planned and implemented marketing campaign will not only tear down the barriers of indifference between you and your targeted prospect, but it also will build a desire in your prospect to meet with you.

If we succeed in this business, it is more often than not because we are marketing ourselves continually and effectively. If you are not attaining the levels of productivity you want, you are somehow failing to market yourself, or not doing it regularly.

Traditional selling involves taking an existing product or service and creating a demand for it. It is a "ready-shoot-aim" process that takes a shotgun approach to prospecting—the more you shoot, the more likely you are to hit someone.

Most salespeople use this type of approach. Products, rates, and service are "sold" without any real knowledge of their prospect's needs. By pushing the product they hope to create a "need."

Professional selling, in contrast, first requires determining what your target audience wants. You then can create a product or service that fills the gap between their desire and what is currently available. It entails aiming before you shoot, and is a much more focused approach. You understand before trying to be understood.

Marketing is a great way to begin to differentiate yourself from other salespeople. A good "marketer" continually produces higher sales results than the "product pusher."

Even if you are successful, you need to consider a Personal Marketing Program. Because it involves a planned, strategic approach, marketing maximizes your effectiveness. It enables you to direct your energies into the areas that will be most productive.

Marketing is integral to the relationship building process. It sets the stage for the relationship because the result of your marketing effort positions you as someone with whom they want to do business. It's hard not to win big when your customers' success is what drives your thoughts and actions.

Like a Business, It Starts with a Plan

Think of your marketing plan as a map. You start with an in-depth analysis that looks at where you are, where you want to go, the competition, and the overall marketplace.

You'll note that certain kinds of business are more profitable than others. Some of your competitors are on the rise, while others are waning. The market is changing due to the economy, buyer's demands, demographics, and new products.

What do you want your image to be in your marketplace? What specific things can you do to create that image? Your marketing strategy addresses those questions.

A marketing plan should have several means that collectively produce a new awareness about who you are and how you work. If effectively implemented, a marketing plan can create momentum for business sources to call you, instead of you calling them.

Establishing a marketing plan enables you to isolate problems, discover opportunities, and set measurable objectives. You will find ways to add value regularly to your business relationships.

After completing the analysis described above, you can begin to formulate your overall strategy. Here are the basic elements to consider.

- Target high-leverage prospects. Maximize high pay-off activities.
- Build awareness of yourself, your institution, and your products, in that order.
- Distinguish yourself, your institution, and your products from the competition.
- Use specific communication tools to build, maintain, and reinforce personal selling relationships.

The strategy you develop will determine the specific tactics you will use to market yourself—whether brochures, letters, or presentations.

To get the benefits you want, set up a timetable for carrying out the tasks referred to above. Also schedule time to assess your program's effectiveness and make any mid-course corrections.

A pre-approach marketing campaign consists of mailing helpful information to your prospect about every four working days for up to six weeks before calling for an appointment. Systematically delivering useful business development ideas encourages your prospect to perceive you as a potential business associate—and thus someone who is worth seeing.

Ideas you can provide are limitless. They need only be concepts or suggestions that can help your prospects. As a salesperson, consider what useful information you can mail that has benefited similar clients.

Our job as professionals is to help our customers make more money and be more successful. A continuing research effort should focus on what very successful customers are doing—and then share those concepts. Sales and work organization ideas, which are universally applicable, are good to use. Articles from your company newsletter or marketing materials, which are helpful—not product pitches—also work.

These mailings do not need to be fancy or professionally prepared. But, they should be legible, informative, and confined to one page. Attach your card with a handwritten note: "Thought you would find this interesting."

Send at least five mailings over a month, followed by a personal pre-approach letter with your résumé or bio attached. If you have a testimonial letter from someone whom your prospect respects, then mail that also.

Keep Going

A superstar should initiate one new approach campaign each week, a good producer needs to start two-a-week, and a beginning salesperson needs five-a-week. If you are already well known, then reduce the number of mailings, but not the number of new approaches.

Our clients determine our success. Too many salespeople waste their time calling on low-producing sources, when their time could be better invested on more productive, targeted opportunities.

STEP 3

You're now ready to call for an appointment. Here are a few hints on telemarketing:

- Concentrate on getting the appointment; don't discuss what you want to talk about.
- Call from a place which has little background noise and where you won't be disturbed.
- Identify yourself slowly so that the person being called learns your name.
- Do not ask, "Did you get my mailings?" Assume that they did.
- Ask the professional question, "Did I catch you at a convenient time? Do you have a moment to speak?" If they don't, arrange a better time to call back.

Once your prospect has said that he or she is ready to listen, state your purpose. "In the past few weeks, I have mailed you several items that I hope you have found helpful. The purpose of my call is to arrange twenty minutes when we may exchange some beneficial ideas. May I suggest next Tuesday—or what is good for your schedule?"

If you get resistance, try a benefit approach: "You are one of the most successful professionals in the area, and I'm one of the more-successful sales professionals. I'm confident that twenty minutes together could be the beginning of a very beneficial business relationship."

Another objection response is: "Gamble twenty minutes of your time against twenty of mine, and I promise not to stay a minute longer unless you invite me to do so." Or, "I can easily understand that, being as successful as you are, you are committed to another company. But, I'm confident that you'll agree that no one has a monopoly on great ideas. Gamble twenty minutes of your time...." These attempts to close on an appointment time will usually result in a commitment.

Every effort should be made to get a prospect onto neutral ground, such as the conference room or a nearby restaurant. Doing so avoids phone interruptions and gets him or her out from behind a desk.

Chances are, by this time you are already receiving business from sources. It is then paramount that you keep the momentum going, so that your visibility stays high.

Probably the most neglected, yet the most important activity a salesperson can perform, is to say "thank you" frequently.

Thank-you cards should be sent whenever a prospect provides you with an opportunity for business—whether you get the deal or not. If you did obtain the transaction, then another thank-you card should be sent at its conclusion.

Be liberal with your thank-you notes. Send them at every opportunity. Thank-you cards should be a permanent cornerstone in your personal marketing campaign.

All this marketing takes time and effort, but the rewards justify the investment. Create more value for them, and they will be your client, instead of just your customer. Personal marketing is ongoing. It is part of professional selling—and lets you conduct your business uniquely and powerfully.

As you develop relationships with your target group, you need to update your database. Every quarter, decide whether or not to keep certain prospects or replace them with other producing prospects. Doing this 90-day upgrading will keep your list fresh, and your business healthy.

How Much Is a Loyal Customer Worth?

All of us are aware that the most difficult thing we do is attract people to do business with us. Knowing what a customer is worth can help us see the value of strengthening hard-won relationships with our business sources.

Studies have shown that it costs six times more to attract a new customer than it does to retain and grow an existing account. Yet our focus is far too often on attracting new customers, rather than optimizing existing relationships. We need to view the customer more as a series of potential transactions, and less as a single deal.

General Motors once estimated the lifetime value of their customers at $400,000. For Taco Bell, try $13,000. Each of us should know how much that loyal customer is worth to us, and then prioritize and target our efforts.

Let me take you through an example used in our selling workshops to bring this point home best, as well as provide an easy illustration on the calculation. For many years I was in the residential lending business, providing home mortgages. Who, then, were my customers? 99% of the time the answers given were: "home buyers, renters, homeowners, anyone wanting to buy a house, and so on...." Then I'd ask the workshop participants to dig harder. Eventually I'd hear "builders, banks, realtors, developers, and financial planners." All of these, then, were potential customers. Each also had differing perceptions of value, and would thereby require different approaches in a marketing campaign.

Now, if I were to limit you to a choice between a realtor and anyone interested in a home mortgage, which would you choose? The answer has consistently been the realtor, given that they are constantly in the market and hold forth more transaction opportunities. Yet, the tendency is to overlook this rich resource for the "obvious." Our concern is that this happens in too many industries with too many salespeople. So, our first task should be to identify and prioritize our customer prospects.

Next, we can see the power of leveraging this focus on the higher value customer. Assuming our customer is a homebuyer with a $100,000 mortgage loan, the salesperson makes $1,500 on the transaction. Too often we have a tendency to stop there in the evaluation. However, if we ask the question of "lifetime value," we then need to determine how many mortgage loans that borrower will do in their lifetime. Again, most people underestimate here, as the national average is seven. If the salesperson were to do all seven, the "lifetime value" would be $10,500. This makes a leap that the customer does all their loans with the same customer/company. The reality is that it rarely happens. Why? All too often the salesperson moves on to marketing toward a new customer and falls out of touch with the current customer.

Here is a key opportunity and lesson for all salespeople. The hardest sale a salesperson makes is typically the first one. That's because the first sale has the least amount of trust imbedded. Once the first sale is made, the salesperson will be well rewarded by maintaining a database and staying in touch regularly. In this way, when the need arises, the salesperson will be considered once again, very often in first position.

Yet, while this borrower/customer is indeed important to us, the realtor is the one who typically brings in this borrower. Assuming we've developed our realtor/customer base with "Pareto accounts" (or the 20% who do 80% of the business), the opportunity for significant production from a relatively small number of accounts is before us.

Let's assume this realtor/customer does two transactions per month, of which we get one. If we maintain an ongoing relationship with this realtor for five years (estimated relationship "lifetime") and combine this production with the previous borrower profile, we get the following value:

Realtor/Client Value

Transactions per month	1
Transactions per year	12
# Years relationship	5
# Transactions over relationship	(12 X 5) 60
Borrower's "lifetime value"	$10,500
Realtor's "lifetime value"	$630,000

In this example, then, one solid relationship is worth over half a million dollars! Given dynamics such as these, it is incumbent not only upon the salesperson but the entire company to be alert and conditioned to deliver differentiated service to customers dependent on the value potential. As well, the salesperson should focus his or her efforts and investments accordingly.

Sam Walton, founder of Wal-Mart said, "There is only one boss—the customer. And, he can fire everybody in the company from the Chairman on down, simply by spending his money somewhere else." More than two-thirds of the time, customers leave a provider of service due to an attitude of indifference exhibited by one employee of the company. We believe that if we communicate regularly to all associates the lifetime value of each "customer" to the firm, then we would display more caring and contact for that client's business.

Focusing on "Share of Customer"

Looking ahead, our business will focus less on transactions and short-term profits, and more on profits realized from long-term customer retention and "lifetime value." To ensure the best possible returns from our efforts, we need to work toward capturing the maximum share of business from each individual customer, rather than looking to increase market share. Retaining a lifetime customer costs less, and returns more, than does constantly marketing for new business.

The technologies needed to track and communicate with individual customers, one at a time, are readily available.

Assuming that indeed your primary goal is to generate business, there would appear to be precious few reasons why database marketing is not an integral part of your marketing efforts. In addition to being easily implemented, organizing your contacts into a database provides you with several tremendous advantages.

1. Your database never forgets. Every potential customer whom you meet this year, and every year thereafter, will continue to receive information about your services as often and for as long as you wish, all at the touch of a key. Never again will a customer be forgotten or allowed to slip through the cracks. Making certain that you're able to provide fast, ongoing marketing to all prospective customers is mandatory in today's competitive environment.

2. It's cumulative and continually grows in power. Because your database doesn't forget, it grows in size and power with every new contact you make. Within a short time, your contacts can grow into thousands, providing you with an enormous pool from which to market.

3. There is no other way to contact as many people so quickly and easily. The power of database marketing enables you to reach thousands of prospects in minutes. Few other marketing strategies can produce such a high rate of effectiveness with such little effort. Obviously, there are more benefits to database marketing than the three we've listed here. Hopefully, these are enough to get you thinking and moving along the right lines.

If you are not using database marketing actively, it's time to start. The business that is slipping through your fingers is a wasted opportunity, and prevents you from realizing your true potential.

The key is to know your customer. Technology helps us both to reach individual customers and to keep updated information on each one.

You need to know which of your prospects are not worth pursuing, in order to keep your marketing costs under control. Stop spending your time and effort trying to get the leads to do something they never will.

Correspondingly, you need to know whom your loyal customers and top prospects are, and take steps to make sure that it's you they do business with more and more.

As a general rule, salespeople call on too many prospects and past customers. We need to better target efforts and time.

Don Peppers and Martha Rogers relate a story in their best-selling book *The One to One Future* that bears retelling:

"Last year a friend of ours on the east coast called a local, independent florist in a small Midwest City where his mother lived, to have flowers sent to her on her birthday. Three weeks before her birthday this year, he received a postcard from the florist reminding him (1) that his mother's birthday was coming up, (2) that he had sent spider lilies last year for a certain price, and (3) a phone call to a specified number would put another beautiful bouquet on his mother's doorstep on her birthday this year."

You can see this florist is focused in getting more of that individual's business. She accomplishes this by performing a service—giving a birthday reminder—and then making it easy to do business with her again.

Such a one-on-one approach works both for the individual sales rep and the overall company. Today, most companies and salespeople are capable of doing business this way, but most don't.

By communicating regularly with customers and adding value on an individualized basis, your relationship with that customer is more likely to be a permanent one. As these satisfied customers tell their friends about us, the ultimate effect can be a gain in market share.

Spending for Results

Our guess is that most organizations are overspending in customer acquisition and underspending on customer retention. Start by figuring how much a particular customer or prospect is worth to you in the long run. We are not suggesting that you do away with mass marketing initiatives. However, recognize these efforts for what they are—simply new customer solicitations.

Our question to you is: What initiatives do you have in place that are aimed toward customer retention and growth of your share of their business?

In our workshops, we illustrate "how to" through something we call our "touch system." Let's take a look.

First of all, each salesperson should maintain four databases: prospects, customers, clients, and other. A prospect is someone with whom you would like to be doing business but to whom you have yet to make the sale. A customer may be an existing or previous consumer but is more occasional in nature, viewed more as "hit and miss." A client is what all professional salespeople yearn for. Someone who does a substantial portion of their business in an ongoing basis with the salesperson would be termed a client. Sales nirvana is when the lion's share of a salesperson's time is spent "looking after and growing" their client's business. The fourth database—other— consists of anyone known by the salesperson, not fitting into the three previous categories, but who could possibly be a center of influence or referral source.

Next, what is a touch? A touch is any way in which the salesperson reaches out and lets the database know they "are out there"/that they exist. Touches can be personal visits, phone calls, emails, voicemails, snail mailings (regular mail), or faxes, to cite a few examples. Key to the touches is they not be all about your company, products, and services. Keep in mind, people enjoy "buying" but don't like to be "sold." The focus of the touch/approach campaign is to ensure we remain first and foremost on the minds of our database. The best touches are those that can help our prospects/customers/clients to grow their business, to help them be more successful. As well, providing targeted items of personal interest or the occasional humor break will help foster a relationship that begins to transcend the business relationships. Along the way, insight into you the salesperson, and your company, is fair game as long as done in moderation.

It's been said that it takes nine touches before the prospect even recognizes you exist. No wonder cold calling is so self-defeating! We say, "Warm up your database" through an effective and ongoing touch system. The odds of success weigh heavily in your favor since most salespeople quit at five or fewer contact points, assuming the customer is happy where they are. The reality is that they just haven't heard you.

Just as all customers should not be treated equally, this is true of the touch system also. Thought should be given as to the proper investment of time and money in our database. Simplistic systems of contact management, when properly installed, will serve to set companies and salespeople apart from the competition, which will result in more business with less work. Let's look at this illustration:

Here we establish four groupings of prospects: A-B-C-D. In real practice, these groupings can be as simple as illustrated or more complex with greater delineation. Regardless, the concepts will be the same.

Prospect	Frequency	Touch Manner
A	Daily	Phone calls, emails, regular mail, faxes, voicemails, and personal visits. As well, alternating the content or value proposition/idea along the process.
B	Weekly	Phone calls, emails, regular mail, faxes, voicemails, and personal visits. As well, alternating the content or value proposition/idea along the process.
C	Monthly	Phone calls, emails, regular mail, faxes, voicemails, and personal visits. As well, alternating the content or value proposition/idea along the process.
D	Quarterly / Event Driven	Phone calls, emails, regular mail, faxes, voicemails, and personal visits. As well, alternating the content or value proposition/idea along the process.

Once we have identified our prospects into the various touch categories, our contact management system ensures the continuity of touches. Over a period of time, the diligent salesperson will begin to win over new business as he or she differentiates from the pack. A similar process should be done with our databases of customers, clients, and other. Key throughout, and not to be emphasized enough, is that the touches should be based more often on helping the target audience than "pitching" you or your company. Beyond the system of frequency, this becomes the true measure of differentiation.

Instead of knocking on "all doors" in their territories, the high-producing sales performers spend more time with their "A's and B's." We call it the value of focus, and focus precedes success. Selling is the transfer of trust. People do business with those whom they trust. They trust the people they get to know. If you call on too many prospects, you dilute yourself in your market and remain an "unknown." Call regularly on the right people and you will gain their trust...and their business!

About The Author

Jack Daly

 Jack Daly brings 20 plus years of field proven experience—from a starting base with the CPA firm of Arthur Andersen to the CEO level of several national companies. Jack has participated at the senior executive level on four de novo businesses, two of which were subsequently sold to the Wall Street firms of Solomon Brothers and First Boston. As the head of sales and production, Jack has led sales forces numbering in the thousands, operating out of hundreds of offices nationwide. His leadership experience was shaped at the Fleet Mortgage Group, Security Pacific Bank, Glenfed Mortgage Corporation, Home Mortgage Access Corporation, and Evans Products Corporation. Jack was born and raised in Philadelphia and currently resides in San Juan Capistrano, California. Jack's education includes an MBA from Wilmington College, a BS from LaSalle University, and the rank of Captain in the U.S. Army. Jack currently wears two hats: COO of Platinum Group, and CEO of Professional Sales Coach, Inc. Professional Sales Coach, Inc. (PSC) is a sales and sales leadership training and consulting firm. As a result of demand world-wide, Founder and CEO, Jack Daly, delivers keynote presentations for industry conferences and company sales events. Jack's custom-designed programs deliver results. On several occasions Jack has spoken to *YEO Universities* and *Inc. Magazine* conferences, garnering highest rated speaker honors.

Jack Daly
Professional Sales Coach, Inc.
5842 La Jolla Corona Drive
La Jolla, CA 92037
Phone: 888.298.6868
Email: jackdpsc@aol.com
www.professionalsalescoach.net

Chapter 3

Make An IMPACT!

Gerry Layo

What is the trick? What is the secret? If there were one thing to which you had to boil sales success down, what would it be? These questions and more are asked by thousands of salespeople across the world as I address them as one of their peers in my Smart Selling seminars and workshops. Although I do not have an answer as simple as most would like, I certainly have great news for those who think that sales excellence requires expertise in every facet of the sales process: You don't have to be the best! You don't have to be the smoothest! You don't have to have all of the answers! You just need to MAKE AN IMPACT in the minds and hearts of your prospects, customers, and clients!!

Think about it. In today's world, there is much greater access to information. Customers know about your company, your product/service, and your prices *before* you walk in the door (or before they walk in your door.) Customers also know about your competitor's company, product/service, and *their* prices. In other words, they are aware of their *options*. And yet, they are still meeting with you; they are giving you and your company a shot. Why?? They are looking for any way to differentiate you and your company in the marketplace. They are looking for a reason to choose you and your company. They are looking for a reason to pay your price, to do business with you! It is up to the salesperson to make that IMPACT! Too many of you do not realize that often, as salespeople, *you are the differentiators* in the minds of the customers.

All a salesperson's job is initially is to get their company and its product/service in the batter's box. If they are working for the right company with the right product or service at the right time, in the right market, with the right price, the rest should be easy. Too often, salespeople go out of their way to try to develop the smoothest presentation or pitch. They are prepared with any and all information that they may feel that they need to dump on their customers, prospects, and clients to get them to buy. They have the PowerPoint presentations in their laptops, and pie charts, flowcharts, handouts, brochures, and other visual aides all ready to unleash the magic that they possess. The unfortunate part is that ALL of their competitors have those things as well. And, those things don't make the sale; they just add some flavor, typically the same flavor that everyone else is offering. Because the perception in the customer's mind is that everyone's offer is fairly similar, the differentiator that they typically turn to is price.

In the following pages, I will outline for you what IMPACT means to me. I have built a very successful career following the wisdom I am about to impart on you. Furthermore, I have been fortunate enough to work with thousands of salespeople throughout the world with whom I have shared these BFOs (Blinding Flashes of the Obvious.) I have seen the lights come on over many of their heads as they realize that they do not have to be the best (although that should always be the ultimate goal), they simply need only to make an IMPACT in the minds, hearts, and guts of the people to whom they are selling.

The Foundation

On of the first things that we need to realize as sales professionals is that *customers don't want to buy what we are selling*! Okay, I can see you scratching your head right now. What I mean here is that customers typically do not want to own your product or your service; *they simply want what your product or service will do for them.* People buy benefits, not features. Think about it! Do you own a drill? If you answered yes, I suggest that, at some point, you simply wanted a hole. The drill was your way to get that hole (the feature)! Correct? When you look at the product/service that you represent in the marketplace—and how you represent it—do you find yourself selling "*it*" or what "*it*" can and will do for the person to whom you are speaking?

There are three sales that need to be made every time that we meet a prospect, customer, or client. I used to think that these sales needed to be made only the first time you them, but quite frankly, with the access to information (options) that I mentioned above, these sales need to be made every time that we have a chance to interact with even our most cherished and long-term clientele as well. These are the three sales that need to be made every time:

1. First, the customer needs to buy you or rather they need to buy *into* you. We define selling as a transfer of trust. If you trust me, it does not guarantee that you will buy from me (or continue to buy from me). However, if you do not trust me, it does guarantee that you will not do business with me! How do you best get a shot to transfer trust? How do you best get the prospect, customer, or client to *buy into you*? This entire chapter will revolve around this. (Let's not spoil the surprise shall we?) If this first sale is not made, there is little IMPACT made in the mind of the prospect, customer, or client, and thus you do not get a shot to earn their business or to keep their business! But, if you do make this sale on a regular basis, you have an opportunity initially to earn their business and to continue to do so for years to come. In addition, if you do this well, you will get the opportunity to earn and re-earn the business of their referrals as well.

2. Second (and only after the above sale has been made), the customer needs to hear about your company, your products, and your services. But, as I mentioned above, they don't want to own these things. They want, instead, to own the benefits that your company, products, or services provide to them and their current circumstances. Be careful that you don't make the mistake of *info dumping* (or, as my partner and mentor Jack Daly puts it, "showing up and throwing up") on the prospect, customer, or client. If you have done an appropriate job while making the first sale (selling yourself), then you should know what benefits they need to hear. Everyone is tuned into the same radio station, WII-FM (What's in It for Me?) Find out what they need in your discovery session and then work your butt off to differentiate your *value proposition* by tying your product/service to meeting those needs.

3. The final sale that is made is on the *price* of doing business with you. That price often goes beyond dollars and sense. Think about it! If I choose to do business with you,

I have chosen also to *stop doing business* with someone else. If I choose to do business with you, it is initially based upon the perception of value that you have created. Any time I change vendors, I run the risks of change. I run the risk of getting something worse than I already have. Although my existing vendor may be the devil to do business with, at least he is the devil that I know! There are real and potential costs of doing business with you that go beyond dollars and sense. But, of course the price of your product is a deciding factor (notice I did not say *the* deciding factor) for every sale. I suggest to you that if you do a good job on making the first sale listed above, if you do a good job in transferring trust, in building a positive perception of difference (okay, that part is coming up), then you get a better *look* from your customer on the second sale. I suggest that if you did a good job making the first sale, then you cannot help but do a better job on the second sale. If both of those have been done effectively (and as long as you are in the game, price-wise) then price will not be a factor. On the flip side of that coin, if you did not do an effective job on sales 1 & 2, then price is all that will matter—and, unless you are the low price leader (and who wants to be that?), you will lose!

Hopefully you are starting to see my point that making an IMPACT starts and ends with you. In reality, all you can truly control is you. That is the good news. We don't have to worry about a bunch of outside influences over which we have very little control. The economy is what it is. All the complaining, worrying, and stressing in the world won't change it either. The competition is who they are, and you cannot affect what they do or say in the marketplace. The price of your product/service is what it is, so deal with it...or don't. You see, it all comes back to what you can control—your choices, your focus, your attention, your preparation, and your *action*!

Make an IMPACT

Let's focus on the letters in the word IMPACT to tell us on what areas we need to focus our attention and preparation with our customers. Each letter will help us form appropriately corresponding keywords that should help create the questions we need to ask ourselves *before* we visit a prospect, customer, or client. If we are aware of the answer to these questions in advance, we have a much better chance of making an IMPACT on our prospects, customers, and clients and thus an IMPACT on their success as well as ours:

I-Impression

"How will I make and leave a
positive IMPRESSION?"

The word Impression is defined by Webster's dictionary as: *A mark, an imprint...an effect on the mind.* If we were to ask ourselves how we plan on making a solid impression on the minds of our prospects, customers, and clients, we would have a much better shot at getting that impression imbedded in the mind of that individual.

As it relates to first time prospective customers, Billy Joel said it right back in the 1970s in his song *Get It Right The First Time* with the lyric "...get it right the first time, that's the main thing. Get it right the next time, that's not the same thing!" Let's face it, the sales business is not rocket science! I did not say it is easy, but it is simple! What words would describe the type of first impression that you would like a prospect to have of you?

- Professional
- Prepared
- Caring
- Knowledgeable
- Interested
- Trustworthy
- Enthusiastic
- Optimistic
- Easy to do business with
- Understanding

Now that's a pretty good punch-list of first impressions, don't you think? What does your punch-list of first impressions look like? I suggest that if you are not acutely aware of exactly what you want yours to look like, it may come across somewhat like this:

- Un-Professional
- Un-Prepared
- Focused on making the sale, not my needs
- Talkative
- Pushy

- Not a good listener
- Non-understanding of my needs
- Untrustworthy

In order to make an IMPACT on your buyers, you need to make sure that you *define the impression* you want to leave with them, *before* you start. Those impressions (whether fair or not) are formed in the minds of your prospects, customers, and clients through your *actions* more so than your words. As sales professionals, we must be careful with everything that may form a positive or a negative impression in the minds of our customers. How do you look? Do you show up for your scheduled meetings with customers early? Late? Do you spend too much time on non-business issues with your customers? Too little? Do you under-promise and over-perform or do you over-promise and under-perform? Are you prepared to answer their questions, regardless what they might be or do you get surprised? Do you anticipate concerns or get blind-sided when they come up? Do you provide value added service? Are you a resource for continued growth or an order taker? Are you there for them when they are not buying? All good questions! You see, your actions indeed do speak louder than your words can ever hope to. What are yours saying about you?

I have seen the careers of many salespeople take a major hit as they lost a long-time client. It is my belief that no client is forever and that there are many forces that are out of our control at work that can and will jeopardize even the strongest of client relationships. The only thing that we do have control over is how we maintain our IMPACT on those clients on an ongoing basis. Again, this starts with the *impression* that we make on our prospects, customers, and clients.

One final thought: Remember that Webster defined an impression as a mark or an imprint? When I read that I think of a brand. Imagine that every interaction that you have with a prospect, customer, or client gives you the opportunity to *brand yourself* with the impression that *you* choose. Just like when branding cattle with the hot branding iron at a dude ranch, that *brand* is your mark forever in the mind of that prospect, customer, or client. What will your *impression/brand* say?

M-Memorable

> "What do I want them to remember about me
> when I am gone?"

In every selling opportunity at every stage of the sales process, whether with a first time prospect, or with a customer or client of some time, we have many things that we typically want to cover. Because of busy time constraints (yours, as well as the customers), lack of preparation, interruptions, and so on, we typically end up *not covering* all that we wish to. Even though we feel that we are thorough with our information, the customer generally *listens* to even less and actually *hears* even less yet! Even beyond this, with everything going on in the life and the business of your customer, there is actually very little that they will remember. We need to ask ourselves this question: "What is it that I want them to remember about me, and thus, about my company, product, or service when I walk out that door?"

When you think about someone who has made an IMPACT in your life, what makes him or her *memorable?* Was it something that they said, something that they did, the way they acted, or a characteristic that set them apart? Too often we hope to be memorable in the minds of our prospects based upon our professional presentation skills that position our product or service in a wonderful manner. Well here's a word of advice: GET OVER YOURSELF!

Put yourself in the customer's shoes. You see about 10 salespeople per week offering a variety of products and services representing an entire host of differing companies. You are polite and cordial with each one and are generally interested in finding out how their particular product or service can help meet your needs. You seek differentiation. You seek a sales professional who cares to ask you what it is that you need. You bristle against the *canned* pitches and the contrived PowerPoint presentations. At the end of the month, you must decide, based upon the information that you have gathered from these salespeople, which company to go with.

Here's the problem: They all sounded alike. Many of them said similar things. Nobody seems to stand out. Nobody was truly memorable. What should we do? Let's go to the bids and check out features and price! Now who wins?

Every sales opportunity is just that, an opportunity! It is an opportunity to make an IMPACT on our customer. We have a much better shot at getting that done if we are in some way, shape, or form standing out positively in the minds of our prospects, customers, and clients. Just how do we go about doing this? Although this entire chapter covers that very question, let's take a look at some specific tactics that will help you be more *memorable*:

Have and Use Appropriate *Power Phrases*

What is a power phrase? It might be defined as a branding statement. I like to think of a *power phrase* as something that, if all else is forgotten or lost, will stand out in the mind of the customer. I want to be known as the guy who had the guts to say what he meant. I want *my power phrases* to appear spontaneous, off-the-cuff, and delivered specifically for that circumstance, that opportunity, that person. Below find an example of one of my *power phrases* that I tend to deliver when a prospect politely tells me that I (or my product/service) am not the cheapest game in town. The objection may come out like we all hear it from time to time. Example: "I like what you have to say, but I think I can get it cheaper elsewhere."

My power phrase response: "I agree! I *know* you can pay less. In fact, if *what you pay* is your main deciding factor, you probably won't do business with me! However, based upon what you have expressed to me throughout this process, it appears to me that your main concern is *what you get for what you pay!* Now, if that is truly the case, then you won't do business with anyone BUT me!"

This power phrase takes strong delivery, a high level of confidence, and a strong conviction that your prospect will be BEST SERVED by doing business with you! You need to deliver this statement with humility, while at the same time looking them square in the eye. This can only be done through extreme levels of preparation and practice.

Focus on the Little Things

Although many books have become very popular recently entitled "Don't Sweat the Small Stuff," it is my belief that when looking to build a solid career in the profession of sales, we need to sweat everything, especially the small stuff! Do you want to be memorable in the mind of the prospect, customer, or client? Try a few of these little things:

Show up on time.	Don't take more time than you said you would.
Focus on them, not you.	Be interested, curious, and *present.*
Take notes.	Look sharp, but not "over the top."
Listen, listen, listen.	Send a thank-you card, immediately.

Have Something to Say

Rather than lump yourself into that forgettable bunch of small talking, time wasting, coffee drinking salespeople who are your competition, I suggest that you get in, get to business, and *have something to say!* Now, don't allow me to confuse you here. I am not saying that you should change your focus back to the old "show up and throw up—info dump" model. What I am suggesting is that you *spend less time going through the typical salesperson/prospect courting ritual where you feel that you have to circle the dance floor with your hands on each other's respective rear ends* before you can get down to business. That wastes time and tends to annoy the prospect. Here are two strong tips to help you in this area:

1. If you don't care about the answer, don't ask the question!
2. Tell him what you're going to tell him. Tell him. Tell him what you told him.

Use *The Customer's Words* to Communicate Your Main Points

Above, I mentioned the fact that note-taking would help you be more memorable. However, what you do with those notes can be one of the all-time best techniques to make you *memorable* to your prospect, customer, or client! Although I do not spend a lot of time on "closing" tactics, here is an absolute winner:

When you are taking notes on the interaction/conversation between yourself and your prospect, customer, or client, pay particular attention to what they say and how it is that they say it. Put quotes around the particular phrases that they use that appear to be important or unique to them or both.

Now, throughout your sales process, but particularly in your attempts to address and overcome objections and subsequently gain the agreement to move forward, (close) use *their words* back with them! It is so much harder to argue with or disagree with your own words or phrases. Although the customer may never realize that you are doing this, there will be also an inherent rapport that this will establish between the two of you when you use this technique. This leads to trust, and this leads to ease of closure. Be careful though, as this requires a tool that many of us have difficulty with called *LISTENING!*

Tiger Woods hits some absolutely amazing shots on the golf course that leave even the most veteran commentators (usually professional golfers themselves) speechless and in awe. Michael Jordan and Kobe Bryant have been dropping the jaws of all observers for years with their gravity defying feats and shows of skill on the basketball court. Jerry Rice has been on more highlight reels and ESPN Sportcenter Plays of the Week than any other athlete due to his repeated feats and accomplishments. What are some of the common characteristics of these individuals?

- High levels of commitment
- Extreme work ethic
- Competitive nature
- Clear desire to be only the best
- Getting lucky by design

Each one of the athletes mentioned above has risen to the pinnacle of their respective careers, set records, and made huge IMPACT! In addition, each one of them is and will forever be *memorable* because they made the impossible possible. They did things that others could not because they did things that others would not.

Many of the best sales pros possess the same talent based upon the same characteristics of commitment, work ethic, competitive nature, desire, and luck (by design.) They go out of their way to be *memorable* on purpose, and they get it done. Try to wrap your head around this concept every time that you spend time with a customer, prospect, or client:

No matter how long you spent with them, the moment that you leave, they are going into a room with 100 of your top prospects for a social event.

> "What is it that you want them to remember about you and your offer that they might share with those people?"

P-PPOD (Positive Perception of Difference)

"What Positive Perception of Difference
will I create?"

Companies all throughout the world spend millions of dollars every year on things such as their advertising and marketing campaigns, their Web strategies, their branding initiatives, their PR efforts, their collateral material, and other areas to grab the customer's attention. In fact, it is not enough that they grab the customer's attention, but that also they create a *PPOD* or a Positive Perception of Difference in the marketplace such that the customer might go out of their way or pay a premium to do business with them or both.

Regardless of all of this effort and focus, the sales professional, in most cases, is *on the point* when it comes time for the customer to make the decision to buy. Even if a company, through its marketing efforts, does a great job getting the customer *in the batter's box,* it is still the responsibility of the salesperson to do their job effectively in order to consummate the sale. In other words, it is equally incumbent upon the salesperson to create their own *PPOD* such that prospect will be receptive to the message regarding the company, product, or service.

It is my contention that many salespeople in the marketplace today feel that they need to follow a style of selling that finds them doing some initial rapport building (small talk) with their prospects, customers, or clients followed by a product/service focused presentation that is filled with the many wonderful features that their company and its products or services offer. At that point, they feel that they need to build value (but wait, there's more), overcome any potential objections, and then move onto the "CLOSE!" We, as consumers, have become so used to this process that we are getting numb to it. In fact, this sale process has become so common in both training and in practice that we tend to "tune out" the salesperson. This cannot be good for the old commission check!

As I have stated above, the sales professional does not need to be the best, but they do need to *MAKE AN IMPACT!* What better way is there to do this than by standing out from the crowd with a *Positive Perception of Difference* over all of the competitors that you face? In fact, this entire chapter, as logical as it may all seem, is about creating an awareness of the need to create your own personal *PPOD* such that your customers will go out of their way or pay a premium to do business with you or both! How can that be done? Here are a few ideas for you. Although none of these is radical (in fact, each is purposefully non-radical) every one separates you from *today's* crowd:

- Send thank-you notes to everyone with whom you meet whether they buy or not.
- Brand yourself by personalizing everything.
- Get there early—stay as long as you say you will, NO LONGER, unless invited.
- Sell, don't tell!
- Make an IMPACT on the gatekeeper too!
- Look sharper than everyone else.
- Leave creative, benefit-rich, upbeat, and *short* voice mail messages.
- Be better prepared...with everything!
- Have the small talk *after* the meeting.
- Don't come in with the answers; come in with the questions.

In today's hi-tech, Internet, cellular, emailed, voice mailed, PowerPointed, need-it-now world, I find that many salespeople have forgotten the lost art of individualism. They seem to feel that it is the snazziest Web site, the flashiest PowerPoint presentation, the coolest email, and the most creative electronic proposals that separate them from the crowd. The fact is that most of this stuff doesn't even get teed up if *the salesperson* doesn't do a good job in establishing his or her differentiation points.

As an example of this, in my speeches, I often speak of the importance of differentiating yourself by the voice mail that you leave for your prospect when you are calling *in to them!* I ask my audiences to imagine that their prospective customer has received 20 calls that day from other salespeople selling the same thing that they are. The prospect will only return three of these calls. *"How do you make sure that yours stands out enough to make the list?"* This tends to spark creativity and benefit-driven thoughts focused on the prospect's needs. Here's the funny part: Many of the audience participants go back to their respective offices and implement these new, out-of-the-box, and creative ideas to the voice mails that they leave their prospects...that's great! However, when the prospect calls back, as he now will more often, they often may get the salesperson's voice mail. When this happens, all the creativity and enthusiasm that went into getting that call returned is answered with the standard,

"HELLO...YOU'VE REACHED MY VOICE MAIL. I'M EITHER AWAY FROM MY DESK OR ON THE OTHER LINE...PLEASE LEAVE A MESSAGE WITH THE TIME YOU CALLED, AND I WILL RETURN YOUR CALL AS SOON AS POSSIBLE."

The salesperson went from out-of-the-box to smack-dab-center-of-the-box with that voice mail. Imagine the prospect having the perception that he was calling back an enthusiastic, creative, and passionate sales professional. Instead, he is met with the standard vanilla flavored message that he has heard a thousand times!

You can create *PPODs* (*Positive Perceptions of Difference*) in every move that you make. Everything counts when you are attempting to make an IMPACT on a prospect, customer, or client. Define the *PPODs* that you would like your customers to have of you and work hard to show them through your actions at every chance that you get!

A-ASK QUESTIONS AND LISTEN

> "What questions am I prepared to ask and
> what am I listening for?"

Throughout our speaking careers, my partner Jack Daly and I define the shortest course on selling as "*Ask Questions and Listen!*" For the purposes of this chapter, nothing is more applicable in creating an IMPACT on our prospects, customers, and clients than this very practice. How many of us in the field of sales feel just the opposite? How many of us feel that we need to be doing all (or most) of the talking in a selling situation? How many feel the need to *control* the sales process by driving it with their words and statements of value? How many feel uncomfortable or even disinterested when they are not doing the talking? How many feel the need to "*show up and throw up*" and to dump all of the information that they know about their product or service or company?

I need you to put yourself in the customer's frame of mind for a moment. How much do you enjoy being sold to? How much do you like the old "Sit down, shut up, listen to my pitch, laugh at my jokes, sales presentation?" Does it endear you to the salesperson or give you another feeling?

Now, each of us, as consumers, is a buyer of products and services. The process of buying in fact, for most, is enjoyable. It is much different from the exercise of being sold to! One of the secrets of great salesmanship (salespersonship) is to put the customer in the right *buying* atmosphere and *to help them* to make the decision to do so with you! This cannot be done without proper ammunition, proper information, proper customer perception, or IMPACT!

Zig Ziglar said it best when he stated, "They don't care how much you know unless they know how much you care." How is it that we can show our prospects, customers, and clients that we care about meeting *their* needs, curing *their* pains, putting peace of mind to *their* fears, or helping them achieve *their* desires or goals if we don't know what those are? How can we show them that we care by focusing on *our* needs, *our* products or services, *our* features, or *our* companies in the sales presentation process?

I am of the belief that 70% or better of salespeople out in the marketplace today are guilty of not being focused on the customer's needs. Because of ever-rising quotas, ever-present pressure to earn commissions, and lack of proper training and focus, they are attempting to *push* customers to *their* (*the salesperson's*) finish line. It is no wonder that the most often used adjective to describe a salesperson is *pushy*! I have news for you. Not only is this practice not effective in most cases, it is more than twice as difficult and time consuming in the long run not only to make a sale but also to build a sales career. Salespeople are always looking for shortcuts. Here is an absolute gem of one. "SHUT UP AND SELL!"

The practice of *ASKING QUESTIONS AND LISTENING* often sounds too simple to get the credit it deserves. Of course there are two parts to this practice:

ASKING QUESTIONS and *LISTENING*

Let's look at the first part. We ask questions for a few different reasons. First of all, asking questions shows respect, interest, and concern. These are all great perceptions for your prospect, customers, and clients to have, wouldn't you agree? Second, by asking questions, we differentiate ourselves from the product focused, self-centered, "close"-driven competition with commission breath. Think about it! As a consumer, how refreshing would it be to have a salesperson come in and leave the laptop closed, leave the pie charts and graphs in the bag, and take out a notebook and pen to take notes on your answers to the questions that he asks? How different would that be? Would that have a shot of positively differentiating that salesperson in your eyes? I think so.

It has been said, "If you are willing to ask the appropriate questions and *truly listen* to the answers, your customer will explain your business to you!" I love that quotation! How true it is! Your customers have the answers—not you! So, the third reason to ask a lot of questions is to find out how your customer will buy from you. You see, your prospects, customers, and clients have all of the answers that you need! Most salespeople just don't ask the questions. *They* will tell you what to say and what *not* to say. *They* will tell you how to deal with them and how *not* to deal with them. *They* will tell you on which benefits to focus and on which not to focus. (That's right, you don't have to sell them the whole farm—they may want only the barn!)

Every time we base the pitch or the presentation only on what it is that *we want* to say, we risk showing the customer that we don't care about them and their individual needs. That shows a lack of respect, a lack of trust, and will end in a lack of sales. The good news is that this really just comes down to one word: FOCUS! We, as sales professionals, in order to make an IMPACT, need only to be focused truly, one hundred percent, on the customer and solving their problems or meeting their needs. Once we take our focus off our own agendas and direct it on the customer and theirs (keeping in mind the end result that we desire), we greatly increase our chances of success.

Ask questions and listen to what your customers have to say. It will change your career.

C-CHARACTER (Have one—Don't be one!)

"How will I show my true professional character?"

It has been said that a well-rounded *character* is square in all of his dealings. In the profession of sales, *character* is often the most underestimated yet vital asset that one must possess. The funny thing is that if you were to ask a random one hundred individual buyers for 20 words to describe salespeople with whom they deal or from whom they buy, I doubt if *character* would make the list.

You see, *character* manifests itself in invisible ways. It is never seen when it's there, yet it is big and bold when it is not present. Consider what happens when a competitor's name comes up in a conversation or presentation with your prospect, customer, or client. What do you usually say? How will you address this? Do you try to shed an unfavorable light on them? Do you tell the prospect how unworthy the competitor is of their business? Do you cast aspersions toward their company, their product, or them?

If you answered *YES* to any of these questions, whether the competition deserved it or not, you have shown a complete lack of *character*. We have all heard the adage that states, "You can't sling mud without getting some on you." I contend that the minute that you start digging a hole in which to bury your competitor, you immediately put yourself in the hole with him in your prospect's mind. You see, by speaking ill of a competitor, you are inadvertently telling the prospect that you and your product alone are not enough to earn and keep their business.

Above, we defined selling as a transfer of trust. If you do not show *character* in every way, especially in the profession of sales—where *character* is many times lacking—you challenge that trust.

How about this one: You are calling on a business account that you currently serve in your territory. Incidentally, you also serve this account's competitors. You are explaining a new product that your company offers. In order to relate to the customer the benefits that he will receive by purchasing your new product line, you let him know just how many that his competitor down the street bought, and what benefit that the competitor is getting from the use of these products. By the way, you are telling the customer this all with the best of intentions to alleviate his fears of making a wrong decision. However, what you are really showing the customer is that you do not hold him or his company's information as confidential. You did this by showing him that you do not hold his competitor's information confidential. He now has a perception that the minute that you walk out that door and call on your next customer, also his competitor, that you will be telling that competitor about what *he* is buying and the benefits that *he* is receiving. You have, in the mind of that customer, challenged his trust in you as a professional, a colleague, and a vendor. You will soon feel that pain in your commission check!

Be careful with every move that you make with your book of business. Your actions speak louder than your words. Everything that you do has the ability to make an IMPACT on your prospects, customers, and clients. It is up to you as to what IMPACT you will make on their perception of your *character*. Here are a few tips:

- Show up on time—early is on time!
- Do more than you promise.

- Don't open your mouth unless you have something of value to say.
- Add value to the relationship—don't just take the sales.
- Treat the customer's business as the most important—no matter how small.
- Take responsibility for EVERYTHING that goes wrong.
- Own up to mistakes and errors.
- Never lie, cheat, show off, tell secrets, gossip, or criticize.

They say that *character is what happens when nobody is looking.* I suggest you're your customers are always looking, so do the right thing. I guarantee that it will make an IMPACT!

T-Touch 'Em

> "How have I touched them before, during, and after the sale?"

The final part of IMPACT is what I like to refer to as *Touching the Customer.* Now, let me clarify that I do not mean in the physical sense but in the "reach out and touch someone" sense.

Too often salespeople rely on being in the right place at the right time in order to make a sale. They come in to the salt mine on a daily basis and swing the old pick-ax the same way, call the same customers, say the same thing, and expect their results to change miraculously. They are calling on the same people that their competition is, saying the same thing that their competition says, and doing so over and over in the name of prospecting.

It is my contention that, as salespeople, we need to create an effective *touch campaign* that, first of all, acts as a way to *soften our approach* to the prospects and, second, keeps us in the *top of consciousness* of our prospects.

As an approach, as my partner Jack Daly has explained in the previous chapter, *touching* the customer acts a personal pre-marketing campaign to ease the barrier to getting in front of the customer. It has been said, "In matters of business, it is not so much *what you know* as it is *who you know.*" Although this is true, I believe that, "It is not *who you know* so much as *who knows YOU*" that truly counts in IMPACT sales.

You see, I have read many, many books on the management practices of Jack Welch, Bill Gates, Steve Jobs, and more. Yet, despite how much I think that I know them and what they are truly all about, they have never hired me or my company to do a speech for them or to work with their salespeople. You see, although I feel that I know them, they don't know who I am!

Instead of calling on thousands of customers *cold* every year, try calling on dozens of customers who are *somewhat warm*. Do this on purpose through the design and implementation of a solid approach (*touch*) campaign.

What if you meet with the customer and they are not ready or are not aware that they are ready to buy? How is it that you can stay on the top of their consciousness? How do you want them to remember you? How is it that you intend to increase dramatically the probability that you get the call when their buying decision changes?

> The only way that you can be sure that the customer thinks of you first is through frequent, repetitious contact!"

There are lots of salespeople vying for the time, attention, and dollars of your prospects, customers, and clients on a regular (even daily) basis. The salesperson who differentiates himself and stands out from the crowd by continually and non-intrusively touching the customer gets the best shot at landing or keeping the account or both.

Customers are looking for value, not price. How is it that you can show them that you provide value? By providing value, that's how! Instead of sending out an annoying email that is pushing them constantly to buy from you, try creating an email newsletter with up-to-date articles and value added tips to help them grow their business. Instead of sending them "special offers" or "hot deal of the month" mailings, send them an article on things that are pertinent to them and their circumstances with a note that says something like this: "I came across this article and thought of you. Enjoy!" Send that to them and think about how you might make an IMPACT. What would you think if a salesperson were to do this to you?

- This salesperson was doing his homework.
- This salesperson cares about me and my issues.
- This salesperson is fighting hard to earn my business.
- This salesperson is thinking about me outside of the sales process.
- This salesperson is different.

Does any one of those sound negative to you? I don't think so! Wouldn't you like your prospects, customers, and clients thinking these things about you? Get out of the box and think of ways to touch those people in your book of business constantly so that you can better have the opportunity to "get in the batter's box" with prospects or, better yet, "hit another home-run" for your existing customers and clients.

And so, it is true! This is the secret of the non-superstars in the field of sales who, despite their lack of smoothness, charisma, and "natural" ability, seem to keep landing and growing accounts. This happens at the same time that the "natural salesperson" is scratching his/her head wondering what happened. You see, making an IMPACT boils down to all of the little things that are the hallmark of the true pros. As long as you know what areas to focus on, the secrets are open to you. Great selling to you...all of you who are out there to MAKE AN IMPACT!

About The Author

Gerry Layo

 Gerry Layo is one of the nations most dynamic and sought after speakers today! As partner in the firm, Professional Sales Coach, Inc., Gerry also heads up the coaching/consulting side of the business where *"We put all the stuff that I talk about on stage into real-world use for our clients! Getting out into the action and working with the salespeople of our clients keeps me current and fresh on the platform and up to date with the changes in today's sales marketplace."* Professional Sales Coach, Inc. is a speaking/consulting firm centered primarily in the areas of sales and sales leadership. Gerry Layo joined the firm in 1999 after many years as a successful salesman, sales manager, and entrepreneur. Gerry comes to the speaking platform from a fresh perspective today as a "been there-done that" sales pro that shares his *simple-not easy* approach with thousands of salespeople every year. "As a member of the audience for hundreds of speakers and trainers over the years, I believe that salespeople need to be moved from the *best practices* model to the *here's what's real out there today* model. My way is easier!" If you are looking for a speaker who can and will **Make an IMPACT** on you and your team, call Gerry Layo at Professional Sales Coach today!

Gerry Layo
Professional Sales Coach, Inc.
3550 Watt Avenue, #208
Sacramento, CA 95821
1-888-298-6868
gerry@ProfessionalSalesCoach.net
www.ProfessionalSalesCoach.net

Chapter 4

Selling Is A Contact Sport

Linda Brock-Nelson, Ph.D.

Selling is a contact sport. If we are seeking to sell, or attempting to influence another person's decision, we must make the first contact, and the second contact, and the third. We must be willing to follow up and carry out any requirements of the job. We must take the lead. After all, we are the experts. We have sold many of these items; the buyer has limited experience.

We must speak the language of our customers in order to make a sale. We can buy in any language, but to be successful in sales, we must be able to pick up quickly on a potential buyer's level of education, values, and culture. Ask questions to determine their needs.

My personal experience in retail sales and advertising form the basis of this chapter, "Selling Is a Contact Sport." For twenty-five years, I was an automobile dealer in Scottsdale, Arizona. As the first woman automobile dealer in the Phoenix metro area, I had acquired four major franchises including BMW, Volkswagen, Oldsmobile, and Dodge. Linda Brock Auto Mall was recognized as the largest woman-owned business in the Valley. When I received an offer I couldn't refuse, I sold it. Now, I teach a course in dealership management, MGT 494, at Arizona State University in the W.P. Carey School of Business. I have the opportunity to demystify the automobile business to enthusiastic students who plan to hold management positions in the industry or to own and operate their own car dealerships in the future.

After the sale of Linda Brock Auto Mall, I entered a new industry. Having bought and sold a number of properties privately, I decided to become a real estate sales professional. I joined Coldwell Banker Success Realty, knowing I would receive world-class training and guidance. In real estate sales, I have the opportunity to meet people from different cultures and with different needs and wants. I truly enjoy the give and take of the interaction and the negotiation process. As successful sales people, we must first understand our customers and ourselves. To be successful, we must master the art of setting goals and designing strategic action plans that determine when and how to achieve our goals. To be successful in any kind of sales, we must first sell ourselves. To sell ourselves, we must know ourselves, our customer, and how to communicate effectively with our customer.

Values, Mission, and Goals

Many people in sales never take time to ask themselves: Who am I? Who are my customers? What do I want to say? What are my values? What is really important to me? For some people it may be God, family, personal achievement, recognition, helping others, or making money.

Now I ask you to seriously consider these questions. How do you instill your values in everything you do and say? Does your advertising reflect your values? Without clarity on these issues, consistent success is impossible. What is your mission? What is so important to you that you will go to great lengths to achieve your goals? What are your goals? What do you want to accomplish in the short term and in the long term? How are you going to achieve these goals? Are they realistic? What is your strategic plan? What is your action plan? When will you reach these goals? How will you measure your success? How can you improve continuously? What kind of organization and team support will you need to achieve these goals?

Teamwork and Networking

Develop effective people skills. The most successful people I know are great organizers and strategic planners. Flee from pettiness; it will absorb all your energy and enthusiasm. Take responsibility for every challenge. Be a problem solver. Learn to manage others. Surround yourself with the best talent in your industry. Hire winners, train them, and pray for the courage to lead wisely.

Build teams, allies, and coalitions. Choose mentors carefully. Teach others by sharing your knowledge and experience, for it is in sharing that we learn most. Sharing multiplies our power.

Successful Selling Requires Hard Work

You must assess market potential. If the economy is strong, sales can be strong; if the economy is weak, sales may be weak. There may be more competition and more confusion for the customer as advertising heats up and the competition for market share skyrockets.

Marketing

Know yourself and know your market. Read current literature and newspapers. Listen to radio and TV. Check the Internet. Commission market surveys or acquire those already done. Ask customers and friends why they bought your competitor's product. Was it because of quality or service? Do you advertise in the yellow pages? Explain why your product or service is the best. How can you improve your visibility? Decide whether to go with the cheaper media or the more expensive. Where are your customers; what is the best media buy to reach them?

Develop your unique market strategy. Know your product upside-down and backwards. Fit it into the market that exists. Define the niche and inject your own personality. Memorize your sales talk, the points that you want to make, and then speak from your heart. Be a walking advertisement for your product.

Marketing is a continuous challenge of packaging yourself and your message into 30 seconds or 15 words, at an affordable price. What messages do you want your customer to remember after they hear or see your advertisement? What media will you use? How can you make it memorable? Most important of all, how can you motivate potential customers to action?

Who and Where Are Your Buyers?

Analyze your buyers. How old are your customers? Are they students and first time buyers, middle-aged with families, or mature empty nesters? Are they inclined to finance or are they more conservative cash buyers? Are they economy minded, middle income, or affluent? Do they own or rent their home? How many people are in the family that will affect each buying decision? The answers will help formulate your marketing and advertising plan. Remember, there is a limited amount of money chasing an unlimited number of possible marketing and advertising opportunities. Choose carefully.

Pick the sector or market niche you want to target. Which is important to you? Are you interested in a broad market with all sectors? Or, do you want to target a specific market with all your effort going into one sector? Imagine that you are interested in buying a specific product. Where would you look for the information? In the phonebook? On the Internet? Make sure you have information available for the customer who is looking for your product or service.

Choose Your Market Area

As a realtor, I know there are many residential areas in Phoenix, Arizona. I must choose where to concentrate my efforts or become a generalist, who spends a lot of time driving. I have learned that defining a geographic market area also helps determine which media to buy. In a large geographic area, electronic media may be the most economical with the broadest reach. However, if you are regional, focus on a specific area and use local print media to contact potential customers. If your customer base is narrow, for example, those making over $500,000 a year, then a targeted direct mail campaign may be the most cost-effective approach.

What Will You Budget for Advertising?

The size of the budget also limits advertising and its frequency. Advertising is expensive; be sure you have an effective message and the best media mix before you spend hard-earned dollars. Plan your advertising. Focus on current events, seasonal holidays, or both. Without careful budgeting, you can advertise yourself into bankruptcy court. Learn to "just say no!" Ask customers how they found you. Track the response to your advertising dollar. Eliminate all advertising that does not bring results.

What Is Your Unique Advantage?

How do you want the public to know you? Are you friendly or professional? Do you have a low cost warehouse operation with low overhead, or a large selection and low prices? Do you have a professional atmosphere dedicated to serving the most sophisticated and discriminating buyer? Are you easy to find, building business relationships on convenience? Tell the public your strengths.

Selling is a people-to-people business. People buy from people they know and trust. How can you build a relationship of honesty and trust with your potential customer? Develop your personal approach.

Develop an Integrated Marketing Approach

Product mix, inventory availability, and sales forecasting must be coordinated. Develop your sales plan, and then design creatively for your advertising. Finally, be sure your advertising supports your inventory in stock or order specifically for the advertised event. Pricing may need to be varied to create an incentive for older products.

Select the best media mix for your customer and your product. There are five types of media: point-of-sale, print, billboard, radio, and television.

- **Point-of-sale** uses brochures, flip charts, rate schedules, and other inducements. In the automobile business this often includes balloons, banners, gifts, posters, and even hot dogs.
- **Print:** Includes newspapers, flyers, magazines, handouts, business cards, direct mail, and so on.
- **Billboards** are expensive and challenge you to give your message in ten words or fewer. They can be effective when placed in front of your competitor's business. Yesterday I saw a billboard for a Ford dealership in front of a Chevrolet dealership, a good media buy for the Ford dealer. It must drive the Chevrolet dealer crazy.
- **Radio** is challenging, and it takes skill to make an impression and bring buyers into your dealership. Prime time is expensive. Use fringe time or late evening to stretch your dollar. Try to create a theater of the mind. Help potential customers get a positive visual image of what you are selling.
- **Television** is even more expensive, due to the cost of production, but it is visual and effective. Since prime time is too expensive for all except the very largest companies with the deepest pockets, you will do well to buy the shoulder times (earlier and later than prime time). These ads may attract your buyer and accommodate your budget. CNN, ESPN, Golf, and movie channels are usually much cheaper than network television.

Polish Your Presentation Skills

Salespeople are made, not born. Salesmanship requires continuous learning, commitment, and practice to stay current and to know the trends in your industry. Some people depend unsuccessfully on the skills they had when they were rookies. Structured selling techniques give you the basic tools, but you must learn to apply your own personality and style on the presentation, or it will come across as canned. Also, you must be well rested, quick on the draw, and able to demonstrate extensive product knowledge.

Today, business is extremely competitive. It is a good time to bone up on new technology. How has the wired world affected your industry? What new training techniques can help you polish your presentation? Role-play with a fellow sales person. Practice in the mirror or on your spouse or date. Sell the organization by explaining why your company is so successful. Develop a strong "why buy here" presentation. Walk through your facility and point out new technology to customers. Then explain how these features benefit your customer.

Work with All the Potential Customers

Many salespeople make the mistake of dropping a customer because the person does not fit the perfect customer demographics. This is a big mistake. If you are working with a customer, you have a chance of selling your product. However, if the customer leaves you to go to a competitor, your chances of that person coming back will range from unlikely to never.

Remember to ask for the sale. Many salespeople get so involved in helping the person and exploring the merchandise that they overcomplicate the buyer's decision-making, thereby throwing the customer into confusion instead of narrowing the choices and helping the customer find the single right item.

Perseverance

Selling is a contact sport. The salesperson is responsible for contacting the customer. Follow up, follow up, and follow up. There are many trite phrases that address the importance of perseverance. "Never give up until they buy or they die." "Persistence eliminates resistance." "Hang in there until something good happens." A positive mental attitude is a necessity for success in sales and is reflected in the following quotations: "When life gives you lemons, make lemonade." "Life is not so much coincidental as consequential." "Develop an attitude of gratitude and multiply your success."

Overcome Your Fear of Mistakes and Rejection

If you haven't made a mistake, you aren't trying hard enough. Failure in nearly everything precedes success. It is not how often you fall, but how quickly you get yourself back up that determines your success.

Communication Is Critical

Listen to your customers. Find out what they want or need and what they avoid. Look for the deeper meaning and not just the words. If you can tie in to their values and goals, they will practically sell themselves. Restate what the customer needs to be sure you have it right.

Question how important this purchase is and how the customer came to the decision to come out shopping today. Slip in the question "By the way," to soften a difficult subject. Then it sounds like a casual statement. Always, listen carefully to the customer's response. Tell everyone you meet that now is a great time to buy.

SELLING IN THE AUTOMOBILE BUSINESS

Keep Merchandise Organized

We kept our reconditioned pre-owned cars clean and ready to sell. Clean trunks, clean glove boxes, and clean engines attract customers. Shiny cars with smiles on their faces have a much better chance of being adopted. Are your products ready to go?

We made it easy for a customer to take a demo ride by having the keys ready and gas in the car. If the customer decides the car is right, then we want him/her to buy it now, and to take delivery today. It must be ready to go. The same principles apply to homes for sale.

Get Involved in the Community: Sell, Sell, Sell

Meet customers wherever you go in all walks of life; I was selling cars at the spa or the golf course. Tell people what you do and ask for their business. I played golf in the Phoenix Open ProAm with Mark Calcavechia and told him all about the BMW 750 as we walked down the fairway. He said, "If I win this tournament, I will buy a BMW 750." He won the tournament that year and bought the BMW 750 from my dealership. You never know.

Give everyone you meet your business card and tell them why this is a great time to buy. Nothing works every time with every customer, but if you work up several approaches you will be much more successful in closing sales.

Practice Your Selling and Closing Techniques

Take time to build value into your product or service, stay off price until the very end when the customer really wants the product. Ask open-ended questions to gather information about the customers and their needs and desires. Ask about what happened with their last purchase. Ask what they like about the one they own and what they would like to have in the new product. Avoid asking direct yes or no questions. Closed-ended questions shut down the conversation.

Gather information continuously to use later in your close.

- Who will be the lucky person, you or Joan?
- Will you be the only driver or will Joan drive too?
- Did you want a four-door or would you rather have a coupe?
- Will you be driving in the city or out on the highways?
- Is this truck for business or pleasure?

Ask leading questions to get your customer saying "Yes."

- Isn't this a great car?
- These special seats are really comfortable aren't they?
- Won't your neighbors be jealous?

Take control of the selling process by reducing the customer's decisions into two or three choices. Let the customers make their decision, after you offer the choices. Either/or questions build to close.

- Will you need 2-wheel drive or the more powerful 4-wheel drive?
- Who will be on the title? Just you or did you want to include Bob?
- Are you going to write a check, finance, or pay cash?

Don't be put off by "NO". No means...not yet...tell me more...keep selling! Tom Hopkins once told me to think of each no as a step closer to the sale. In the automobile business, 100 ups = 10 to 15 sales. (Ups are contacts with prospects.) In real estate, it takes 20 calls to get an appointment. Half of the appointments don't show up, and it takes 5 appointments to get a listing. One of two listings will expire or get canceled, and then 50% of the sales fall out of escrow for some reason. So, it takes a lot of work to put a deal together, and every bit as much to hold it together until closing. Don't be discouraged. Think of the millions of sales made every year. First do the footwork...sales will follow.

Another way to help customers make a decision is to ask them to make two lists. Put "Yes" at the top of the left side of the paper and "No" on the right side. Help your customer create the "yes" list, but let them figure out the "no" list by themselves. When they are finished, ask which list is the longest. This often works to narrow the choice to a single product, car, or house.

Narrow the customer's objections by saying, "Then the red Viper is okay, and you are satisfied with stick shift? The engine is the most fuel-efficient even though it is not as fast as you wanted. Are you satisfied with this engine? Then price is your only objection?"

Selling is a commitment to make something happen. I realize that if I don't do anything today, nothing will be sold. "If it is to be it is up to me." Next, I must decide what I can sell and who wants to buy it.

How It Works in the Car Business

As an automobile dealer, my first franchise was Volkswagen. We sold the cute little VW bugs that everyone wanted. It was a toy car, especially when compared to all the tanks that General Motors, Chrysler, and Ford were building. The biggest challenge we faced was how to contact our customer and how to get them to visit our showroom in Scottsdale. We wanted market share, but in sales, nothing happened just because we wanted it to. We had to plan a strategy to move us from wishful thinking" to a SALE. That strategy always involved contacting potential customers, building trust, and asking people to do business with us.

In the automobile industry there were several ways to contact customers: television, radio, newspaper, direct mail, personal friendships, clubs, and organizations. The first step was to get the attention of a person who had an interest or a need for our product. That wasn't too difficult. Everyone needed a car, especially in Arizona. There was very little mass transit, and it ran infrequently. The Phoenix metro area is spread out, so there are miles and miles between where you start and your final destination. Therefore, people needed cars. They wanted a car that fit their lifestyle and their pocketbook. It was our job, as automobile dealers, to help them satisfy their needs and fulfill their dreams at a price they could afford.

The next goal was to help the customer select a single car that he or she was interested in buying. Then we demonstrated the product. We took them for a ride and explained the benefits to the customer...then we asked for the sale!

Market research helped define the demographics of potential customers and the media and message to which they would be most receptive. Different cars attract different folks. Therefore, the advertising must be targeted to the customers likely to choose the particular type of car or truck. To sell, we first had to get the potential customer's attention. We contacted the customer using a variety of media, giving them enough information to whet their curiosity. When the customer came to the dealership, we encouraged him or her to share as much information as possible to enable us to find the best vehicle at an affordable price that fit their lifestyle and self-concept.

How It Works in Real Estate

Automobile sales involve mass marketing. With automobile sales, the more people you contacted the more sales. Real estate sales are targeted more in terms of demographics and geography. In real estate, similarly, the more leads that are followed and worked, the more listings, and the more opportunities there will be to sell.

As I transitioned into real estate, I wondered how many times I should call a person. What should I say the fifth or sixth time when they never return my call? Should I give up or will they finally say yes after the seventh or eighth contact? Sometimes it is that last call, when the person finally says, "Yes, I am ready to sell my home," and I would immediately forget how many times I had called. It only takes one "Yes" to forget all of the "No" responses.

Selling real estate is more complicated than selling cars, and each transaction requires more time. It is so much more personal. When you get in to someone's car, you get some idea of who that person is, whether he or she is neat and clean or sloppy and disorganized. You learn something about their personality by the type of car they drive. In real estate, you walk into a client's home, and you meet their children, their dog, and their extended family. You read their loan approval, and their insurance report. You know what problems they have because, in the time it takes to sell their home, you will have an opportunity to become well acquainted. There is a greater feeling of intimacy.

Real estate requires perseverance and follow up that is timely, but not too aggressive. A realtor must work days, nights, and weekends (especially weekends). It takes knowledge, skill, and patience to earn the trust of a client. There is a lot of money to be made in the real estate industry, and there are many interesting people to meet. But, it isn't easy.

Personal Selling Experiences

I never knew there were so many questions with so many conflicting answers as I found the first time I took an Open House assignment. I was so excited. It was a gated community, which meant that I had to go down to the gate to fetch everyone who wanted to come and see the home. I asked the owners to show me around the home. Before they were able to say much more than Welcome, my cell phone rang. It was the gatekeeper. He said there were customers, and that I must come and get them. I left the sellers and drove ten minutes to the front gate and retrieved the couple that was waiting for me. We drove back to the home, and I noticed to my chagrin that the sellers had left before I had learned anything. I panicked. The buyers wanted to know how much the taxes were. I shuddered, as I reached for the MLS listing and scanned nervously to find the needed information. Finally, spotting it, I announced proudly, "The taxes are $535.00." Before I could relax they asked about the homeowners fees. Again furiously, I scanned the listing, without my glasses. Finally, I discovered that homeowner's fees were $600.

"Was that monthly?" they asked incredulously. They looked shocked! The phone rang and off I went to fetch another customer. Much later I discovered that the homeowner's fees were paid annually. The customers never returned my subsequent calls. I learned the importance of product knowledge.

Another couple from out of state was looking at open houses because they just happened to see the sign. So, they got in my car and I drove down the hill. We arrived at the house. I called over my shoulder to the new couple just entering the house, "I will return soon, make yourselves at home"...then I remembered that there was no furniture in the house. The phone rang and it was a woman. She was eager for me to come to get her. So, I went to the gate and picked her up. She wanted to know all about the area. Whoops, I forgot to get that information from the owners. This lady wanted to see every house that was "For Sale" in the complex. We started looking. I took her into all the homes with lockboxes. I learned the importance of knowing the inventory before meeting with perspective clients.

By the fifth house, I asked, "How long have you been looking at homes?"

"Four or five months," she replied. My heart jumps into my throat. I asked, "Are you working with another realtor?"

"Oh yes," she replied. All hope drained from my dreams. From this customer, I learned the importance of asking questions up front to find out all I can about the customer before we spend a lot of time going to homes.

Another couple came to my open house, a Midwestern couple that was looking for a retirement area. I made an appointment and the next morning I took them to see 12 houses. They could not agree on anything. He wanted a horse farm, and she wanted a suburban neighborhood. They did not like any of the same homes. After they left, I wondered how I could have found a home that would work for both of them, but realized that it would require marriage counseling.

Selling is a contact sport. It requires incredible courage and patience in the face of a wide variety of customers. I learn fast, and it did not take me long to realize that the only way I would ever get a sale would be to spend time with customers and build rapport. Get to know them and let them know a little about me. Find out what their plans are and how I can help them realize their dreams.

Salespeople as Authorities

The customer expects the salesperson to be an authority. The buyer asks questions, and the seller guides the process through answering the questions. The salesperson asks fact-finding and end-use questions to find which product will match the needs and the financial ability of the buyer. If conversation lags, it is the salesperson's responsibility to reinvigorate the discussion, because he/she sets the pace. However, if the salesperson talks too much, he/she may miss the important information the buyer might have given to help him/her find the perfect product.

The Socratic approach is particularly effective in selling. Ask questions that help people come to their own conclusions. Ask questions to determine needs and wants. Ask questions to help a person narrow their choices. For example, "Would you rather have a large yard or be closer to the city?" "Of the first two homes we have seen, which do you like best and why?" "On a scale of one to ten, what would you give the first one? What would you give the second? What would a home need to get a ten?"

I love to work with buyers. I enjoy the buying process and especially enjoy buying houses. I have the opportunity to help buyers find their favorite home in the area of their choice at a price they can afford. When I work with a buyer, I help the person through the decision process by asking probing questions that narrow their choices and help them focus on what, for them, is most important.

Listings

Getting a listing is selling my company, my negotiating skills, and myself. It is building rapport and trust. I will be working with the seller over a longer period of time, so it is particularly important to establish trust and to explain the working relationship. It is how I work with sellers and what they can expect from me.

Selling a listing requires a different focus. The goal is to reach as many agents and potential buyers as possible. To price it right at a competitive price, to take the best photos that enhance the home, and to design an attractive flyer. A well-designed brochure is the silent salesman that goes home with potential buyers or agents. Because I may not have the opportunity to meet the potential buyer until the contract comes in, the design of flyers and brochures will be important. They answer questions when I am not there. These are point of sale flyers that are left in the home for prospects to take with them.

As a listing agent, the homeowners are my clients. I owe them obedience, full disclosure, and continuous contact. I will present all offers. I will keep in touch with the sellers, contacting them at least weekly to let them know what I have done that week to sell their home. I will arrange open houses and meet potential buyers. I will respond to questions quickly. I am working for the sellers to get them the highest price in the shortest time with the fewest contingencies. After we have a contract, I will shepherd the sale through the escrow process until the close of escrow, and I will still be there for anything they may need after they move out of their home to finish the process. I promise to assist in resolving issues as they arise.

I subscribe to a win/win philosophy for negotiations. I seek the best outcome for all parties. This is a business transaction between a willing seller and a willing buyer. Therefore, when it closes, everyone should be satisfied. As a seasoned negotiator, I look for ways to make the purchase as smooth as possible for all concerned. My reputation depends on it and because I care about my customers.

Know Yourself and Be Aware of the Impact You Make on Others

To be successful, you must like and respect yourself. You get out of life what you put into life. If you are angry and cynical, people will react to you with anger and cynicism, and may avoid spending much time with you, much less buying from you. If you are happy, joyous, and free, people will seek you out because they feel good about themselves in your presence. How you feel about yourself is a sure tip-off for how you will treat other people. If you are kind and forgiving to yourself, you will be kind and loving to others. If you are harsh and demanding on yourself, you will be harsh and demanding on those around you. First you must build a loving and caring relationship with yourself.

The following poem had a tremendous impact on me. It helped me learn the importance of being consistent in everything I did and said. I care about my customers and I want everything I do to reflect my concern. This requires constant awareness of what I am saying and doing. As you read the poem, reflect on how your customers and friends see you. How can you become more consistent in your actions and words?

You Tell on Yourself

You tell on yourself by the friends you seek,
By the very manner in which you speak.
By the way you employ your leisure time,
By the use you make of dollar and dime.

You tell on yourself by the things you wear,
By the spirit in which you your burdens bear.
By the kinds of things that make you laugh,
By the records you play on your phonograph.

You tell on yourself by the way you walk,
By the things of which you delight to talk.
By the manner in which you bear defeat,
By so simple a thing as how you eat.
By the books you choose from the well-filled shelf,

In these ways and more, you tell on yourself.
So there is not a particle of sense
In trying to keep up a false pretense.

Author Unknown

80

Attitude Determines Altitude

People must want to be with you and respect you before they will listen to your message. The depressed person walks with head bowed and low energy. Stand tall and hold your head up and your shoulders back. Make sure your confidence shows. Be a positive thinker. Develop a "can-do" attitude. It will serve you well during the high points and the low valleys of your life. Be happy and grateful. Make today count.

Yesterday is a memory and tomorrow is a dream. Live today! Live in the moment. Do you spend so much energy feeling guilty about the past or worrying about the future that you miss today? We crucify ourselves between two crosses: the guilt of the past and the fear of the future. Sadly, we lose today. I invite you to live today! Yesterday is gone, and tomorrow is not here. Today is the only time you can make a difference. Be like a child. Rekindle your childlike enthusiasm, curiosity, and wonder.

Choose your friends and associates wisely. Avoid the whiners of the world. They will absorb your energy, and you will soon be whining, too. Shun those who give up and tell you why you should give up. There are many people who blame others and can tell you all the reasons why they are not successful. You don't need their help.

Remember the old saying "Birds of a feather flock together"? It is true. If you hang around with losers, you will learn the way of losers, and you will never break away for success. If you spend time with winners and achievers...guess what? You will find yourself successful and achieving your goals proudly.

Find a friend who is enthusiastic and optimistic. Share your enthusiasm. Charge each other up. Challenge each other to reach out for more of life's treasures. Make a contract with each other, based on something you want to do. If you want to make three cold calls a day, make that commitment, then touch base with your friend to report the success of your actions. Accountability is the greatest motivator for most of us.

Faith and Fear

Develop a strong faith in your God, yourself, and others. Faith will carry you through many difficult situations. Keep faith that you will succeed, even when you have just lost a sale or an account. Develop a positive attitude about the future. What is the best possible outcome? What do I need to do to be ready for it?

Fear paralyzes many people. The three worst fears most people have are the fear of making mistakes, fear of failure, and fear of rejection. If you have not made any mistakes, you are not trying anything new. Your life must be awfully boring and repetitive. I used to wonder why my life was so dull. I was a perfectionist, shunning anything that I had not mastered. I was a dull person with a dull life, but I found a way out: Try something new and so what if you make a mistake! Learn from your mistakes.

Faith breeds courage and confidence. Fear undermines our energy, enthusiasm, and creativity. The fear of failure keeps many people from stretching their boundaries. It is fear of the unknown. Step up and face it. Try it out. Have faith that you will survive, no matter what happens. Happily, the world does not keep score of our mistakes and failures, only our successes.

Success is earned day by day. We do not suddenly awaken to find that we have succeeded. We must plant the seeds and then plant more seeds. If we keep busy planting, the day will come for us to harvest those plants, and people will think it is magic or just good luck. Deep down we know that it took many knocks on doors to sell one item. We know how many people we talked to before one finally bought the product. This is the perseverance that leads to success.

Be persistent—never give up. My friend Tom Hopkins always says that he is happy when someone says "No", because he expects to receive ten no answers before he gets a "Yes". The closing ratio varies from industry to industry, but the concept is the same. We must overcome our fear of rejection because, if we are in sales, we will be rejected, and we must get back up and go ask someone else to buy from us. That is how we can make the big bucks in sales. The losers are people who cannot or will not get back up and make another call or knock on another door.

On a personal note, I remember asking my sister how she survived when life knocked her down. I will never forget what she told me. She said, "I just pick myself up, dust myself off, and tell myself that I am OK.... No matter what."

Put yourself into the sale. Widen your outlook toward people, places, and things. Get over childhood prejudices that get in your way. We may think we can hide our prejudice, but the other person will always pick up on it. It is our responsibility to work through why we put people into boxes, and open our eyes to everyone. Do not say that there are no bad people in the world, because there are. We must learn to look at the behavior of the individual person and not to a group of a particular color, race, or religion.

Think of yourself as successful, confident, courageous, fortunate, intelligent, attractive, and enthusiastic. If you believe it, you will begin, however slowly, to absorb it. Gradually, your life will change. People will begin to notice, and one day you will wonder why you spent so many years feeling sorry for yourself. There are many ways of explaining that what you do to others will come back to you. Your attitude will come back to you in all your relationships. Remember, "What goes around comes back around."

Customers for Life

As an automobile dealer, I purchased hundreds of copies of the book *Customers for Life*. I had all my employees read that book, and we talked about how to implement many of Carl Sewell's approaches in our dealership. As an adjunct professor at Arizona State University, teaching dealership management, I again turned to Carl Sewell's book as part of required reading for all students in my class. Many students reported that it was the most important book they had ever read. *Customers for Life* stressed the concept that businesses must be customer focused. Sewell encouraged us to think about what the customer would want. We must ask ourselves how we can completely satisfy the customer. (Sewell, Carl, 1991, 1998, Simon & Schuster, NY).

Develop Your Listening Skills

Learn to listen...really listen to what your customer is saying and to what he may never be able to say. Many of us make the mistake of trying so hard to compose our rebuttal while the other person is talking that we miss the essence of his/her dialogue. Listening is the most important component of learning. Take lots of notes. Rewrite them later. Every time you write them, they will get clearer in your own mind, and you will be putting them into your memory bank.

Practice active listening. When I was earning my master's degree in counseling, we practiced many ways to let a person know that we had heard what he was saying. First, listen. If you can, write it down in your own words; you will have better retention. However, you must be sure you heard it loud and clear. If you are not sure, ask the person to say it again. If you do not understand, there will be no communication.

Smile, nod your head, ask questions for clarification, and probe for deeper meaning. Fools rush in.... Wait until you hear where the other person is going and what they are interested in. Use words that focus attention on the other person. Use simple words, but avoid slang and weasel words. Slang is local so it is easy to make a mistake thinking people understand when they have no idea what you mean. Weasel words hedge and help you avoid making a real commitment. Words such as perhaps, maybe, and sometimes are weasel words. A weasel invitation would be: "Why don't we get together sometime?" A clear invitation would be: "Let's meet at the Cork and Cleaver at 5:00 p.m. on Tuesday."

If it is critical that you understand what the other person said, repeat it. Restate as closely as possible what the person said, and then ask if you have it right. If you have missed something, the other person will correct you. Another skill is to reflect what the person said and how they said it. The goal is to be a mirror for the other person. "When you talk about how you lost that last sale, you seem really upset." Avoid profanity. It never improves your speech and will appall your listener.

Exercise your memory. Memory skills are learned. Take time to practice remembering important details such as peoples' names. Ask the person to repeat her name. Then use it in the next sentence. Think of your memory like your bank account. File those memory chips where you can find them for later use. Practice using word associations to describe a person. This may help you recall his or her name if your paths should cross again. Use colors, data, or visuals to describe what you are trying to remember. Try repeating the name and writing it down. Repetition is your friend.

Keep your mind busy. Remember to avoid cruel words and harsh acts. Make only positive deposits in your memory bank account. Be sure you file them for retrieval later. Clear your memory slate daily; don't bank clutter. Write things down and keep notes to refer to later. Avoid those little white lies. It is just too hard to remember them later.

Keep every promise you make. It is a contract between you and the other person. Let that person know that she can count on you and on what you say. Stand behind what you say. Don't exaggerate or cover up. This will backfire, and you will be left embarrassed when the truth becomes known. Be true to yourself.

Avoid gossip at all costs. Small minds talk about other people; great minds talk about ideas. My father's favorite saying was: "If you can't say something nice—don't say anything at all." He was a man who believed that if you have something good to say, tell everyone. If you know something bad, it is usually better to let it go.

When you are overloaded and life just seems overwhelming, take time to set your priorities. Simplify by asking yourself which is most important and must be done today? Then ask yourself what is going to make a difference in five years. These questions help in sorting what can be postponed and what is urgent. Once priorities are set, break the task into smaller components, and it will be much easier to complete.

Everyone you know is a potential customer or knows someone who is—if not today, sometime in the future. Keep in touch. Contact people to remind them that you are in the service business and hope to have the opportunity to help them. Be assertive and tell people about yourself and what you sell. If you are not proud of yourself and what you sell, then you will not be successful. Either change your frame of mind or find another service or product to sell.

Selling is a contact sport. It takes a real sport with staying power to make as many contacts as it takes, with the closing ratios that exist in most industries. However, selling is one profession in which you can succeed, if you are tenacious. It is an equal opportunity employer, regardless of the product or service you choose. A successful selling career requires knowledge of yourself, your values, your product, and your customers.

My hope is that you are interested in sales as a profession and will make the effort to be successful in this field, whether as a salesperson, a manager, or the owner of a company that sells. In fact, I would be hard-pressed to think of any company or organization that does not sell either a concept, a product, or a service. Think about it.

Everyone is selling something. Make it a point to watch them in action and learn from their presentation. We are all teachers, and we will all be learners for our entire lives. Success comes from developing a focused approach with the knowledge and skills to convince others that you know your business and are willing to help them in their decision making process. "Nothing happens until somebody sells something."

In closing, I want to share an often quoted variation of my favorite poem, which was originally written by Bessie A. Stanley in 1905. It has been an inspiration to me over the years. I wish you success in selling.

SUCCESS

To laugh often and love much;
to win the respect of intelligent people
and the affections of children;
to earn the appreciation of honest critics
And endure the betrayal of false friends;
to appreciate beauty; to find the best in others;
to leave the world a bit better,
whether by a healthy child,
a garden patch,
or a redeemed social condition;
to know even one life has breathed easier
because you have lived.

This is to have succeeded.

About The Author

Linda Brock-Nelson, MC, MBA, Ph.D.

 Linda delights in helping people reach new levels of success in their personal and corporate life. She is a natural motivator. With four degrees, Linda Brock-Nelson may be the best educated real estate agent in town. To her Bachelors in Business, she has added a Masters Degree in Counseling, a Masters in Business Administration and a Ph.D., from Arizona State University. Linda has had extensive experience in sales. As co-founder of a Volkswagen dealership, she built the largest woman owned business in the state of Arizona. She expanded her dealerships to include BMW, Dodge and Oldsmobile and operated the business for twenty-five years. Following her successful experience as an automobile dealer, Linda chose to apply her sales, marketing and management experience to real estate. She joined Coldwell Banker Success and now specializes in luxury properties in the Paradise Valley, Northeast Phoenix and Scottsdale area. Linda loves to share her knowledge with others. Currently, Linda teaches an undergraduate course entitled Dealership Management at Arizona State University. She motivates people to improve their personal and corporate lives. Her subjects include sales, management, leadership and inspiration.

Linda Brock-Nelson, PhD.
P.O. Box 9220
Scottsdale, AZ 85252
Tel. 480.991.9596
Fax: 480.990.8036
Email: LindaBrockNelson@aol.com
www.LindaBrockNelson.com

Chapter 5

The Art of Closing Sales

Howard Kellman

When most people see the letters ABC, they think of television. Some people think of the Alcoholic and Beverage Commission. To other people, ABC means the American Bowling Congress. However, to those of us in sales, ABC means <u>ALWAYS BE CLOSING</u>. Plain and simple. When you consider that 62% of salespeople *never* ask for the order, then you realize why you always should be closing. Do you know why 62% of salespeople never ask for the order? It is because they fear rejection, the salesperson's number one fear.

When I say <u>Always Be Closing</u>, please do not misunderstand me. I do not mean that you should try to close the moment you meet someone. I mean that once you have established value and gained the client's trust, then you should always be closing. Be ready for any opportunity to close from that point on. You must establish value as soon as possible because, until you do, any price you give will be perceived as too high. This is why, as professional speakers, we never give our fees up front.

Did Not Plan Sales Career

Before we get into the various ways to close sales, let me tell you how I got into selling. Like most people in sales, I did not plan a career in the field.

At the age of fourteen, I decided I wanted to be a sports announcer. This was my dream. It has worked out beautifully and truly has been a dream-come-true. In addition to broadcasting baseball in Indianapolis on radio and television, I announce a High School Football and Basketball Game of the Week on television and have filled in on the Chicago White Sox and Cleveland Cavaliers broadcasts.

Here is how I got into sales. I was hired to broadcast the Indianapolis Indians games in 1974 at age 22. I was rehired the following season, however no radio station wanted to broadcast the Indians' games in 1975. Without a radio station, there is no need for a radio announcer. Even though the team asked me to announce the games in 1975, there were no games to announce. I was out of work. The following year, the Indians found a radio station that wanted to broadcast the games, so I got my announcing job back. Moving to mid-February of 1977, again no radio station wanted to broadcast the games. The idea of being unemployed once more was not appealing to me.

Then came one of those magical, defining moments, although I did not realize it at the time. My employer, Max Schumacher, the President and General Manager of the Indians, called me into his office. Max said, "Howard, I have an idea. It probably will not work, but we might as well go down fighting. Go to the radio station that broadcast our games last year and tell them that you will sell the advertising for them. The station does not want to broadcast the games since they were unable to make any money selling advertising."

My response to Max was that I never had sold anything and that I was an announcer, not a salesman. He told me that, as I already had found out, without a radio station to broadcast the games, I was not an announcer, I was unemployed. I told him that I thought he had a pretty good point.

I agreed to approach the radio station WNON in the town of Lebanon, Indiana. I met with owner Warren Wright, and he agreed to let me give it a shot.

Make no mistake about it, I did not want to do this. I only agreed to sell the advertising in an effort to save my announcing job.

Breaking Into Sales

Max and I met, and he explained to me that I had to sell eight minutes of advertising for the season at $1,000-a-minute. Max suggested that I get four advertisers to buy two minutes each.

I started knocking on doors. I called people. I sent out proposals, and I got absolutely nowhere. Minor League Baseball was not very popular in 1977. There were no beautiful new fan-friendly ballparks as there are today. Our games were not broadcast on a major AM radio station as they are now. I did have enthusiasm for baseball, and I was very determined to sell the advertising, but I knew nothing about selling.

It was March 15th, and I had not made one sale. I felt pressure because, if I did not make a sale soon, I was quite certain that the whole thing would come to an end and that I would be out of work.

On Friday of that week, we had a beautiful, warm spring day. I was downtown and decided to eat an ice cream cone at a place called Morrow's Candy Kitchen. I started talking to the proprietor, a man named A.J. He asked me what I did for a living. I explained to him that I was trying to save my announcing job with the Indianapolis Indians by selling radio advertising. He said that he would like to help me. He asked me how much it would cost, and I told him that for two thousand dollars he would get two minutes of advertising in every game. He told me that he was sorry, that he could not afford to spend that much money. I then asked him how much he could afford to spend. He said somewhere in the neighborhood of five hundred dollars. I thought for a moment and said to myself that five hundred is 25% of two thousand and that 25% of two minutes would be one thirty second commercial per game. I told him that that would work. He said that he would get his neighbor, Morrow's Nut House, to do the same thing. This was my first successful close. I then went back to Joseph's Shoes, the St. Moritz Steak House, and Windsor Jewelry, all of whom had turned me down at two thousand dollars for two minutes. I pitched all of them at one thirty second spot for five hundred dollars, and they all accepted. Wow! My confidence level soared! I was closing sales. Instead of getting four people to spend two thousand dollars that first season of selling, I got sixteen people to spend five hundred dollars. I sold all eight minutes. The moral of this story is that it pays to eat ice cream cones. Seriously, if I had not met A.J., I do not know what would have happened. In fact, I might not be able to afford ice cream today.

I saved my announcing job. Then, whenever I had some free time, I got my hands on every book and audiotape about sales. I grew to love the challenge of closing sales and very quickly became the Indianapolis Indians' top salesman.

I did not want to sell at first. As I stated, I reluctantly agreed to do it just to save my announcing job, and it turned into one of the best things that ever happened to me professionally. There is a moral to this story. When you are faced with a difficult task, always give it your best shot because it could turn into something big as it did for me.

Let us discuss the various ways to close sales.

Various Closes

About ten years ago, when I was trying to close a sale and having no luck, I discovered a way to close sales that has been tremendous. In fact, at one of my sales seminars, a fellow said to me that I ought to label it the "Helpful Howard Close." I was going nowhere when I instinctively said to the potential client, "I want you as a client of the Indianapolis Indians for life. I know that the only way that you will renew this radio advertising package for next year is if you are happy with the way things go this season. I will do anything I possibly can for you to make this a success. Please come with me this year, and I will work as hard as I can for you...." Sold! A successful close! I promised and delivered great customer service, and I used it here to close successfully. In fact, I am very proud of the fact that I have never lost a client due to poor customer service, and I guarantee you that I never will. Too many salespeople make the mistake of taking their clients for granted.

I have heard and read many theories about closing sales, but nobody ever mentions closing your sales with your sense of humor. It can work wonders for you in tense situations because humor disarms the other person, enabling you to close.

Let me give you some examples. One of my close friends and neighbors in Indianapolis is a man named Floyd Whitesel. Several years ago, Floyd was selling door-to-door with Fuller Brush. No matter what you may be selling for a living, I do not see how it could be more difficult than going door-to-door. A salesperson's biggest fear is rejection, and you are going to encounter a great deal of rejection when selling this way, so this is no easy task.

Floyd knocked on the front door of this one woman's house. She opened the door and immediately read the riot act to Floyd, "Don't you ever bother me again," and so on, and she then slammed the door in his face. Floyd then noticed that there was a side door; he knew the same woman would answer it, but Floyd Whitesel has courage. He knocked on the side door, showing determination and persistence and completely overcoming the fear of rejection. After all, he reasoned, the worst thing that could happen would be that the woman would say no again in a quite definitive manner. At least, he hoped that was the worst thing that could happen!

He knocked on the side door, and the same woman answered it. She was ready to let him "have it" again, but before she said anything, he quickly said, "I hope you are nicer than the woman at the front door. She was nasty. You are not that way, are you?"

The woman broke up laughing and invited him in, and do you know what happened? She bought just about everything he had to sell. Persist until you succeed. I love this story because it illustrates the determination that often is necessary to close sales. 99.9% of salespeople never would have persisted because of the initial manner in which Floyd was rejected. His sense of humor totally disarmed her and enabled him to close the sale.

Here is another story about closing and your sense of humor. These days, David Halberstam is a regional sales manager for Westwood One and a cousin of the renowned writer David Halberstam. Let us go back to the 1970s when David was a student at Hunter College in New York. David put together a "Game of the Week" basketball package on radio involving the various colleges that compose the City University of New York.

At that time, there were approximately 250,000 students enrolled in the City University of New York. Hardly any of them cared about the basketball games. One of the colleges, City College, was a basketball power in the late 1940s and early '50s, but the college basketball betting scandals brought that program down, and it never recaptured those glory days. David needed another radio sponsor to keep the broadcasts on the air, so he brought the local Vice President of a bank out to a game with hopes of making the bank a sponsor. Much to David's chagrin, there were only twenty people in the stands. The gentleman from the bank was not very impressed. "David," he said, "250,000 students attend the City University of New York, and there only are twenty people in the stands. This is not good!" "No," David replied, "It is good." The bank Vice President said, "Wait a minute. How in the world can this be good?" David countered, "There are twenty people here, and the other 249,980 students are all at home listening to the broadcast of the game." The man from the bank broke up laughing. He knew David was kidding, but David so disarmed him with his humor that he closed the sale on the spot.

One of David's responsibilities these days with Westwood One is selling advertising for Monday Night Football on radio. When he is about to close, color commentator and former Cincinnati Bengal's quarterback Boomer Esiason will write a letter to the potential client. When you are closing, you look for an edge, and this letter often gives it to David and helps him close.

Too many people do not close sales because they fail to create a sense of urgency. More often than not, if you give someone forever to think about something, he or she will think about it forever.

One of my responsibilities with the Indianapolis Indians is to sell season tickets. Selling season tickets in November and December when the season begins in April can be difficult. People are not thinking about baseball at that time of the year. The way to close successfully here is to create a sense of urgency. I explain to the potential client that if they buy the season ticket now, come opening day, they will be able to walk *down* to their seats instead of up to them. The best seats still are available, but they will not be right before the season. This close works a great deal of the time.

One of the major mistakes that too many eager salespeople make occurs when they are trying to close. The potential client is struggling with the decision and the salesperson tries too hard. What does the salesperson do? He starts talking, trying to close, and the potential client immediately backs off from a decision. The lesson here is that, when you are trying to close and the person is thinking it over, you should *not* say anything. Let the party make the decision, and hopefully it will be a yes and you will have closed. If you get a no, then you talk and try to overcome the objection. One of the best ways to close after someone has voiced an objection is by getting that individual to restate the objection. When the party restates the objection, there is a good chance that they will talk themselves out of it. I have seen it happen many times. In fact, some of the times when I have seen this happen, I was the person doing the buying.

Over 80% of sales are closed after the fifth attempt is made to get the order. Unfortunately, most salespeople quit after the first try. Do not get pushy or aggressive; just keep trying in a friendly, relaxed manner, and many times you will close.

We have gone through several different ways to close. Now I will tell some stories about specific closes that I have made and then I will get into other closing techniques.

There was a chain of auto repair stores in Central Indiana in the 1970s and 1980s called Guarantee Auto. I pitched them on sponsoring

Opening night with the Indianapolis Indians. The Indians would give Guarantee Auto some tickets for some cash. I met with Doug Branch, my contact there, and laid out the proposal. I tried to close there, but Doug insisted that he needed more time to think it over. As disappointed as I was at not being able to close on the spot, I realized that I had to give him the time he requested. I asked him when he would like me to get back to him. This is something I do on every sales call. It has proven to be very helpful. He asked me to give him about a week before calling him back. I called Doug a week later, and he immediately told me he was not interested. The vast majority of salespeople will quit at that point and not try to close by overcoming the objection. The good salesperson will not quit here. He or she will not get confrontational either because this only gets the other person on the defensive. The good salesperson, the one who always is closing, first will acknowledge the other person's feelings. When you do this, you are not committing to anything, you simply are listening. I acknowledged Doug's feelings by saying, "Doug, I understand how you feel." These are great words because they made him feel at ease despite giving me a "no." Then I asked Doug a question to try to get to the source of the objection.

I said, "Doug, I am curious as to why you do not want to sponsor opening night."

He said, "Howard, it might rain on opening night since it is in April."

"Doug, if it rains, we will play the game the following evening."

He responded by saying that there is not much interest on the team on opening night, so he did not want to do it.

"Doug, I would just like you to know one thing. The President of the United States throws out the first ball every year on opening day. He used to do it in Washington, D.C., and now he does it in Baltimore. Doug, that is a tradition that goes all the way back to William Howard Taft in 1910."

He said, "Wow, I did not know that."

I said that, for the Indianapolis Indians opener, Mayor William Hudnut throws out the first ball.

"That is great; let's do it!", he said.

A successful close! This was a very satisfying close since I overcame the objection by: a) acknowledging his feelings; b) asking questions to get at the source of the objection; and c) providing some new information to completely alter his perspective and then close successfully.

You can close sales if you keep communicating with people when most salespeople would have quit. Example: There was a Mr. Dan's Hot Dog stand across the street from the Indianapolis Indians old ballpark. Mr. Dan's was getting a lot of business from Indianapolis Indians fans, and I felt that, with all the business it was getting, the least it could do would be to up its ad in the Souvenir Program from a quarter to a half page. You see, the minute I shook the owner's hand, I was thinking about closing, since I know him well. I could tell immediately that he was not going to change the size of his ad and that nothing I could say or do would get him to change his mind. My years of experience told me not to leave his office and to keep communicating with him. You just never know what might happen. We talked for quite a while and were having a great conversation, and then I got all excited and said, "John, I would love to talk about Mr. Dan's on the radio broadcasts." "Howard," he said, "As you know, Mr. Dan's usually does not do radio advertising. But, I enjoy talking to you so much that I will buy a half minute of radio advertising from you." This was really great. I made a bigger sale than I initially sought. He did not go from a quarter to a half page in the magazine, but he bought a half-minute of radio. That successful close can be attributed simply to communication skills. Yes, ABC means Always Be Closing, but in situations like this, it also means Always Be Communicating, too.

Here is another example of a successful close and one that I achieved by staying on top of my game. There was a business in Indianapolis several years ago called Hoosier Coal and Oil. I met with Paul, the fellow who handled the company's advertising, on a cold, blustery December day. I pitched him on doing some radio advertising with the Indianapolis Indians. He said that he needed time to think it over, and he wanted me to call him after the first of January. My instincts told me not to press him for a decision and to do what he asked. I know that many successful salespeople will say that I should never have walked out that door without getting a decision from him. I feel that there are times when you must back off and give a person more time if you feel that he is sincere. You realize that there is no way that you can successfully close at that moment. I have heard many salespeople say that the worst thing you can get is a "maybe." Their feeling is that you get a decision one way or the other and you move on. With a "maybe," you cannot move on, so they feel that they are wasting their time. I completely disagree. Many, many times, I have gotten no answer but successfully closed with the follow up. This experience with Hoosier Coal and Oil was one of those times. Since

Paul told me to call after January 1, I called him on January 2 at 9:00 a.m. He started laughing when I told him that he had asked me to call him back after the first of the year. I said that, to be prompt, I thought I should call him at this time. After he stopped laughing, he said, "You know, by calling me now, you have shown me that you are on top of your game, so I am going to buy this advertising package from you. My guess is that you will provide good customer service if you are this determined to succeed." A successful close!

Here is another example of a successful close. I was trying to close a potential client on a radio-advertising package. It was an automotive business in Indianapolis called Stan's Auto Electric. Nothing was working. I decided to call Stan from spring training while I was in Florida, hoping that would impress him. It worked. I did not realize that he also had a home in Vero Beach, the Los Angeles Dodgers spring training home. We talked for a few minutes about Florida, and I closed successfully with no trouble at all simply by asking for the business. The lesson here is to be open minded about any ideas that can help you close. Keep on charging, but do it in a friendly, relaxed manner.

There was a chain of family owned jewelry stores in Indianapolis called Goodman Jewelers. They advertised on the Indiana Pacers and Indianapolis Colts games, and I felt that they would be a natural to advertise with the Indianapolis Indians, too. I just could not close. Proprietor Ray Goodman met with me or talked with me on the telephone every year but would not do any business with me. Still, I kept trying because I felt that it would be a good fit. In the fourteenth year, I closed, not because of something I said, but because of my determination, which Ray said he admired. No two people sell alike, and no two people buy for the same reason. I talked to Ray recently; he is 87 and still full of energy and enthusiasm though retired. I asked Ray his feelings on closing sales. He said that the only way to overcome objections and close successfully is through persistence. Ray said that people change over time and that if the salesperson is persistent, he can close when the person has changed his feelings about things. If the salesperson lacks persistence, he will not be knocking on the door of the person who is receptive to buying now because his feelings have changed. He added that, when a salesperson fails to close, he should never take the rejection personally. If he does, that potential client probably will not do business with him even when his attitude changes about things. If that is the case, the salesperson's persistence will not be rewarded.

When you try to do nice things for people, with no ulterior motives, your ability to close will be enhanced. For instance, I approached one potential client about radio sponsorship with the Indians, and he was so definitive and self-assured in rejecting my proposal that I felt that it would be a waste of time to approach him again. He also told me that it would not be worth my time or his time to call upon him again. I took his advice and moved on. Several years later, tragically, his wife passed away. I called him to express my condolences, and he asked me to call him in a few weeks. I did, and he told me that he had changed his mind about advertising with the Indians. I met with him, and all I had to do to close was ask for the business.

Let us get into some various closes that have proven to be successful for many people over the years.

First, let us start with the alternative close. I think this is a great close because people love choices. You will have so much more success closing if you offer a person a choice between x and y as opposed to "do you want to buy x?" In 2003, I am selling a thirty second commercial in each Indianapolis Indians broadcast, for $2800 for the entire season. Most of my sponsors who buy radio advertising with the Indians buy that package. A few buy two or three thirty second spots per game but most stay with the $2800 package for budgetary reasons. Even knowing that, I still use the alternative close. There is a much greater chance of the potential client buying the $2800 package if I give him a choice of that one or the $5600 package for two thirty second spots than if I just try to sell him the $2800 proposal. Yes, the alternative close is great because people love choices.

Next, let us discuss the assumptive close. There are many salespeople who have had great results with it. I must admit that it is the only close that I do not like used on me. The salesperson starts writing the order while the two of you are conversing and then says something like, "Will that be cash or charge? Do you prefer delivery Tuesday or Thursday?" Yes, you can have success with this close, however you also can rub people the wrong way because this is a bold way to close.

Now let us go to the relevant story close. This close requires you to be able to give examples immediately of people who have bought from you and have been very pleased with the results. Stories are a great way to illustrate a point, and the relevant story close can be an excellent way to prevent that client from walking out the door and shopping around. Have several stories of satisfied customers up your sleeve and your closing ratio is bound to improve.

The ascending close works very well for the astute salesperson. This salesperson is very well prepared and knows that, if he or she asks question after question and gets a yes to these questions, the potential client is getting in the habit of saying yes and is on the way to closing. A good rule of thumb is that, if the salesperson can get six or more yeses, he or she is on the way to getting the big yes and closing. The key is that you better have your questions well thought-out, and you have to get those yeses because, if you do not, you have dug yourself a very big hole. Let us say that I am trying to get an advertiser involved with the Indianapolis Indians, and I am going to use the ascending close. If my first question to that person is "Do you like baseball?" then I have a very good chance of getting a "no" and failing immediately. If, on the other hand, my question is "When you have gone to a baseball game on a beautiful summer evening, with some friends, have you enjoyed yourself?" the odds are very strong that the person will say yes, and I am on my way. You see, almost everyone has been to a baseball game whether or not they are fans of the sport. Baseball's leisurely pace lends itself to conversation, and everyone can have an enjoyable time. The ascending close is a great way to make sales, but you have to be very thorough and on top of your game to use it effectively or else you will not get the stream of yeses needed to make it work.

The puppy dog close works very well and is a very safe way to make a sale. If you are selling cars, the puppy dog close enables the potential client to test drive one. If you are selling baseball like I am, you do your best to get the potential client to go to the ballpark and see the beautiful grass and experience all the sights and sounds. This close is so basic that, unfortunately, many salespeople overlook it. This close really appeals to a person's senses.

The Ben Franklin close will work wonders for you as long as you are well prepared. It is similar to the ascending close in that regard. It is called the Ben Franklin close simply because Ben Franklin used it to his advantage many times. The salesperson draws a vertical line in the center of a piece of paper and on one side lists "pros" and on the other side lists "cons." Assuming that the salesperson knows his or her stuff, the "pros" certainly will outnumber the "cons." This can really impress the potential client when he sees his potential objections listed in the "con" column. The salesperson can overcome the objections right then and there.

With the summary close, the salesperson goes over all the benefits and tries to close simply by asking for the order. The benefits in the summary close will be similar to the "pros" in the Ben Franklin close. This is another close where the salesperson has to be well prepared. The alternative close, the puppy dog close, and the relevant story close do not require the same kind of knowledge and preparation as do the ascending, Ben Franklin, and summary closes.

There is one other close that I would like to mention. It is very good and should be used only in certain situations. It is called the "no" close. The "no" close works best on people who like to say no. I am serious! Great closers are great listeners. If you are dealing with someone who is very negative, use this close. At the opportune time, say, "Is there any reason we should not go ahead with this?" The potential client, who loves to say no, says, "Well, no." Closed! This close has worked wonders for me. It can be used on anyone, but works best with people who tend to be negative.

There is an old expression "Seeing is believing." This is true for the majority of people. The salesperson can say whatever he or she chooses, but must have a pen and paper handy to close. This is one reason that the Ben Franklin close works so well. It is in writing and this enhances its credibility.

Let us remember what we discussed at the outset. To close successfully, you must eliminate or push aside the fear of rejection. If you can do that (and it is not easy), you are on the way! Success shall be yours!

I think it is time to "close" this chapter.

About The Author

Howard Kellman

Howard Kellman has been a sports broadcaster, professional speaker and salesperson for more than 25 years. He has filled in on the Chicago White Sox and Cleveland Cavaliers broadcasts and is the radio and television voice of the Triple A Indianapolis Indians Baseball Team. He has been the Indians top salesperson more than two decades selling radio advertising, souvenir program advertising, billboards, season tickets, group outings and promotional packages. Originally from New York, the Indianapolis Indians brought him to the Midwest right out of Brooklyn College. He announces the High School Football and Basketball Game of the Week on television in central Indiana and gives speeches and does sales seminars. Despite a busy schedule, Howard still finds time to run and lift weights almost every day.

Howard Kellman
501 West Maryland
Indianapolis, IN 46225
Phone: 317.824.1035
Fax: 317.269.3541
Email: howard@howarrdkellman.com
www.howardkellman.com

Chapter 6

A New Selling Commitment

Charles J. Clarke, III

Portions of this chapter are excerpts from
Charles J. Clarke III's "Bulls, Owls, Lambs and
Tigers®: Personality Selling,
Personality Marketing—How to Sell More
New Homes," ©2003.

How many of you ask each and every person you give a sales presentation,

"What do you think about going ahead with this today?"

or some "call to action"?

What is your guess as to the percentage of salespeople who do? Interestingly enough, only about 50% of salespeople report that they even ask their "A" buyers to "go ahead with this today," much less everyone.

The "New Selling Commitment" is two-fold. It means asking everyone, 100% of the time, always, **"What do you think about going ahead with this today?"** *and* **matching your personality to the personalities of your prospects** 100% of the time, as well. Let's begin by discussing the first element—the commitment to ask, **"What do you think about going ahead with this today?"**—and end with the **personality matching** aspect of my "New Selling Commitment."

You can divide the entire selling process into my Critical Path of Selling's five basic steps regardless of what you sell.

1. Meet, greet, and connect with the prospect's "animal" personality.
2. Qualify for (a) **ready**, (b) **willing**, and (c) **able**.
3. Demonstrate your product (presentation).
4. Selection—determine which product they like best, and whether it is something they would like to own.
5. Overcome objections and close the sale.

All five steps are critical, but in this chapter we will focus on only two—step one (connecting with the buyer's personality, which we will discuss at the end of the article), and step four (selection). Step four includes asking the crucial question "**What do you think about going ahead with this today?**" You may at first think that asking, "**What do you think about going ahead with this today?**" is a part of step five (overcoming objections and closing the sale). However, "**What do you think about going ahead with this today?**" is actually an extension of the demonstration or presentation, and what we refer to as the **selection process**.

If you ask this question, and the prospective buyer says yes, then you obviously proceed to step five and close the sale. You don't need to overcome any objections at all—just close the buyer or prepare the purchase agreement. If the prospective buyer says no, you inquire, "Why?" which will flush out one of only seven objections[1] no matter what you are selling. When you ask, "**What do you think about going ahead with this today?**" three possibilities could unfold.

1. You may get the sale.
2. You flush out one of the seven possible objections.
3. You shorten the buying process. You now know what the prospect's objection is even if you don't close the sale today. Knowing the objection gives you a better opportunity to close the sale the next time.

---

[1] NOTE: All buyer objections ultimately are rooted in just seven objections, which is the topic for another chapter: "The Only Seven Objections with Specific Strategies to Overcome Them for Each Personality." ("Bulls, Owls, Lambs and Tigers®: Personality Selling, Personality Marketing—How to Sell More New Homes," ©2003.)

The Four Magic Questions

There are four questions salespeople should ask everyone after completing the qualifying, demonstration, and presentation (whether a salesperson's demonstration or a self-demonstration). Of course, this line of questioning can be varied and made specific to the product you are selling.

1. How do you like everything you have seen or heard so far?
2. Which do you like best, according to your needs?
3. Is this something you would like to own?
4. What do you think about going ahead with this today? **or** How do you feel about going ahead with this today?

Again, the first three questions will naturally vary depending on what you are selling, but the fourth question can be the same, regardless of your product. Most salespeople don't have a problem with the first three steps, but many resist the fourth, which is the most important and vital step—"The Call to Action."

The Seven Reasons

Why a salesperson would not ask 100% of the time, "What do you think about going ahead with this today?"

Salespeople everywhere avoid asking their prospects, **"What do you think about going ahead with this today?"** or any form of asking for the sale. Instead of closing, they offer explanations, rationales, and endless excuses. It may seem as though there would be as many different excuses for not closing the sale as there are salespeople. Actually, each of the reasons fits in one of the following seven categories.

1. FEAR OF REJECTION or I don't want to look foolish.

You develop a scenario in your mind in which you ask for the sale, and the prospect responds with something like, "Are you crazy? What kind of idiot are you, asking me that?" So, you decide maybe it's not worth the risk to ask, and that maybe if you're nice to them they'll just tell you when they are ready to buy, as they would a clerk.

2. I don't want to come across as too pushy.

This excuse is especially prevalent if you don't make decisions quickly yourself and would not want to endure a pushy salesperson if *you* were the buyer. Some salespeople would prefer sincerely to earn less money and preserve their image as a nice person, rather than appear pushy.

3. MY JUDGEMENT or I don't think the prospect is ready.

This mindset is "prejudging" the prospect. It's the attitude that says, "I've been doing this many years, and my experience tells me that a person like this is not ready to buy." Why not ask the *prospect* and stop judging other people?

4. I'm not ready.

If reason number three is "I don't think *they* are ready," number four is "*I'm* not ready." Maybe you do not think you have given the prospect enough information. Or, perhaps you're convinced certain things must be done before a sale can take place. Is your idea of the perfect sale one in which you complete your entire presentation without interruption? Sometimes this excuse comes in the form of, "I have not earned the right to ask, '**What do you think about going ahead with this today?**'" This is a BIG misconception. When the prospect is in the same room with you, you have already earned the right to ask.

5. I believe I'll have another opportunity when I come back or the prospect comes back.

You can always sell them next time. The prospect seemed so sincere that you truly believed you really would get another opportunity. "The 'Be Back Bus' does not stop here if they meet a closer along the way" (...*that Big Bus that has all those people on it who say, "We'll be back...*").

6. I simply didn't feel well, or wasn't in the mood.

Sometimes, if you're feeling out of sorts, you won't want to make the effort to cause the sale to happen. Maybe you are dealing with a family crisis at home or issues with a co-worker. Whatever the excuse, Master Closers will not allow personal feelings to interfere with the performance of their job with excellence. Your buyer *does not care* if you didn't feel right that day. Yet, having said that, we have all been there and had this happen to us. It is in this situation, however, that we must *"REFRAME"* immediately or lose the sale.

7. I forgot to ask.

Simply forgetting may seem like it would never happen, but it's something that *can* happen to anyone given the right distractions. A salesperson can become so involved with the buyer that sometimes the salesperson just "forgets to ask." When that happens, the salesperson often reverts to reason number five and believes "I'll have another opportunity." The solution is to have a system in place that ensures that all steps in the selling process are addressed with *every* prospect, and that every prospect is asked, **"What do you think about going ahead with this today?"**

The element that all seven reasons share is that they are all "I" centered. They are each based on the *salesperson's* opinions or feelings. One of the foundational principles of my BOLT system ("Bulls, Owls, Lambs and Tigers®") is that, as salespeople, we need to take the "I" out of the selling formula. Again, this chapter will delve more deeply into that concept in its second half.

Consider this...

> Which of the seven reasons affect *you* the most and hinder *you* from asking for the sale 100% of the time, all the time, with everyone, always, no exceptions? Why not rank *your* top three?

I have had the opportunity to see first-hand the remarkable effects of my "New Selling Commitment" in action, through my observations of and experience with a broad cross-section of industries. Unfortunately, I have also witnessed examples of sales lost when it is *not* implemented.

The Automobile Industry

The "Yo, Vinny" Story ("Yo, let's do it!")

Once when I was in Philadelphia, I visited a new Cadillac dealership that had a memorable salesperson named Vinny. He had Rocky Balboa's Philadelphia accent, and he said "yo" at the start or end of every sentence.

I was looking at the new Cadillacs when Vinny approached me and said, "Yo, I'm Vinny and you are?" After I introduced myself he asked, "Yo, how do you like this particular Cadillac?"

"I love it," I said.

Vinny replied, "Yo, let's do it." When I declined, he asked, "Yo, why?"

"I live in Tampa," I said, because I lived there at the time.

"Yo, we ship." I said no again and Vinny asked, "Yo, is there any chance of your *ever* buying from me now or later?"

"No", I said, "there's no chance." He dismissed himself by simply saying, "Yo, have a nice day." (I now refer to that as the "Vinny dump.")

I followed Vinny around for the next 15 to 20 minutes and found that he basically used this methodology with *everyone*. By the time I left the dealership, he had someone in the closing room. In actuality, Vinny was the dealership's most successful salesperson. He had created a very strict time management system, which included a "call to action" 100% of the time—"**Yo, let's do it.**"

Granted, "Yo, let's do it," will not play in most cities, but the point is that Vinny was *always* asking for a decision. In some cases the person said yes. When the prospect said no, Vinny was able to determine whether the objection was one he could overcome. As I mentioned before, keep in mind that Vinny's technique does have one great advantage—its inherent time management. He never wastes time giving a lengthy presentation to someone who is not truly interested. He weeds out the non-interested prospects within the first couple minutes, and politely excuses himself. No, I do not recommend his specific technique, but I do endorse his *always* asking for the sale.

The Homebuilding Industry

In the new home sales industry, as well as in many other industries, a perpetual myth exists that says that people do not buy during their very first visit. Therefore, many companies actually teach their salespeople that generally they should **not ask** for the sale the first time a prospective buyer visits a model home. Salespeople and sales managers who would not buy the first day themselves believe that others would not buy the first day, and so perpetuate this myth. This myth also links to reason number two—the salespeople's fear of being too pushy.

I have devised closing questions for each particular industry with which I work. The questions I recommend that new home salespeople ask after their demonstrations are:

1. How do you like our community?
2. Is this a community you would like to live in?
3. Which of our homes do you like the best for you needs?
4. Is this a home you would like to own?
5. What do you think about going ahead with this today?
6. (If they say no, the new home salesperson asks, "Why not?" which will expose one of the seven buyer objections.)

An interesting and highly accurate "rule of thumb" in the new home sales business is that approximately **90% of the total traffic that comes through new model homes never comes back.** For example, out of every 1,000 people who come through furnished models, roughly 100 return. Another interesting statistic is revealed when we ask the people touring new home communities: (1) Would you buy a home the first day you saw it? (2) Have you *ever* bought a home the first day? (3) Would you *prefer* to buy a home the first day if you had decided to move (i.e., **ready**), liked the home and community (i.e., **willing**), and were in the price range and could afford the home (i.e., **able**)?

Thousands of potential buyers nationwide have completed this survey, and 50% of respondents answered yes to at least two of the three questions. (This percentage comprises mostly Bulls and Tigers, which we will discuss later in more detail.) My BOLT system is founded on this idea: "If I always sell the way I would like to be sold, I could be losing at least ½ of my potential sales." Why would anyone want to take the chance of waiting for their prospects to "come back" to ask, **"What do you think about going ahead with this today?"** if 90% of the people are *never* coming back? Yet, that's the trend in one major industry after another, and countless sales are lost as a result.

A large western community homebuilder and developer with whom I consult and for whom I provide sales training shared the following story. I had conducted my Master Closer Trilogy for that company. At the end of the three-day seminar, I asked how many of the salespeople would sign the Charles Clarke Commitment, which simply says, "For the next 30 days I will 100% of the time, all the time, with everyone, always, no exceptions, ask, '**What do you think about going ahead with this today?**' (or some facsimile)." Usually when I ask for this commitment after the Master Closer Trilogy, about 50% of the sales staff signs the commitment, and about 50% of those who sign it actually *do* it. The salespeople who do follow through, however, are on their way to becoming Master Closers, and historically literally double their sales.

One of the salespeople at this particular home building company had committed to asking *everyone*, "**What do you think about going ahead with this today?**" Before the community's official opening, she was in the model, and one of the sub-contractors (the grout man) was on the bathroom floor, grouting tile. Recalling her signed commitment, the salesperson asked him: (1) How do you like our community? (2) Is this a community you'd like to live in? (3) Which of our homes do you like the best for your needs? (he had already been doing work on the three other models); and (4) Is this a home you'd like to own? (*Keep in mind, these were $800,000 homes to well over a million dollar homes, and she had already "judged" the grout man as not earning more than $20 per hour*). Would *you* have gone on and asked, "**What do you think about going ahead with this today?**"

She did, and the grout man said no. When she asked, "Why not?" the grout man responded that he would have to bring his wife by. That didn't encourage the salesperson because she "knew" (see reason number three) that the couple couldn't afford the home. Finally, not knowing why, the salesperson asked the grout man what his wife did. He said that she was Executive Vice President of a large national company and was earning a considerable salary. It also turned out that the grout man owned his own company and was only doing a favor for the owner for the grand opening. Incidentally, the grout man and his wife bought a home there the following weekend.

After that the salesperson started asking "**What do you think about going ahead with this today?**" to *everyone*, even the UPS man. By the way, the salesperson had never sold any homes, new or existing before, nor had she worked in sales. She had previously worked in customer service. Yet, she became one of the company's top salespeople by asking everyone, 100% of the time, "**What do you think about going ahead with this today?**"

The Retail Industry

Selling Suits

I was in upstate New York working with a company when, on our lunch break, the president of the company said he needed to see his attorney and asked that I travel with him. To pass the time during his appointment, I went to a men's clothing store that displayed a banner reading, "*$1,000 suits for $300. Moving to the Suburbs Sale.*" I made clear to the salesman inside that I had only 15 minutes to spare, and warned him that I was browsing only and had no intention of buying any clothing.

He quickly convinced me to try on five suit jackets and eventually one pair of pants that matched the last suit coat I had on. As I was admiring this last suit, the salesman asked me, "How do you like our suits?" I said I really liked them.

"Which one do you like the best?" I said I liked the one I had on best. He asked if I liked any others, and I said yes, I liked the other two as well. He said, "Fine, I'll tell you what I'll do. I'll put these three suits on hold for you. You told me earlier you could come back at 5:30, so I won't let anybody get these suits until 6 p.m."

I said, "Absolutely, guaranteed. I'll be back at 5:30."

So, how many of the suits did I end up buying?

None. I had every intention of buying those suits—all three, in fact. But, I found myself on the airplane that night at 11 p.m., and suddenly I thought, "The suits!"

The salesperson "knew" I was coming back, and so did his sales manager. I myself planned to go back that day, and yet I didn't (see reason number five). I became distracted and focused on something else.

This is how the scenario *could* have gone. The salesperson could have said, "So, how do you like our suits?"

"I love your suits."

"Which one do you like the best?"

"The one I have on."

"Do you like any of the others?"

"Yes, I do. Those other two."

"What do you think about going ahead with this today?"

I would have said no. That may surprise you, but I say no to everything at first, and I had planned on coming back and purchasing them later. Yet, after I refused to buy, he could have said, "You really like and are impressed by these suits, right? And, you see high value, right? Why don't you give me your credit card, and by the time you're out of the dressing room, I will have all three of the suits wrapped up for you." Then I would have said yes to all three suits. Everyone needs a nudge! That salesperson didn't even *try* to close the sale, but just went directly for the *appointment*. How about you? Do *you* sometimes just go directly to the appointment? One of the definitions of a Master Closer is a salesperson who **convinces** prospective buyers to do something beneficial for them that the buyers would not have otherwise done.

"Bulls, Owls, Lambs and Tigers®: Personality Selling and Personality Marketing"

One of the keys to successful selling and marketing.

In the beginning of this chapter I said we would deal with two aspects of my Critical Path of Selling—step number one (meeting, greeting, and connecting with their "animal" personality), and step number four (the selection close). We have dealt just with step four, the first aspect of the "New Selling Commitment." Now, we'll examine briefly the second aspect with a summary of my "Bulls, Owls, Lambs and Tigers®: Personality Selling."

One of the questions I am always asked at my seminars is, "Wouldn't you offend someone by always asking, 'What do you think about going ahead with this today'?" I always respond, "It depends!" It depends on how you present it to the prospects. Remember, "it's all in the presentation," and that means connecting with *their* personality.

If you are a salesperson, do you sell the way you would like to be sold? If you are in marketing, do you market the way you would like others to market to you?

Consider this...

> If you answered yes (as most people do) to either or both questions, then you are possibly losing at least ½ to ¾'s of your potential market and potential sales.

As salespeople and sales managers, what, then, is the best way to market or sell a particular product or service? The answer, quite simply, is that **IT DEPENDS!** It depends on the prospects' personality, or what I call their Bull, Owl, Lamb or Tiger®.

The concept of "Bulls, Owls, Lambs and Tigers®" is based on two variables:

1. How "tell-oriented," "bossy," and "**assertive**" a person is (or is not)
2. How much **positive emotion** (all emotions except anger) they display or do not display to other people.

Those two "predictors" have a high degree of accuracy in predicting *how* prospects buy, *what* they buy, and *when* they buy. Moreover, these two simple variables provide a clear and accurate picture of other aspects of the prospects and their personalities. I first began developing "Bulls, Owls, Lambs and Tigers®" while completing my masters degree in sociology and psychology at the University of Hawaii. I continued researching and working on this concept while working toward my Ph.D. at the University of Arizona and the University of Maryland. My adult life's work has been dedicated to "Personality Selling and Personality Marketing," and "Personality Motivation."

Look at the chart below and decide which two animals you think you are. As you consider your personal levels of assertiveness and emotion, which animal emerges as most like you? Which would be second? For instance, if you were a highly assertive and *somewhat* emotional person (perhaps a 4 on assertive and a B on emotion) you would be a Bull with Tiger, which indicates a dominant "Bull" personality with visible "Tiger" characteristics. A highly *un*-assertive, somewhat emotional person would be classified as an Owl with Lamb.

As you consider the make-up of your own personality, consider also what animal personalities are hardest for you to sell. Generally, **salespeople have the most difficult time selling a prospect of**

the opposite animal personality. Bulls have a difficult time selling Lambs; Lambs have a difficult time selling Bulls. Conversely, Tigers tend to struggle selling Owls, and Owls often struggle selling Tigers. **These personality differences and difficulties translate into _lost_ sales.**

Bulls, Owls, Lambs and Tigers®

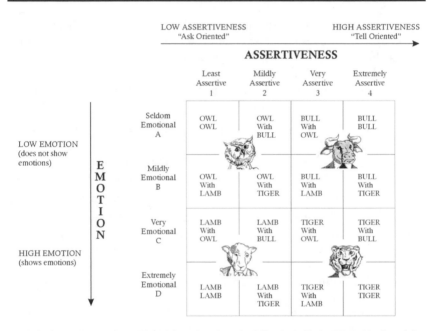

		LOW ASSERTIVENESS "Ask Oriented"		HIGH ASSERTIVENESS "Tell Oriented"	
		ASSERTIVENESS			
		Least Assertive 1	Mildly Assertive 2	Very Assertive 3	Extremely Assertive 4
LOW EMOTION (does not show emotions)	Seldom Emotional A	OWL OWL	OWL With BULL	BULL With OWL	BULL BULL
	Mildly Emotional B	OWL With LAMB	OWL With TIGER	BULL With LAMB	BULL With TIGER
HIGH EMOTION (shows emotions)	Very Emotional C	LAMB With OWL	LAMB With BULL	TIGER With OWL	TIGER With BULL
	Extremely Emotional D	LAMB LAMB	LAMB With TIGER	TIGER With LAMB	TIGER TIGER

Bull, Owls, Lambs and Tigers® is a registered trademark of Charles J. Clarke, III. ©1994 Copyright, Charles J. Clarke, III. All rights reserved. No reproduction allowed. Charles Clarke Consulting Seminars, 770-287-7878, Fax 770-287-8994.

The population as a whole comprises approximately 25% of each animal personality. Bear in mind that the BOLT system is not sex-biased. Approximately half of all Bulls are women and half of all Lambs are men. It is also important to note that the system has no value judgment. No animal is better than the other. My BOLT system is not foolproof, but it has roughly a 90% probability of being accurate. (Wouldn't you love to take 90% probability to Las Vegas?)

The following chart is a summary of my BOLT system and the unique characteristics and buying habits of each animal type. All of the information included is based on 30 years of my research.

	Definitions	Questions They Ask	When They Buy

The Bull	1) Bottom line, get to the point, business first
	2) Somewhat abrasive personality
	3) **Control** oriented
	4) "Hurry up"
	5) **Highly assertive, low emotion (except the emotion of anger)**
	6) Bull "turn-offs":
	  a) Answering a question with a question (Bulls *hate* that)
	  b) Imagination, testimonial, and trial closes
	  c) Salespeople who are too emotional, and too "nice"
		1) How much?
		2) What's your **best** price?
		3) What does it come with? (Interested in knowing what "extras" they can get.)
		4) How soon can I have it?
			1) When they want to
			2) When *you* get out of their way
			3) When they are assured they have the best price, and that you won't lower the price
			4) Bulls say their preference is to buy the first day, even for extremely expensive items (homes, automobiles, and private airplanes)
			5) Sell the "steak" not the "sizzle" with Bulls
			6) **Fast decisions makers, high risk takers**

The Owl	1) Extremely analytical, detail oriented, business first
	2) Person who corrects almost everything you do
	3) Loves **order** and systems
	4) **Low assertiveness, low emotion**
	5) Owl "turn-offs":
	  a) Too much excitement, and too much emotion
	  b) Salespeople who do not stay on track
	  c) Urgency closes
		1) Tell me about the manufacturing process
		2) What materials are used?
		3) What kind of warranty does it include?
		4) Questions about value
		5) Questions about everything
			1) When all of their questions have been answered
			2) Answering all of an Owl's questions could take several visits or appointments
			3) Owls buy with logic and justify with logic, not emotion
			4) **Slow decision makers, low risk takers**

The Lamb	1) Wants to **please** everyone, social before business
	2) Takes a long time to make up their mind
	3) Dislikes confrontation and arguments
	4) **Low assertiveness, highly emotional**
	5) Lamb "Turn Offs"
	  a) Pushy sales people
	  b) Urgency and take-away closes
		1) Which do **YOU** like best?
		2) What is your best seller?
		3) Lambs ask friendly, non-threatening questions
		4) "Mr. Rodgers" or "Neighborly" questions
			1) When the purchase has been validated by someone else
			2) Validation could take several visits or appointments
			3) **Slowest decision makers, low risk takers**
			4) **Highest level of buyer's remorse**

The Tiger	1) Dominated by wanting **fun and excitement**, social before business
	2) Extremely talkative
	3) Distracted by "shiny objects"
	4) **Highly assertive, highly emotional**
	5) Tiger "Turn Offs"
	  a) Too much detail
	  b) Ben Franklin closes
	  c) Not enough emotion
		1) Tigers ask completely unrelated questions, due in part to their distraction by shiny objects and/or "shiny thoughts."
		2) Tiger questions often have "nothing to do with anything"
			1) When they are excited
			2) Tigers buy on their first visit (or not at all) even for expensive items. If they don't, they rarely return for a second visit.
			3) Sell the "sizzle" and not the "steak" with a Tiger
			4) **Fastest decision makers, highest risk takers**
			5) **Impulsive, compulsive buyers**

Product Has a Personality

You and your prospects aren't the only members of the selling process who have animal personalities. *Everything* you sell has a Bull, Owl, Lamb or Tiger® personality, as well. As salespeople, we need to **match the personality of the product to the personality of the buyer**. Think for a moment—why do some people walk into your place of business or showroom and immediately love a particular product while other buyers dislike it? Or, why is it that some people appreciate particular features of your product or services that others do not? It is often due to a "personality conflict" between the buyer and your product.

Just as you must match your personality to the buyer's, the personality of the product *must* match the personality of the buyer; if not, the buyer will not like it, and thus, will not buy it. This simple principle applies to every part of the business world, no matter what you are selling or marketing. **The benefit of a feature is different for each personality**. Different people see things differently, but a Master Closer has learned to speak the "animal talk" of potential buyers in order to market to them and make the sale.

Consider this...

> All products have personalities. No matter what you are selling— automobiles, clothing, furniture, or computers—these concepts apply to you.

Homes

An example of product personality.

Homes are a powerful example of product personality as it relates to *all* industries. For example, does everyone like an "open space" home where the kitchen flows into the family room, and where ceilings are vaulted into a cathedral effect? When I ask my seminar attendees, "How many of you personally like an 'open space' home with a flowing kitchen and family room, and cathedral ceilings?" around half respond positively. A past issue of the National Association of Home Builders national survey of buyers' preferences reported that only 15.8% of home buyers prefer "complete openness" in their homes' kitchen and family room arrangement; 45.9% prefer the arrangement to be visually open but with a divider; 20.9% prefer the rooms to be side-by-side, but with a wall between; and 17.4% prefer the kitchen and family room to be completely separate areas. Clearly particular buyer personalities tend to connect with the "personalities" of particular homes and reject those of other homes.

For example, Tigers and Bulls would look at a home with an 18-foot ceiling and a plant shelf 12 feet up, and love it because it's fun, exciting, and different for the Tiger, and striking, impressive, and statement-making for the Bull. Yet the Lamb could feel that it is too overwhelming, and the Owl would question the loss of heat or air-conditioning and ask, "How would I dust up there?" (Tigers might comment, "Dusting...interesting concept!")

What often happens is that a Tiger selling homes will walk a prospective Owl buyer into an "open space" home and *praise* the virtues of the cathedral ceilings, along with the beauty of the window at the apex of the ceiling, and the skylight in the kitchen. The more the Tiger salesperson emphasizes the openness, the more they are "unselling" the Owl—turning away a population of buyers who report that they prefer low ceilings and completely separate, or partially separate, areas for the kitchen or family room.

Each Animal's Favorite Room

	Bull	Owl	Lamb	Tiger
Favorite Room	"Me" room or den, and an impressive front entrance	Practical kitchen, separate living room and separate dining room	Family room with a cozy fireplace, or a great room	Sexual and sensual master bedroom and master bathroom (owner's retreat)

Automobiles

What kind of automobile does each animal prefer? Which one prefers large automobiles to small automobiles even in times of higher gasoline costs? Which animal prefers the darker colors of brown, black, and dark blue in terms of the exterior and interior packaging of the automobile? Which likes pastels? Which likes red and jewel tone colors? Which likes neutral colors like beige? Every year color experts try to convince the population that "the color of the year" will be mauve or some other exciting color by which Bulls and Owls are usually not motivated. The following chart outlining the animal personalities' preferences examines these questions.

Summary of Preferences

What the animals want products to accomplish, and the animals' favorite colors

	Bull	Owl	Lamb	Tiger
Wants Product To Be...	Striking, impressive, and statement-making	Practical, efficient, and functional	Warm, cozy, and comfortable	Fun, exciting, and different
Favorite Color	Black, dark brown, dark blue, and hunter green	Beige, light gray, and neutral colors	Pastels (light blue, yellow) and soft colors	Red, primary colors and jewel colors (ruby, sapphire, emerald)

Charles Clarke III's "100% COMMITMENT"

Tying both concepts together

What if you were to, 100% of the time, all of the time, with every-one, always, no exceptions, ask, "**What do you think about going ahead with this today?**" and actually *become* **the personality of your buyers 100% of the time**? Do you believe that if you consistently did these two things your sales would increase? You know the answer is yes. In fact, these two selling concepts in concert can literally **more than double your sales**.

If you are ready to make both of these commitments for 30 days, e-mail us at Bolt@personalityselling.com with your commitment. Also, let us know how your sales increase during and at the end of your commitment. For more information, on "Bulls, Owls, Lambs and Tigers®," review our Web site: www.personalityselling.com.

Good luck and great selling!

About The Author

Charles J. Clarke, III

Charles J. Clarke III, world-class speaker and sales and marketing consultant, is author and creator of "Bulls, Owls, Lambs and Tigers®: Personality Selling and Personality Marketing." Charles's BOLT selling system consistently and dramatically increases sales and profits in diverse industries worldwide. His impressive résumé includes having been an instructor at the Universities of Arizona and Maryland, department Chairman and Professor of sociology at Mount Mercy College, President of Clarke Property Management and Clarke Investments, Inc., first Vice President of Sales Training for Century 21's Texas and Louisiana Region, and President and Regional Director of Florida's Today's American Builder. The scope of Charles' speaking and sales training includes over 200 engagements yearly with companies of every size and industry. Described by one client as a "Johnny Appleseed...spreading good will and increased sales and profits wherever he goes," Charles' sales techniques and concepts are renowned for consistently increasing the confidence and sales of the salespeople he trains. A member of the National Speaker's Association and numerous other related organizations, Charles is currently a builder and developer, and President of Charles Clarke Consulting, Inc., located near Atlanta, Georgia. Charles Clarke Consulting, Inc., is an internationally recognized, full-service consulting firm serving diverse businesses across the nation and abroad.

Charles Clarke
Charles Clarke Consulting, Inc.
PO Box 2817
Gainesville, GA 30503
Phone: 770.287.7808
Fax: 770.287.8994
E-mail: bolt@personalityselling.com
www.personalityselling.com

120

Chapter 7

Against The Wall

Jim McCarty, CLU

Some say the cards falling from his grasp that hot summer afternoon were aces and eights; a full house—two black aces, two black eights, and the red eight of diamonds. Others say that the last card wasn't the eight of diamonds at all, but rather the queen of that same suit. Most people just don't know for sure. What is known, however, is that before he slumped sideways and fell to the floor due to a fatal head wound, James Butler Hickok was seated in the wrong place.

"Wild Bill," as many frontier historians reference him, had cheated death many times before. As a highly feared gunfighter, well-respected lawman, and avid card player, James Hickok had "dispatched more men to the shades of Hell than any other man who ever lived." This, according to Henry Onsgard, who wrote about Bill in his 1926 bestseller, *The Romance of the Black Hills*.

Due in part to his living legend, which was promulgated by local newspapers, dime novels, and various national publications, "Wild Bill" had developed a long list of men who swore they would kill him at the first opportunity. Because of this, he always insisted on sitting with his back against the wall while participating in any game of chance. On August 2, 1876, however, the seating arrangements were different. Engaging in a serious game of poker, Bill lost the wall seat to a fellow gambler, Charlie Rich, and was forced to settle for one that would position his back to the open door of Nuttall and Mann's #10 Saloon located in Deadwood, South Dakota.

As the game ensued and the cards were played, a twenty-five year old drifter named Jack McCall, seeking revenge for one of Hickok's past misdeeds, put a bullet in the back of "Wild Bill's" head, thrusting him into history as one of the most colorful figures in Western lore.

What do you suppose was the underlying reason that James Butler "Wild Bill" Hickok lost his life that Wednesday afternoon, at the tender age of thirty-nine? Was it the particular cards he held, frequently referred to as "the deadman's hand," or was it the position in which he was seated, which exposed his back to the saloon front door? I think we will all agree that it was his poor position at the gaming table that caused him to pay the ultimate price. Salespeople can learn a valuable lesson from Bill's demise. That is, positioning is everything!

When you think of positioning in the sales process, visualize a large "X" representing the expenditure of time and energy. The center of the "X" represents the least expenditure and the separations on the left and right reflect the most. Picture "positioning" occurring at the extreme *left side* and the "close" taking place at the intersection. This graphic clearly illustrates that successful selling begins by devoting maximum energy and time to the "set up," or positioning, well in advance of any attempt to close. If this positioning is done effectively, there will be little or no resistance when you ask your prospect to buy. Conversely, if little time and energy are devoted to proper positioning, your closing efforts will be fraught with objections, frustrations, and delays. These obstacles and hindrances are reflected by the ever-widening gap as you move to the right of the intersection on our diagram.

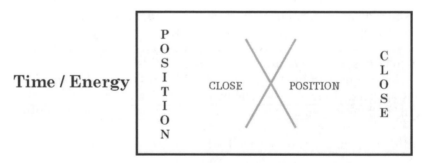

When resistance and hesitation are met along the way, don't forge ahead. Instead, identify where you are on the "X"-shaped model.

Then, employ the "back-up" strategy. That is, back up and reposition before making another attempt to close.

Effective positioning in the world of sales enables you, the salesperson, to pique interest, generate curiosity, and create an atmosphere in which people feel compelled to buy. This positioning begins with how you think of yourself, that is, how you picture yourself in your mind's eye.

In September of 1993, I attended a delightful and thought-provoking business seminar that featured a fascinating presentation by Mr. Allen Bloom. Allen is the Executive Vice President of marketing and public relations for The Ringling Brothers and Barnum & Bailey Circus, a division of Feld Productions. In his speech entitled "Marketing Can Be a Circus of Fun," Allen told how he and his staff of 75 employees regularly draw over 25 million people each year to worldwide, spectacular live productions of the "Greatest Show On Earth." Interestingly, Allen said, even though the sign on his office door reads "Marketing and Public Relations," he has never thought of himself as being anything other than a promoter! This self-image was evidenced quickly during his presentation by the fact that everything Allen does is done with panache, the dashing elegance of manor and style. Allen "big deals" everything! He truly thinks of himself as a promoter, and that is exactly what he is. Allen's speech and mannerisms were proof-positive that if you hold a vision of yourself as anything, including a prosperous salesperson, that vision will become a reality. We do, in fact, become what we think about, and even the scriptures agree for they tell us, "As a man thinketh in his heart, so is he." Therefore, begin your quest for sales success by first positioning that successful vision of yourself firmly in your own mind's eye.

The truth of the matter is, however, you cannot promote anything enthusiastically unless you yourself consider it to be a thing of great value and become excited about it first. You must exude a high level of passion and conviction for what you sell. There is no question about it, conviction sells! And, in this hi-tech, electronic age, salespeople should remind themselves periodically that this conviction must come from their heart, not from some "box" they have plugged into the wall, called a computer. On the pathway to sales success, there is no substitute for a deep-seated belief in yourself, your products, and your services! Allen Bloom is excited and passionate about "The Greatest Show on Earth," for example, and his enthusiasm clearly shows.

Just because your products and services appear to be exciting and valuable to you, however, doesn't mean that they will always appear exciting and valuable to each and every one of your clients. A story told by Dale Carnegie in the mid-1930s illustrates this point well. Dale said, "I go fishing up in Maine every summer. Personally, I am very fond of strawberries and cream. But I find, for some strange reason, the fish prefer worms. So when I go fishing, I don't think about what I want, I think about what the fish want. Because of this, I don't bait the hook with strawberries and cream." Mr. Carnegie points out in his timeless and meaningful message that, just because something is important to us, it doesn't necessarily mean that it is important to all consumers. As you wouldn't waste your time baiting a hook with strawberries and cream, don't waste your time offering the advantages of your particular products and services to prospects who can't truly benefit from them.

On a recent flight aboard Delta Airlines, I listened as the flight attendant demonstrated various features of the aircraft and safety procedures. Upon completion of a visual demonstration detailing how the seatbelt operates, gesturing toward the emergency exits, and pointing out the aisle path lighting, she went on to state, "In the unlikely event of loss of cabin pressure, oxygen masks will fall from the panels above your head. Reach forward, grab your mask, place it over your nose and mouth, secure it with the elastic band, and breathe normally." Concluding her message, she said, "Secure your mask before assisting others." The attendant's admonishment to "secure your mask first" reinforces a message that I convey on a regular basis while conducting skill-building sessions for salespeople. Working with insurance agents and financial advisors nationwide through my business, Showbizselling.com, I constantly advise that they protect themselves, their families, and their business partners first. This should be done before offering their products and services to others. Make your conviction and enthusiasm evident. Sell your products to yourself first! Position your products and services as valuable to you, and set an example by owning them first.

To begin positioning for maximum sales achievement, there are four questions that you must initially answer. They are:

1. What do you sell?
2. Do you sell your product itself or do you sell what your product or service will do for the customer?
3. Do people purchase what they want or do they purchase what they need?
4. Do they buy tangibles or intangibles?

To answer these questions, I offer the following vignette from an article I published in February, 2002. In this manuscript, I referred to a young salesman, W.C. Coleman, and detailed a major turning point in his prosperity that was brought about when he came to a clear realization of what he actually sold. This enlightening discovery caused him to position his product in such a way as to lead toward exceptional sales success.

In 1901, during his travels to Alabama, "W.C.," as he was referred to by his friends, met another talented and energetic young man who had invented and manufactured a highly efficient, brilliantly luminescent lantern that was fueled by clean-burning, pressurized gas. This new lamp was offered as a replacement for the smoky oil burners that were in common use at the time. Consumers, however, failed to share the young entrepreneur's enthusiasm for the revolutionary product and, consequently, didn't exactly beat a path to his door.

Sales were terrible to the point where the young man offered his entire company, complete with inventory, to W.C. at a bargain price. Being a talented visionary and wise businessperson, W.C. seized upon the opportunity and quickly became the sole purveyor and builder of this marvelous appliance. But, alas, in spite of the fact that he was the consummate promoter and brimmed with excitement for his revolutionary lighting device, W.C.'s own sales efforts floundered miserably.

One evening, after months of disappointments, W.C. retired to his modest hotel room facing a particular mercantile store where the proprietor had rejected his sales attempts several times that very day. As darkness fell, W.C. lit one of his lanterns to illuminate the room, which had no electric lights. Immediately, his quarters were filled with a lustrous glow. Clean radiant light was everywhere! Instantly revealed was the secret that would lead to worldwide fame and great riches for W.C. and make him one of but a few multi-millionaires in existence at the turn of the century. The secret lay in discovering what he actually was selling. Running from his hotel, he crossed the street to make yet one more sales call on the store's reluctant owner. This time, however, W.C. was no longer selling the lanterns. He was now selling the light!

W.C. stressed that the clean, bright light would allow the proprietor to extend the hours customers could shop in his store. In addition, his goods would look radiant in the newfound glow. Colors would come alive, glasses would sparkle, and jewelry would glisten. Chrome fixtures would appear brilliant because of the new white light and shoppers would purchase more merchandise, which is exactly what the proprietor wanted! The owner immediately bought six lanterns for his personal use in the store and several more for his sales inventory. W.C. was on his way!

W.C.'s sales prowess and intense focus on selling light eventually progressed to the point where today, no matter where we are in the world, when we purchase lanterns, regardless of the actual brand, we commonly refer to the device by his name. We call it a "Coleman"!

When W.C. positioned light as his primary commodity, he conveyed a clear and powerful message to all salespeople. That is, people don't purchase tangibles, they purchase *intangibles*—what a product or service will do for them. Through your creative imagination, position your products and services as W.C. did, in such a way as to focus prospects' attention on the intangible benefits they provide. Don't sell the lantern, *sell the light!*

Position your wares emotionally. Connect them to your prospects' dreams, and success will quickly come. In his recent book *Selling Dreams*, author Gian Luigi states, "We are all drawn to various products and services because of their emotional link to our imagination. This intangible connection actually transcends the product or service's functional purpose." A good example of this emotional link is found by observing a motorcycle owner as he purchases a pair of Sampson Ripsaw exhaust pipes. Don't be fooled for a minute! He is not buying an extremely efficient, well-designed exhaust system; he is buying the emotional sight and sound. The exhaust system is merely the means to his emotional dream—to look and sound really "cool."

When W.C. discovered his true product, light, he was then able to position it as the key to the shopkeeper's dream of increased sales. When positioning during the sales process, remember that dreams are not products, they are experiences.

Many insurance agents and financial advisors frequently fail to sell their wonderful life insurance products because they attempt to sell the "lantern." Instead of focusing on the "light," they stress tax-deferred cash value growth, cost of insurance, internal rates of return, sub-account performance, dividends, sales charges, and the tenth year interpolated terminal reserve. They exacerbate their sales problems by telling clients that they *need* life insurance in spite of the fact that psychologists tell us that, at a certain hierarchy, people buy what they *want*, not what they need. There is an interesting story told of Bill Gates, founder and CEO of Microsoft, that reinforces this point. The story relates how, in 1999, Bill purchased the *Codex Leicester*—Leonardo da Vinci's notebook. Bill reportedly paid $31 million dollars for the manuscript. The question you might ask yourself is, did Bill *need* the notebook, or did he *want* the notebook? Successful insurance agents and financial advisors cause prospects to want their products by positioning them as the "light," the pathway to the dreams prospects are naturally drawn to because of strong emotional ties.

A few years ago, *Financial Services Journal Online* published one of my articles on sales achievement. In it, I offered an example of this emotional link as it related to life insurance. The article referenced a client whose deceased husband had owned a large sum of life insurance when he died. On one occasion, while speaking affectionately of her late husband, the widow mentioned that the greatest gift he ever gave her was the ability to visit her children without ever having to stay with them on a permanent basis. Her late husband gave her freedom, the emotional link to her dream of financial independence, which is exactly what she wanted.

Challenging your prospects' imaginations and connecting your products to their dreams is imperative for sales success! The purchase of life insurance, for instance, has nothing to do with the fact that it is good risk management or sound protection. But, it has everything to do with quality, choice, independence, and dignity—*dreams*. People want their dreams to come true. Life insurance is the only financial instrument that creates money where none existed before, and it is this money that brings those dreams to fruition. Life insurance won't keep people from dying, but the policy proceeds will keep their dreams from dying with them. Isn't this what most people really want? Position life insurance as such and great rewards will follow.

Just as a hammer must be effectively positioned to drive nails successfully, each of your sales tools, products, and services must be effectively positioned to drive results successfully as well. For example, if your prospect offers an objection or simply hesitates to implement your sound recommendation to purchase municipal bonds that will provide tax-free income during his retirement, your proposition must be repositioned, in such a way as to generate enthusiasm and cause your prospect to take action.

Effective positioning implements include analogies, token gifts, storytelling, and an intriguing, surprising one that will be revealed later in this chapter. Of these tools, the use of an analogy is the most expedient way to generate intrigue and develop a sense of urgency in your prospects. An example of using this strategy to position municipal bonds as a source of tax-free income during retirement would be:

"Mr. Prospect, there seems to be only one three-part rule for successful investing in real estate. The first part is 'location.' Would you happen to know what the other two are? (Of course, he answers, "Location, location.") The same rule applies to other successful investing as well. To achieve maximum tax-free income during retirement, it simply comes down, once again, to location, location, location, the particular place you invest your money.

Just as real estate developers build hotels in beach locations to attract tourist money, downtown locations to attract business money, and airport locations to gather travelers' money, we too have three locations in which to invest as well. They are locations that produce income that is taxed now, locations where income is taxed later, and some locations that will produce income that is never subject to income taxation at all. My job as your investment advisor is to make certain that we take full advantage of this tax-free location and maximize net-spendable income for you and your family during retirement. Isn't this what you want me to do? Just as success in real estate investing is highly dependent upon location, success found investing in other financial instruments is dependent upon location as well. Mr. Prospect, municipal bond investments occupy a coveted tax-free location. Let's relocate some of your assets there and increase your spendable income during retirement, fair enough?"

Superior sales results are often achieved with similar analogies that begin usually with questions that lead prospects to discover for themselves opportunities that they often overlook and ones that will improve their existing circumstance or situation. Turning a prospect's complacency and lack of interest into a burning desire is the real game in professional selling. Analogies will help you do this.

On the other hand, the use of an analogy to position yourself for the initial sales call is seldom effective. There is a better way. If you desire to telephone a prospect and schedule a face-to-face appointment, you must first position your call in such a way as to gain the maximum opportunity for sales success. You can accomplish this by sending the prospect something of minimal value before making the phone call. Send something that will flatter them, appeal to their ego, and bring a smile to their face. Tall order? How about an article cut from your local business journal that names them to a short list of "The Top 50 Most Successful Business Executives in the City of Orlando"? Prior to sending the small souvenir, make it special by laminating it in plastic at your local office supply store. Your cost for such a memento will be minimal, and your prospect will proudly show it off to others before you make your initial contact. Catch your target prospects doing something good and show them you are aware of it! This act of sending a token keepsake will favorably position you and enhance your reception when you make the call.

A third way to position your products and services is to tell an interesting story, one that raises curiosity, makes your point, and causes your prospects to buy in to your suggestions and recommendations. The most powerful type of story to tell is called a "signature story." A signature story is one that relates an experience that actually happened to you, and one in which you play an important part. My favorite signature story was told a short time ago by Tommy Gioiosa, prolific salesman and leading Herbalife distributor from Ormond Beach, Florida.

I met Tommy about two years ago and was fascinated early on by his masterful selling prowess and his quick journey to prosperity. Tommy's trip to the top of the sales profession began only eight short years ago in 1995. Destitute, with only 47 cents to his name, he entered into an agreement that offered unlimited success as a distributor for the nationally acclaimed Herbalife product line. His current level of success as one of the country's leading salesmen came about not because of his extensive product knowledge, engaging personality, or ability to set and achieve ambitious sales goals. Rather, it was due to a single-minded focus and dedication to just three basic habits that he developed early on in his career and continues to practice even to this day. Justifiably proud of his accomplishments, Tommy loves to relate his personal experience.

When I first heard Tommy's story, I was visiting with a young couple I met just minutes before. My new friends, who were also Herbalife distributors, recognized Tommy immediately as he turned his bright yellow Porsche into the driveway where we stood conversing that hot summer afternoon. Filled with excitement at the mere sight of this renowned purveyor of health products, they couldn't wait to engage him, listen to his story, and glean the secrets to his success.

With minimal encouragement, Tommy entered the conversation and happily related his personal Horatio Alger "rags to riches" signature story.

"A friend of mine and I," Tommy began, "launched our Herbalife careers by each placing ten pennies in one of our front trouser pockets every day. After each face-to-face interview during which we asked someone to buy, we would move one of the pennies to a different pocket. When all of the pennies were re-located, we took the remainder of the day off and relaxed. We talked to everyone, moved the ten pennies, and went to the beach. It was as simple as that!"

As his saga continued, Tommy explained, "It was essential that I personally used the merchandise I sold. Early in my life, I went through a period where I was considerably overweight, out of shape, and lacking the energy I thought I should have. Through the encouragement of my wife Sandy, I became a distributor for the Herbalife product line and an avid consumer as well. After demonstrating a high level of conviction by implementing the diet myself and achieving the physical fitness and energy level I desired, I became more confident and closed more sales. In addition, I encouraged my downline associates to 'walk the talk' by consuming Herbalife products themselves. As a result of this new-found enthusiasm, my total sales volume soared."

Next, Tommy emphatically told the young couple, "Wear the button! Always wear the button! I constantly wear a two-and-one-half inch diameter, shiny button that reads, 'LOSE WEIGHT NOW, ASK ME HOW!' You don't need expensive ads or billboards, but it is imperative that you promote constantly! Everyone must be reminded continually of the services you provide and the products you sell. If you firmly believe that what you sell provides great value to your clients and prospects, you should never stop asking them to buy! Because of your vigor and tenacity," Tommy continued, "you will be paid well now and handsomely rewarded in the future. The initial sale produces pennies, but there is a fortune in the follow-up! Of course, in spite of your passion, conviction, and persistence," Tommy said, "not everyone will make the purchase. So, if someone isn't interested, move on to the next!"

The two Herbalife distributors in attendance on the driveway that sunny afternoon clung to every word of Tommy's enlightening and enriching personal story. Mesmerized, they wanted the conversation to last forever. Unfortunately for all, at some point, Tommy had to leave. Before departing, however, he graciously summarized his three secrets for sales success:

1.   Set a specific, measurable level of daily activity and immediately reward yourself when that goal is achieved!
2.   Personally own the things that you sell!
3.   Constantly promote!

Tommy's signature story caused the young couple to desire more encouragement and direction from him as they searched for success. Tommy's story not only revealed three powerful "secrets" to help them achieve their goals, it also excited, invigorated, and motivated this husband and wife Herbalife team to put their newly acquired wisdom into practice and take action immediately. This is exactly what a well-told signature story will accomplish. Selling is nothing more than communicating. Positioning locates that communication in such a way as to encourage your prospects to listen carefully, implement your advice, and do things you want them to do. Storytelling has been the most effective form of communication since the beginning of time and gives the salesperson of today a distinct advantage in the highly competitive sales arena. As important as it is to have a story to tell, however, it is just as important that you know how to tell it well. Exude your emotions and let your feelings show when using signature stories as effective positioning tools.

Interestingly, a plethora of manuscripts, books, and articles have been written and published on the art of closing a sale, but very few have been penned on the art of opening one. This brings us to our fourth technique of positioning, the "surprising one" referred to earlier. The most powerful and effective positioning tool of all—*YOU!* Most sales are actually "closed" when the first contact is made. Every time you interact with another human being, whether by telephone, fax, email, or face-to-face, there is only one thing you bring to the table—feeling. You can actually cause a person to feel better about themselves by virtue of your interaction with them, or, conversely, this interaction could truly leave them feeling worse. Either way, they will not be left with the same sentiment as before you made contact. Bottom line? Prospects who feel better about themselves because of their interaction with you will buy more products and services than those who feel worse. It is up to you to set the stage through your friendly and engaging personality to tip the scale in your favor. This first contact occurs, as you recall, at the *far left* of our positioning model. How you position *yourself* at the first "hello" will definitely determine your ultimate sales failure or success. Your engaging personality, sparkling charm, genuine interest, and sincere broad smile favorably position you when your initial contact is made. These personal attributes clearly define you and tell the prospect just who you are. They are the keys to opening the sale!

Psychologists suggest that there are three events that must take place before a person will do business with you. Further, these occurrences must happen in the following order:

1. Prospects must like you.
2. They must trust you.
3. They must feel that they are receiving value for the time or money they spend with you.

We live in an information age, an age in which anyone can email, fax, or voice mail us. Consequently, people crave communication that is face-to-face with those whom they like and trust. Malcolm Gladwell, author of the current bestseller *The Tipping Point*, reinforces this message when he tells us that the only kind of persuasion people eagerly respond to anymore comes by word of mouth brought forth in person, face-to-face.

Because trust and value cannot occur until "likeability" has been achieved, I devote the majority of my time and energies to this facet as I develop high levels of prospecting and client-building expertise within professional salespeople. There is no question about it. When a prospect first makes contact with you, you are the most important "product." As a result, you must be likeable and present yourself as a commodity that your prospect will want to "buy."

Moving forward in the selling process, prospective clients must want to hear more from you, rather than less; and likeability is the ticket! Possessing a good sense of humor, being fun to be around, complimenting easily and often, and listening actively are all characteristics possessed by a person who everyone wants to hear more from and, frankly, spend more time with.

Likeability should not be something you exude only during the first hello. It should be an ongoing trait of all salespeople. There is an old story that makes this point quite well:

A salesman died and found himself standing before St. Peter, seeking admission to the Pearly Gates. In a rather unusual move, St. Peter gave the salesman an opportunity to view both Heaven and Hell to decide for himself where he wanted to spend eternity. Looking around Heaven, the salesman noticed a rather tranquil atmosphere with many angels gently floating around playing harps and meditating all alone.

To the contrary, when the salesman descended into Hell, he was welcomed by Satan and several other wretches who gave him a wonderful greeting complete with a brass band, dancing women, and free-flowing libations. Everywhere the salesman looked there were parties and merriment. This, without a doubt, looked like just the place for him!

Heading back up to St. Peter, the salesman announced his decision to live 'down below.' "So be it," St. Peter decreed, and soon the salesman found himself at Hell's doorstep. This time, however, things were quite different.

There was no one to greet him but the devil himself. There were no dancing women, no libations, and no parties, and no one paid any attention to him. He saw only fire, darkness, and misery. Shocked, the salesman asked about the great difference from when he visited less than 24 hours previously. The devil replied, "Yesterday you were a prospect, and you were important to us— today you are merely a client!"

To be perceived as honest and sincere, likeability shouldn't terminate when the courtship ends. When a prospect becomes a client, it is not an ending, but rather a beginning. A beginning that could possibly lead to an add-on sale or a profitable referral at a later date. If a prospect chooses not to do business with you today, stay in touch— they might place a large order with you tomorrow. Because of your ongoing personal interest, you will be well-positioned when the window of opportunity opens again in the future.

Contrary to popular belief, prospects are not attracted to you because of your competitive products or fast delivery. They are, however, attracted to you because of your engaging, magnetic personality. This is an emotional connection, not a logical one, and salespeople who are charismatic infect others with their emotional charm. Harvey Mackay, in his best-selling book *Swim with the Sharks Without Being Eaten Alive*, says it best when he advocates, "Once you attach your personality to a proposition, people start reacting to your personality and stop reacting to your proposition." In the competitive world of selling, emotions rule the day. We do not live in a logical society. If we did, *men* would ride sidesaddle!

So, there we have it. Effective positioning in the world of sales is everything! Take a genuine, warm interest in your prospects, and they will want to hear more from you rather than less. Properly position your products so clients will want to purchase more versus less. Use analogies, send token gifts, tell stories, and just be nice. Take a valuable lesson from history as you recall the fatal mistake of legendary gunfighter "Wild Bill" Hickock. Being poorly positioned can prove to be deadly! Keep your back *"against the wall"*!

You will be happy you did!

About The Author

Jim McCarty, CLU, RFC, RHU, LUTCF

A master salesman, constant promoter and ambitious entrepreneur, Jim has mowed lawns, washed windows, delivered newspapers, merchandised electronic components and successfully sold life and disability insurance products. After 36 highly rewarding years in direct selling, Jim now shares his expertise with other success seeking sales people as he conducts an extensive array of dynamic, results producing, highly acclaimed sales achievement seminars and workshops. Frequently in demand as a professional speaker, Jim has addressed numerous trade association meetings and company sales conventions throughout the United States and Canada. Three times he has addressed Million Dollar Round Table (MDRT) annual meetings and has held the stage at the National Association of Insurance and Financial Advisors as well as the National Association of Health Underwriters annual conventions. Jim is a dynamic presenter, motivating sales coach, premier storyteller and a proud member of the National Speakers Association, the National Association of Insurance and Financial Advisors, the General Agents and Managers Association, the United States Marine Corps Association and the International Association of Registered Financial Consultants. Jim is the author of several books on effective selling techniques and has published many nationally recognized sales achievement articles.

Hire Jim now for your next sales extravaganza!

You will be happy you did!

Jim McCarty, CLU
2545 S. Atlantic Avenue
Suite 2003
Daytona Beach Shores, FL 32118
JimMcCarty@Showbizselling.com
(FUN) 304-9684

Chapter 8

Driving Sales Success While On Remote Control

Denise Koepke

Closing business, making money and moving into your next sale-nothing is more exciting! If you are one of those people who desire to close more business or want to increase your closing ratios, (and who doesn't?) you are reading the right chapter!

Becoming successful in sales doesn't have to be hard. In fact, it can become an ingrained skill, like driving a car. You just need to learn the basic skills and repeat them every day. Soon you'll be driving sales success--while on remote control!

We won't be talking about fancy closing techniques or, for that matter, any "techniques" at all. We'll be discussing behaviors that will help us work smarter, not harder. I've closely studied the behaviors of the top people in the field of sales and I've identified 5 distinct areas that can help you increase your business. These areas are: Analyze the Best, Listen to Learn, the BRIDGE Strategy, Avoid the Feature Dumps, and Feedback for Champions. Every successful salesperson uses these strategies as a foundation for success and now you can too!

Everyone wants to know what makes a salesperson successful. Some might answer that it's a salesperson's "maturity" in the industry. Or maybe the person was lucky and had great mentors to help them. Or perhaps business was just handed to them. But I've found that there are many people with a lot of years in the industry who aren't successful. Also many did have business handed to them, and when the business was done, so were they. They couldn't sustain their success.

Why don't many salespeople do as well as they could or should? Let's think back to when you started in sales. How were you taught to sell? Most of us began with some product knowledge and general how-to's. .We were then most often sent out to ride with a sales rep from the company. We were told to watch what they do and they said soon we would be ready to be on our own. In the behavior world we call this modeling-- "monkey see, monkey do" activities that help us all learn. With whom did you ride? The best rep? Probably not. They are usually too busy and frankly don't want to share their information or their secrets of success. We ride along with whoever is available-- someone who's been with the company for a while and can show us the ropes. Maybe they make their quota, but I'll bet you that most of them did not explain a single solid sales strategy to you. What did they show you? Most likely it was exactly what they learned when they started. It probably had a lot to do with "feature dumping". They show up and talk all about the products and services that their company could offer, without asking a lot of questions. We'll be looking at how to avoid this most negative type of behavior later in the chapter.

So you see, it's easy to gather a history of bad habits, passed down from generation to generation of sales people. No wonder it's so difficult to be the best. Thankfully, that's not true any longer! The most successful reps look at what they're doing and analyze what others do, so that they don't reinvent the wheel.

Analyze the Best

The secret is to become a detective and find out how the best reps in your business are actually staying successful. Ride with, question and interact with as many top reps as possible. Some areas to explore include the networks they belong to, the books they read, and the people they know. Ask if they are working closely with consultants outside the business. Watch the process as they call on their accounts. How much time do they talk about personal items and then business items? How do they orchestrate the next step in the sale process? Ask them if they follow a certain process that they think makes them successful. You may have to leverage the law of reciprocity, which says that if you ride with them, you do something equally nice back, such as buy lunch. Writing a glowing letter about them to the CEO of your company would also work.

Next, you be the consumer. As you learn these skill sets, go out and be on the other end of the sales process. Listen as the sales person asks questions and then matches your needs to the solution. You may note that they missed some important areas you said you wanted, indicating they didn't listen well. You may also find a great listener who matched your needs to their solutions. Note how they did that. Be aware of who is doing most of the talking during these interactions.

When they talk about their product, do they match the product to what you said you wanted? Or did they talk mostly about what *they* would want? Bring up some objections and see how they handle those. Analyze the way they answered you and take note of it as soon as you leave the store so you don't forget. The real learning is in applying what you observe to your own sales process.

Listen to Learn

Go back to the last time you built a new relationship with someone. How did you begin to trust them? Most of us find that the relationship was built with communication. Getting to know someone and trusting them begins with them asking questions about you. Socially, this is a very common practice. Typically, the more you talk and reveal yourself, the closer you feel to that person and the more you find yourself "trusting" them. Couples in love will say (and you most likely felt this way too) that the other person really "understands" them. They could talk for hours about their lives, current events etc. Questioning and Listening is the key to building relationships in any area of your life. This holds true in most cases when we are dating, finding a new doctor, developing a new friend, or (hopefully) building a relationship with a new client.

Questioning to learn about your client's situation is a key skill all successful reps possess. Listening almost always requires taking notes. If you are "actively" listening, that means that you're sitting forward, head nodding at the right times and note taking. Think about what someone looks like when they are really listening to you. "Paraphrasing" is a form of listening where after the person stops talking, you begin to clarify by telling them what they just told you. Most people will paraphrase by saying "What you're saying is.....and then phrase back what they just said, using as many of the other person's words as possible. They "check for understanding", which is a professional way to let the client know that you are really listening to learn.

How do we know if we are listening enough? One way to know is to check your questions. Are you asking the types of questions that will draw out from the client what their problems are and how you can help? Are you deliberately designing these types of questions before you go on the call?

Let me share with you a very common sales scenario. I was observing 2 sales reps that were employed by a Fortune 500 company that specializes in freight. The freight company was changing sales reps within many of their major accounts due to a realignment initiative. Their reps had been on the job with the same customer for many years, and the freight company knew that their customers were worried about the change. The incoming and outgoing sales reps each had over 20 years of experience in the freight business. They decided that they would call on this very big customer together to ease the changeover concerns. That was the extent of their pre-call planning for the meeting.

We all met the customer and made our introductions. The customer was telling the new sales rep how worried he was about this change. The new sales rep nodded her head in understanding and reassured the customer that she would do a great job for him. She told him "I have big shoes to fill but I'll do my best." He voiced his concern about the change again, and she continued to reassure him that she understood that it was difficult, that she would do her very best and that she had a lot of experience with the company. She also had a very good relationship with the inside support team. The customer would state again that he was worried, but relieved that she knew the support person, because they were key to finding out where the freight was and when it would be delivered. The new sales rep assured the customer some more and I noticed he wasn't feeling very reassured. Then the new sales rep promised she would "drop by" every week to make sure that things were running smoothly. Hesitantly, he agreed that at the very least, he wanted to see her every week. That was the end of the call.

This sales call could have been much stronger. Let's analyze what happened. First, no real questions about the client's concern with the changeover were asked. Second, the new sales rep never inquired about her new customer's business nor if any changes in his business have occurred. The new rep didn't discuss any industry information to indicate that she knew something about his business that could have eased his distress. She also never asked point-blank, "Tell me the areas you are concerned about in regard to this new change?" If she would have asked these questions, clarified his concerns, listened and responded, she would have found out what took over 45 minutes to uncover (and I can guess that this was only part of the customer's concerns). The customer stated that he wanted to make sure she knew and worked well with the inside support person, especially when there was a problem. This would have been a perfect time to *ask* some questions instead of *telling* the client that all would be OK. And to add further pain to this process, this rep never took a note of any type. If I were that account, I'd be worried. And if I were the competition, I'd be trying to win that business, because I believe it is very vulnerable.

How could we have helped this rep? Easy, we could have done a much better job at pre-call planning. The major part of that planning would have been the development of intelligent questions. What types of questions could we have asked that would have helped us uncover the client's concerns, thereby bridging our solutions to their needs? A technique that I call The BRIDGE Strategy can help us hone this integral selling skill.

The BRIDGE Strategy is an easy process that most successful consultants follow in order to *stay* successful. Use the letters in the word "bridge" to help you remember the qualities that each of your questions should possess.

Based on research

Relevant to the business or industry

Intelligent and original

Deliberate

Geared to uncover needs

Engineered beforehand

Let's explore each area of the BRIDGE Strategy and then apply it to your business.

Based On Research

You should know the industry trends, stock prices, challenges the industry is facing and any uniqueness or quirks. Explore the areas that touch on your products or services.

For instance, if you sell telecommunications, you would want to know the trends in your prospect's business around international expansion. It would also be helpful to know if the salespeople, field support, or customer support teams are traveling more to international locales. This type of information can be gathered before the call and built upon as you gain more knowledge about the account. The longer your sales cycle, the more you can uncover.

Let's say you want to meet with the VP of Sales for your target company. Before you meet you could contact the sales managers and sales reps to attain pertinent information that would support your questions. The marketing department could also give you insights as to their changing marketplace, their future strategies and possible sales challenges. With just a little bit if footwork on your part, you can obtain valuable information about your target company's problems.

Relevant

Questions should be relevant to the information you discovered. Ask yourself if your product fits their current or future state of business. What is happening in their industry or business that your product could influence and how? This area will help us to create questions that we can use with our research.

Intelligent

List possible relevant areas of their business that the "average" reps won't ask about. These are designed to set you apart from the competition, so eliminate any run of the mill types of questions here. This is the area in which your research can really pay off. If you find a quirky piece of their business, or a problem area that isn't commonly known, this is the time to take your place amongst the professionals and showcase your knowledge and research with your outstanding questions.

Deliberate

What areas (based on your research) do you want to explore at this meeting that would give you the most leverage? Using the information gathered to this point, what is your best guess strategy?

Geared To Uncover Needs

To uncover needs, your prospect must have problems they want to fix. Your research (and experience) will have uncovered some problem areas for which you have solutions. Which of your product offerings will create the greatest impact so far?

Engineered Before Hand

Once we have collected our information, we can begin thoughtful construction of our questions. These questions will verify that a problem indeed exists and that the prospect feels it's serious enough to fix. Engineered questions are best asked as open-ended so that we can obtain the largest quantity of information. (Open-ended questions require the prospect to elaborate on the answer).

When you use the BRIDGE Strategy, you'll find you ask better, more in-depth questions and obtain better information. And most of all, you'll be perceived as a consultant, which you are!

Pre-Call Planning

How do the professionals pull all the information together and then utilize the BRIDGE Strategy? They perform pre-call planning, all the time, every time.

One sales professional I know who is a master of pre-call planning is Bill Taylor. He always does his research on every call, plans his questions based on the BRIDGE Strategy and executes his calls with utmost professionalism. He truly listens to learn and always take notes during every call, whether he's on the phone or there in person. He knows the "dullest pencil is better than the sharpest memory". As a result, his follow up is the best I've ever seen (and his customers resoundingly echo this sentiment). By properly planning his calls, he moves to the next steps smoothly with his clients.

Using the BRIDGE Strategy and planning your calls will also help you avoid falling victim to the "visiting rep syndrome". This describes all the reps out there who just drop in on their clients. They check in to see if everything is okay, and usually it is. Then one day they drop by and find the competitor's product sitting right there in front of them. Things are definitely not OK, but the client never let on that they were looking at the competition.

Remember that it is our job to help solve problems, but we have to constantly work at uncovering them or someone else will step forward to solve them. That includes fixing the problems our products might cause. But not to worry, the evidence shows that if someone has a problem with your product and you solve it for them, they are more loyal to you than if they never had experienced a problem. This is good news, however finding and solving problems even before the client may recognize they have them is what separates a mediocre sales person from a great consultant!

Pre-call planning is easy to do but it takes a bit of time and some thought. There are basic questions that will help you in uncovering problems so that you can bridge your customer's needs to your solutions. Some thoughts to consider before every call:

- What do you want to gain from this call? (Call objective)
- What information do you need to obtain that you can't find out any other way?
- Using your research, where do you think the problems are based?
- If everything goes well (they don't say "no") what would be the next steps at the end of the call?

Let's use the changing freight rep scenario as an example.

First, research on the account would give us trends in their industry and their business. For instance is there a seasonal fluctuation or flat periods of business that need to be considered.

What do we think the customer is most worried about with a new rep? (For example, knowledge of their business and their processes, the new rep's accessibility to them, etc.)

Is the current rep doing something for them that might now be discontinued?

Based on our research, we could then ask the following questions:

- I read that your industry is growing by 13%. What growth plans do you foresee in your business?
- I noticed more shipments to Europe over the past 12 months. What do you anticipate for the next 12 months?

- When it comes to shipping your freight, what are your top three priorities?
- Tell me what the existing rep does that you want me to continue?
- What concerns you most about changing reps?
- What happens in your business that affects what we do on the freight side?
- Describe what happens when you have an emergency and what is the ideal way to resolve it?

Think about areas that could be sticky for this customer, and plan how you will handle it. Plan for better and for worse.

Remember that if they don't admit that they have a problem, you don't have a basis for a solution. You may have to plan several different ways to approach the problem areas. Once the prospect admits they have a problem, only then may we offer up our solutions. In a long sales cycle, you may have to do a lot of research before you have earned the right to suggest a solution. If they ask you about a solution first, you can say that you have that solution but then drop back into asking what problems they are experiencing. In this way you can better help them choose exactly the right product with the correct features. The more complete the picture is, the more appropriate your solution will be.

What problems do you think exist for the freight company? What questions could you ask that would uncover them? This is the type of activity the professionals use and below is a tool that helps when constructing these questions.

What Problems May Exist	Questions To Ask
My service level will drop	What concerns do you have about your level of service?
Concerns about new rep	Tell me your immediate concerns about changing reps.
Pricing may change	Explain your concerns about pricing
Internal processes may change at our company	When internal processes change at our company, how does that impact you?

The next follow up questions depend on their answers. In many cases, you'll need to dig deeper to understand their full meaning. This is critical to bridging your solutions to their need. Keep asking yourself if you really understand what the root of the problem is, so that you don't assume. I've noticed that we hear the same answers so many times we just assume that "everyone" knows what the problem really is. However when interviewing the seller and the buyer, we have found that in fact they differed widely in what the real problem was. This puts you at risk by missing the solution to their root problem.

After you have created a list of questions following the BRIDGE Strategy, the next step is to think about your products and services and in what way they could solve these problems. Focus on your uniqueness and differentiate your product from the competition's. If you create a solution that *any* vendor can solve, the sale will typically default to the lower priced product.

Computers are a good example of a price-driven product. I needed a new one for my business and went out shopping. I checked the Internet for prices and also went to a nearby computer store. The sales rep at the computer store asked me a lot of questions about how I intended to use my new computer? What types of programs would I be running? I explained my business and the programs I primarily used. He then asked me if I had an IT person on my staff to help if my computer went down. I said, "No". And then he asked a great question. "What happens to your business when your computer goes down? Can you continue working?" I replied that I couldn't work at 100% because I rely on email communications and also need my computer to create presentations. He then asked, "If your computer goes down, what will you do to fix it and what is the time table around that?" This was a great question because it allowed me to figure out that it takes a lot of time and work to get my computer fixed—2 or 3 days. When he then suggested the special 24-hour turnaround time offered on their special service agreement, I was all ears. I was feeling a lot of pain around my computer going down and putting me out of commission. The other computers I was looking at were cheaper, but they didn't have service guarantees. I suddenly HAD to have an extended service agreement. He differentiated his product, making price a lesser issue. And he got the sale.

We can reenact this exact sales scenario and have a completely different outcome. Imagine that I walk into this same store. The sales rep asks me questions about what programs I run and what I use it for. I tell him I use it for my business. Then he tells me all about the service warranty and the 24-hour turnaround time and how all businesses that don't have an IT person should have it. This now changes the scenario because he is *telling* me about a feature that I don't have a clear need for. My reaction could easily be that he is trying to make money off of me on this expensive service agreement that I don't really need.

Asking questions to help the customer define the seriousness of their problems so that the customer, not the sales rep, makes the linkage, is the key to uncovering needs. The solution is always more powerful if the customer makes the connection between their problem and solution rather than the sales person *telling* them they have a problem that needs to be fixed.

Defining your call objective seems obvious. You want to make a sale, right? That makes sense, but how often does anyone make a one-call close? Probably not very often. There are many steps we need to take before the sale is made. That is what the call objective is about when pre-call planning. In many first calls, the objective is to discover if problems exist and to determine whether we can solve them. Another objective may be to find out if our prospect is the decision-maker and who else may be involved in the process. Another objective may be to do a demonstration before they buy. (This happens much later in the sales cycle, after problems are uncovered.) All of these steps lead to a sale, but no sale is made without many of these steps.

When we find out that they indeed have problems we can fix, what is the next best step to keep the sale progressing? This is our next step that we suggest to the customer. If you will plan for 3 possible next steps, you'll almost always get one of them, keeping the sale on track. First, plan a next step for when the call goes the best it possibly could. Then, plan a next step for the call going pretty much to plan. Finally plan a next step if things didn't go quite as well as you expected. Decide what would be the minimum you'd want to walk away with?

By thinking in this manner, you will almost always keep the sale moving forward. The result will be a shorter and more valid sales cycle. *You* are in control of what is happening, not the customer. If we allow the customer to be in control, they will ask for a proposal before all the problems are uncovered and then what happens? Your product becomes too expensive. Or some of my customers have actually handed my proposal to the competition to drive down the price.

Therefore, no proposals should be given until you have accomplished the needed steps in your sales cycle.

Here's a tool that will help you plan your questions, think about the objectives and determine the next steps if things go well. This pre-call planning tool will also help you build on the information you find out and create a history to follow for each sales call you make. (This is available electronically)

BRIDGE CALL PLANNER

Company _____   Company _____

Background _____
_____
_____
_____

Industry Information _____
_____
_____
_____

Business Challenges _____
_____
_____
_____

Areas to Explore: _____
_____
_____
_____

Call Objectives

Advance

Follow Up

Avoid the "Feature Dump"

Top sales reps understand that "telling isn't selling." All of us have the urge to tell our customers, friends, and family about all the great stuff we have. For some strange reason, we actually think that since we are excited about our new widget, everyone else will be excited too. Unfortunately, this isn't true and if you have ever done this to a group of your friends or relatives, you might have noticed the bored look on their faces or lack of interaction in the conversation. One of my customers, a CEO of a large corporation explained to his group, "There is nothing worse than hearing about a lot of stuff you don't care about."

To make matters worse, talk about unneeded product features and guess what the customer thinks? *"Boy, this must be expensive"*. We are now making our job even harder by creating more objections than ever! We all know that there's "no free lunch" and "you don't get something for nothing". So when we start adding all the features of our products, we get the customer thinking, "How much would I save if I didn't have that?" Or, "My, that sounds complicated. It would be too hard to operate." There we go again, creating objections that will be tough to overcome. If there's no need or expressed problem that the feature solves, don't talk about it no matter how wonderful you think it is.

I wondered how I started this bad behavior of "Feature Dumping" when I spoke with clients. As I reflected back, I realized that every time I was introduced to one of our new products, I was told about the features. A typical product launch would include touting the product's great features (features *the company* thought were great), what was included in the package and then the price. So I would go out to my prospects and repeat excitedly all the great features that this new product had. They would listen and then say, "Gee, it seems too expensive." (This is the first reaction to a Feature Dump.) I would then counter with, "It only costs x amount, just pennies a day," (or some type of objection-handling process) and then they would "think about it".

Next, I would go back to marketing and tell them the price was way too high. Marketing would tell me I just didn't know how to sell. I would go back to Marketing and complain that the pricing was all wrong. Then they would come back to me saying the pricing is fine, it's you and well, you see the pattern.

Now I know they were right. I didn't know how to sell because *telling isn't selling*. And I was *telling* my customers all about features they didn't care about. I fell into the classic Feature Dump mode commonly seen in sales.

Sometimes we think that if we talk enough, something will spark the interest of our clients. This is the equivalent of throwing spaghetti against the wall and hoping it will stick.

How do we stop the Feature Dump? It's easy. We focus on questions that help uncover the problem. Here's a strategic way to help avoid the Feature Dump.

Let's use a new product that is advertised quite a bit lately— Stay-On All-Day Lipstick. It's main feature is it won't rub off.

First, think about the problems that may exist for the customers (Most products are developed around a common problem your customers have and would be willing to pay for).

The problems with regular lipsticks are:

- Lipstick comes off on clothes and it may not come out.
- It wears off so you always have to reapply.
- It comes off on other people which can be a nuisance or embarrassment.

We may not know which problem your particular customer is experiencing, so we'll design questions that hit on these prime areas. You may think of even more problems that are specific to you or your industry.

Questions to uncover if a problem exists:

- What problems do you experience with wearing lipstick?
- Do you find that lipstick comes off on your clothes?
- Is it a concern that when you kiss someone, it comes off on his or her face?
- What is the typical reaction of someone who has been kissed by a wearer of lipstick?
- Have you ever ruined a blouse because you couldn't get the lipstick out?
- Is it annoying to always be checking your lipstick to see if has worn off?

If you experience this problem from either the wearing end or the receiving end of the lipstick, the all-day lipstick sure sounds good! There are, in fact, several ad campaigns on TV that ask these questions and then provide the solution with their product.

Consultants don't talk about features of products or services until they've helped the customer uncover problems and needs. By asking great questions, based on the BRIDGE Strategy, you help the customer uncover their problems, and then you make the linkages to your solutions. Avoid the Feature Dump with pre-call planning and remember, "No one wants to hear about stuff they don't care about."

Feedback for Champions

The best sales reps get better by consciously working on their skills in a variety of ways. They read books about sales as well as books their customers would read. They use the pre-call planning tools to make their questions the strongest they can be. They challenge themselves to increase their questioning vocabulary.

They also thrive on having someone they trust watch them and give them relevant feedback. Analyzing what you do in front of a customer is the most important way you can achieve the skill sets of a professional.

This is the same method that professionals in any field use to get better. Think about basketball. In order to get into the pro circuit, one would have to be really, really good. What percentage of players actually makes it to the pros? Maybe .0001% of the great basketball players. And when they make it, they already know how to play a very, very excellent game of basketball. Yet they have coaches that help them with everything they do, from running to shooting to rebounding. Those coaches are giving them constant feedback.

Yet most of us obtain very little valuable feedback in our careers. How much feedback do you get on skill set development? The majority of sales professionals would agree that it isn't enough. And it's not because the sales managers don't want to help-- these days their plates are way too full.

How then can we get feedback? Find a skillful salesperson who you really trust and ask them to watch you on a call. Pre-call plan the meeting with them using the tools I've given you and tell them which part of the call you want them to give feedback on. Choose an area you want to focus on. It could be questioning or listening or suggesting next steps. But remember, you can only change one thing at a time, so ask them to give you feedback on just one area. There may be others areas you'd like to work on, but you'll need to focus on one thing at a time to really improve.

Another way to get feedback, if there is no one to actually watch you, is to take a recorder and record the call. (Check with your attorney for any legal questions about this. As long as you do nothing more with the recording and it is for your own personal use, it should be okay.) This is a great way to listen to the call and decide what you did well (to reinforce the good areas) and what you'd like to work on. Pick one area for 2 weeks and work on it. You'll be amazed at the results you'll see in one year's time!

Modeling is another way for all of us to improve. By watching someone else who is doing well, you will pick up on some finer points that you can incorporate into your own style.

Consider teaching the skill to others. The saying, "Who learns more the student or the teacher?" is true. If you really want to learn a skill in depth, teach it to someone else.

Receiving valuable feedback is the way the ordinary become extraordinary.

Make these practices your own today. They will soon become second nature to you. These skill sets are the foundation to becoming the best and staying the best. If you utilize these steps as the professionals do, you will never worry that your success was a fluke, or that you were handed the business. Your sales success will be accomplished consciously and effectively with your own effort and steam. You are behind the wheel of your career, driving your sales success while on remote control!

To obtain the Pre-Call planner tool go www.r-c-m.com and choose Pre-Call tool.

About The Author

Denise Koepke

Denise Koepke founded Remote Control Management and delivers proven sales and skills-based programs to entrepreneurial and Fortune 500 corporations that generate measurable results. Ms. Koepke is a dynamic, internationally known speaker, author and consultant with over 20 years of successful sales and sales management experience. After interviewing and researching America's top-performing salespeople, Ms. Koepke offers "inside information" and simple yet powerful tools that anyone can apply to immediately double or triple their sales. Ms. Koepke brings vast knowledge and real-world experience that when applied, can take any participant to the next level in their sales career. You can order her best-selling audio program, "Driving Sales Success while on remote control" or bring her to your next meeting by contacting her at 949-709-2699 or ddkoepke@aol.com. Make sure to visit www.r-c-m.com for your free "Pre-Call Planning Tool" guaranteed to shorten your sales cycle and close more business.

"Denise Koepke trained and developed the representatives in my area and largely contributed to making it the #1 sales region for a multi-billion dollar company. I highly recommend Denise Koepke if you're serious about taking your company to the next level."

- John Combs, Southwest Region President Nextel Communications

Denise Koepke
Remote Control Management
27758 Santa Margarita Pky #339
Mission Viejo, CA 92691
Phone: 949.709.2699
Fax: 949.709.2688
Email: DDKoepke@aol.com
www.r-c-m.com

Chapter 9

How To Outsmart Your Competition

John Boyens

Have you ever had a situation in your sales career in which you knew you were going to close a sale only to have it unhook in the 23rd hour? If so, then you were a victim of being "outsmarted" by your competition. I say you were outsmarted because you were sure that you were going to win, and your prospect never gave you an indication that you were going to lose. As a matter of fact, you were so sure that you were going to close the sale that maybe you spent some, if not all, of your commission dollars in advance! What would it be worth to you to have known some of the warning signs that you were in danger of losing the sale long before the final decision was made?

How to outsmart the competition is an overview of BLC's best practices research and buyer surveys regarding how the best salespeople "outsmart" their competition on a daily basis. Let me start by sharing a general concept with you. In today's complex, business-to-business sale, we know that there is a small percentage of your prospect universe who will buy from your company no matter what. They buy from you because of previous positive sales experiences, faith, or confidence in your product, great service, and so on. There is also a small percentage of your prospect universe who will buy from your competition for the exact same reasons. Our research shows that the two segments who have already made up their minds to buy account for less than 10% of the opportunities to be sold. That means that 90% of the accounts in your prospect universe still need to be convinced in order to make them buy your product or service. What we have found is that people/companies buy for one of two reasons. They buy either to satisfy a need or they buy to fulfill a vision. If you cannot get your prospect to admit a need or if you are unable to create a vision with a bias toward your product or service, you WILL NOT make the sale. It doesn't matter how low your price is or how many features your product has. The bottom line is No Need or No Vision equals No Sale!

I have divided this chapter into eight sub-chapters to make the concepts easier to integrate into your day-to-day selling activities. The golden rule in being able to "outsmart" the competition is to have a wealth of prospect knowledge. Prospect knowledge includes knowing the names and titles of key players in your prospect's organization, the industry, and marketplace that your prospect serves and the competition that you are likely to encounter.

The eight keys to outsmarting your competition include:
1. Creating a competitive advantage in your market place
2. Establishing and implementing a consistent account planning process
3. Developing product capability knowledge
4. Effectively targeting your prospects
5. Knowing the secrets of how organizations buy
6. Knowing how to sell to different buyer personalities
7. Selling value, not price
8. Standing firm during negotiations

Key Number One
Creating a Competitive Advantage in Your Market Place

Based on our research, here are the steps that you must follow in order to create that advantage. The best salespeople today spend a fair amount of time being introspective about their selling successes and selling challenges. What I mean by being introspective is that they look at how their industry has changed over the past 18 to 24 months (e.g., increased competition, poor economy, budget cuts). They look at how their marketplace has changed over that same time (e.g., stores or businesses that have closed, increasing numbers of layoffs, delays in decision making). They also identify the selling challenges that they have faced over the past 18 to 24 months (e.g., inability to cost justify their solutions, inability to connect with senior-level decision makers, inability to get decision makers to take action). Once they have completed their introspection, they create a road map (with specific action steps) that will allow them to address these changes and challenges in a proactive manner.

One way to address these changes and challenges is to understand how your prospects view your company as it relates to your competition. We know that all companies have specific needs in order to be successful in their own marketplace. We also know that these companies have a perception (right or wrong) about your ability to address their specific needs versus your competition. In some cases, they believe that your capabilities are stronger than your competitor's capabilities in addressing their needs, and in those cases you should "win." In some cases, they believe that your competitor's capabilities are stronger than your capabilities in addressing their needs, and unfortunately in those cases you will probably "lose." Your job is to maximize your strengths and minimize your weaknesses to increase your probability of success. It is important to note that what I have just discussed is the perception of your prospect, not necessarily the reality of the situation. In any event, their perception IS your reality. In order to "win," you will have to change their perception of you, your product offering, or your company. Our research shows that perception can change only when two things occur: new experiences or new information over time. You can't just tell a prospect something is different. For instance, you can tell your prospect about the improvement of your customer service function, but until they can experience that improvement first-hand and actually believe that it is sustainable, their perception will not change.

Another way to create a competitive advantage is to use BLC's three "W" strategy. The three "W's" are: identify **who** you are targeting, **what** product or service you are targeting, and **why** he or she would use your product or service. When communicating why he or she would use your product or service, it is helpful to articulate your company's unique value proposition. You may have heard this referred to as an "elevator pitch." In other words, what would you say to a prospect when riding two floors on an elevator with them? A value proposition is normally one or two sentences that identify what it is that your company does that your competition doesn't do, can't do, or won't do in the marketplace. Please note, after you complete your value proposition, if you can replace your company's name with the name of one of your competitors and the statement is still true, then it's not your unique value proposition, and you must start over.

Key Number Two
Establishing and Implementing a Consistent
Account Planning Process

The first step in establishing a successful account planning process is effective pre-call planning. Whether your sales cycle is two hours, two days, or two years, there is a series of events that must take place in order to generate the desired results (i.e., a mutually beneficial business relationship between two or more parties). There are various ways to create and organize a successful account strategy. There are also a myriad forms, processes, contact management systems, and software tools available in the marketplace to help you. No matter what format or process they choose, all top-performing salespeople use some type of account planning process to organize account information (both prospects as well as clients), to help with the pre-call planning, and ultimately enable them to manage the sales process proactively to a successful close.

One essential step in gathering account information is to have an IDEA of whom you are selling to. In other words, what is the role or responsibility of the person to whom you are speaking at the account? Is your point of contact the influencer (I), the decision maker (D), the end user (E), or the approver (A)? I realize that in most businesses people may wear multiple hats. Your job is to discover which hat is primary so you will be able to stay in alignment with their specific business issues and needs. We have discovered that in order to be successful in today's economy, you probably need to sell to all four points of contact, but you must know how to sell to each one of them very differently. For instance, you shouldn't reveal pricing or terms to an end user at any time during the sales process because the end user doesn't care how much it costs; they just want to make sure that it helps them address their issues. The price discussion should be saved exclusively for the final decision maker because they control the power of the pen. Conversely, you shouldn't demonstrate your products or services to the final decision maker because they don't care about the nuts and bolts of your solution; they just want to make sure that their people are satisfied and that the payback is fair. It is better to save your product demonstration for the influencers and end users because they are the ones who will be using the product or recommending the purchase.

In addition to having an IDEA of whom you are selling to, the best salespeople do pre-call research on their prospects. Much of the success of a live sales call is dependent on how much you already know about your prospect, their industry, and their marketplace before you make your first contact. Today, buyers expect you to be prepared and to have done your homework. There are many resources available to you for collecting this important background information. Visiting their Web site is an excellent research tool. Trade publications, industry journals, and the business section of local newspapers are good resources. If your prospect is a large publicly traded company, reading their annual report is also a great way to gather critical data. If you read their annual report, you should focus on three key areas: the President's message, their value proposition, and their mission statement. Also, make sure you that understand their sales and revenue numbers, their year-over-year trends, how much market share they own, who their competitors are, and what new products are being developed or marketed. In addition, make sure that you know their history with your company (both the good and the bad).

After you have done your research, it's time to establish the objectives for a successful call. We recommend that you should establish three objectives for every call to ensure buyer/seller alignment. For instance, your objectives could include uncovering their needs, identifying the decision maker, and identifying your prospect's decision-making process. Prior to making the call, make sure that you identify what potential needs your prospect may have, decide which of your solutions you are planning to introduce during the meeting, and are prepared to share a customer success story that would be relevant to their current situation. When crafting your customer success story, make sure that it is peer-to-peer (e.g., one VP of sales to another), and make sure that you identify the problem he or she had before purchasing your solution, two or three reasons why this problem existed, what their vision was of a solution, and what the measurable results were after purchasing your product or service.

During the live sales call, top performers ensure buyer/seller alignment by focusing on four steps during the discovery process. Those steps are:

- Discover your prospect's true needs, critical business issues, or both
- Analyze the reasons and costs for those issues
- Link your unique capabilities to those needs
- Unveil proof that by using your solution they can solve their critical business issues

After navigating your prospect through the four steps mentioned above, top-performing salespeople are able to weave a web of impact through the influencer, decision maker, end user, and approver in order to establish buying authority and then get them to agree upon next steps and timelines. Please note: when weaving the web, make sure that you use your products to prove your capability rather than demonstrate your products at the beginning of the call.

Key Number Three
Developing Product Capability Knowledge

Product capability knowledge is the blend of knowing what your product is, what it does, who would use it, and how the use of it would benefit your prospect. We have met too many salespeople who have great product feature knowledge but poor product capability knowledge. How do you gain that knowledge? One way to do this would be to create a one-page reference sheet to use when making sales calls. Divide the sheet into three columns. In the first column, make a list of all the various products (along with their features and capabilities) that you currently sell. In the next column, list the job functions or titles of all the people in your prospect's organization who could benefit from each of your specific products. In the third column, answer the question, "What bad thing would happen to each job title if he/she didn't have access to my products?"

For example, let's say you sell an accounting software package that has an automated commission-reporting feature that can be sorted by customer, territory, or salesperson. How would this feature benefit district sales managers? Perhaps it could help them compile their monthly status reports more quickly. Maybe it could help measure their team's performance. Perhaps it would enable the managers to realign sales territories. What bad thing would happen if the sales managers didn't have this feature? They could waste time and lose productivity because they couldn't compile their monthly reports in a timely fashion. They could increase administrative costs because they would have to track their team's performance manually. They couldn't realign their territories with automated tools, which would cause current negative sales performance to continue.

What would this feature mean to the finance managers? Maybe it could help them pay commissions accurately and on time. It may provide for backup documentation and audit trails. Also, it may enable them to accurately project cost-of-sales on a monthly basis. What bad things would happen if they didn't have this feature? Commissions might be paid late, or paid incorrectly with inaccurate supporting documentation, resulting in an increase in the cost-of-sales month over month.

What would this feature mean to human resources managers? Maybe it would allow them to increase employee satisfaction. Perhaps it would enable them to reduce turnover in the sales force. It also may help them improve morale. What bad things would happen if they didn't have this feature? Employee satisfaction could deteriorate even more. Sales force turnover could increase, which would have a negative impact on the morale of the entire organization.

What would this feature mean to marketing managers? Maybe it would enable them to better understand the profile of their existing customers so that they could create products that their customers would buy. Perhaps it could help them with their market messaging based upon region, location, or size. It also may empower them to create an advisory board to improve communication with their customers. What bad things would happen if they didn't have this feature? Product marketing could create and introduce new products that fail in the marketplace. Marketing communications could send the wrong message to the wrong prospects at the wrong time causing customer dissatisfaction. That dissatisfaction could cause companies to lose their best customers.

Key Number Four
Effectively Targeting Your Prospects

Top-notch salespeople target a minimum of three specific titles (i.e., the VPs of sales and marketing and the CFO) to whom they want to sell in their prospect's organization. They know the day-to-day responsibilities of each job title and know what challenges are faced by not buying his or her solution. In addition, these top salespeople target specific solutions that they want to introduce to the prospect and how that solution would make their jobs easier. Lastly, the best salespeople today are masters at positioning their solutions as they relate to helping their prospect increase their revenue, decrease their costs, or improve their operating efficiencies.

For years, salespeople have been told the importance of calling at a high level within their prospect's organization. However, too many times salespeople have connected with senior-level decision makers only to be delegated instantly to the end user level. Why does that happen? Chances are that the salesperson was leading with features and industry buzzwords in an effort to describe who they are, what they do, and how they do it.

Our research tells us that salespeople are delegated to the person that they speak most like. Let me give you a real-life example. A salesperson from one of our clients sells technology solutions to Fortune 1000 businesses. He was fortunate enough to get an appointment with a CEO at one of his largest prospects. As soon as the meeting started, the CEO said that he was pressed for time, so the salesperson went right into demonstrating the features of his product before uncovering needs or creating a vision of how things could be different. Five minutes into the demonstration, the CEO stopped the salesperson and told him to set up a meeting with the Director of IT to show her his solution. In less than 10 minutes, the salesperson was delegated two levels lower in the organization to the end-user level.

How should you avoid being delegated to the end-user level? Salespeople must first understand the business issues from the prospect's perspective, determine the reasons these issues are happening along with their associated costs, and then be able to paint a picture of how the prospect personally could become a "hero" by using your company's solutions. What does it mean to be a hero? That varies from individual to individual. In some cases people just want job security. In other cases, people want an increase in salary, a promotion, or just to be recognized as a valuable member of their organization.

Key Number Five
Knowing the Secrets of How Organizations Buy

It is imperative to understand how to position a new solution if there's already an existing vendor in place or if the buyer already has a vision toward another vendor. We also have to be able to create a new vision for the prospect to choose our offering.

If somebody were to ask you how your company compares to your number one competitor, your response should be, "I'm not sure how to answer that question. How do you plan on using, or how are you using, the competitive offering?" What you want your prospect to do in asking them that question is to articulate their vision of a solution or to identify the need that they are trying to satisfy.

We have found that the more expensive the product you sell, the more likely it is that you're going to have to sell to a committee, and the more likely it is that that committee is going to request proposals from multiple vendors to be able to cost-justify their decision.

While the committee's request may sound encouraging, the fact is that they want you to show your hand by having you issue your proposal in somewhat of a vacuum. That being said, let me share with you the following warning signs that will let you know that you are NOT the vendor of choice:

> **Warning sign #1:** Overly-friendly buyer to an unknown salesperson (e.g., you receive a very friendly call from a prospect whom you've never spoken to before).

> **Warning sign #2:** Compresses timeframe for a decision (e.g., the buyer says, "We're going to buy a new software program by the end of the month").

> **Warning sign #3:** Buyer has a list of requirements a mile long (e.g., the buyer says, "We want a software product that is PC-based that can be put on a server that accepts 50 users access at the same time with state-of-the-art firewall protection, and so on"). That list was not created by accident; someone (probably your competition) helped create that vision for him or her.

> **Warning sign #4:** No access to the decision maker (e.g., all of your communication is with a low-level decision maker or an end user). The ultimate decision maker instructed a member of his or her team to contact three to five vendors to get price quotes that they could use when negotiating with their vendor of choice.

Key Number Six
Knowing How to Sell to Different Buyer Personalities

It is important to know what buyer personality types you will be facing and understand what would motivate each one of those different personalities to buy from you. By knowing this type of information about your prospect, you will be able to adapt your selling strategy on the spot, using the approach that is most likely to pay off. You will also be able to get your prospects, of all types, to work with you during the sales process. In addition, once your prospect becomes a customer, you will be able to manage "problem" customers no matter what their problem is.

Let me identify three different personality types and share with you the secrets of getting them to buy. The three personality types include someone who is a "price" buyer, someone who is a "risk adverse" buyer, and someone who is an "egocentric" buyer. Before I detail each type of buyer, please note that it is best to employ empathy with each type of buyer so that they will "trust" you throughout the sales process. The buyers whom we interviewed used the words trustworthy, sincere, and competent when we asked what it was that would cause them to buy from salesperson "A" versus salesperson "B" if products, pricing, and services from both salespeople were similar.

The "price" buyer is someone who says, "I buy exclusively on price. I want the lowest price. Price is the only thing that is important to me." What we have found is that price is never the main buying criterion but rather a smokescreen for the salesperson to overcome. We have discovered that the value differentiation between your products and services and your competitor's products and services really drives all buying decisions. The only time someone will actually buy on price is when the buyer can't see any difference between what you are offering versus what your competition is offering. Your job as a salesperson is to communicate and document your value differentiation so that your prospect will buy from you even if you have the higher price.

The "risk adverse" buyer is someone who doesn't want to make a decision for fear that he or she could be wrong. They are very conscious about how they are viewed by their boss and by their co-workers. They believe that the "pain" of making a change is greater than the "pain" they are enduring today. The best way to sell to this type of buyer is to help them see the consequences of not buying your product or service. In other words, what bad things would happen to them if they didn't buy? For instance, their costs could continue to rise, operating efficiencies may be slowed, or worse yet, they could be terminated. If you can create a transition vision in their mind of how they can go from where they are today to where they need to be, along with specific steps of how to get there, the risk adverse buyer can be sold very successfully.

The third buyer I mentioned is the "egocentric" buyer. They're the type of buyer who talks about how important they are and what a powerful name their company has and may even go as far as to say, "You'd be lucky to have someone of our stature as a customer." The best way to sell to this type of buyer is to detail the successes that are to be gained by buying your product or service. In other words, how can they be made a "hero" by buying from you? For instance, maybe they would get a raise or a promotion by buying from you, perhaps they would get recognition from co-workers or from their boss for a job well done, or maybe they would be able to do their job more efficiently, eliminating the need for overtime. In any event, the "egocentric" buyer needs to see proof of how others have successfully used your product or service, and they need to see proof that it will work in their environment as well. Successfully negotiating with the "egocentric" buyer can pay big dividends when it comes to cross-selling additional services at a later date.

Key Number Seven
Selling Value, Not Price

The most successful salespeople today are skilled a uncovering the buyer's need, analyzing the costs associated with that need, creating a vision with a bias toward their unique capabilities, and then offering proof. They use their products to prove their capabilities rather than demonstrate what their products do.

Our research shows that one of the primary reasons that people don't buy is because they cannot justify the cost of the investment nor begin to calculate a feasible payback. If salespeople demonstrate their product before buyers have a chance to create an internal vision of how they see themselves using it, or if the salespeople quote prices (even under pressure) before the buyer has seen value, it is almost guaranteed that a price war will ensue. Salespeople often mistakenly believe that they lost the deal simply because their price was too high, and that just isn't the case.

Let me give you an example. Let's say you demonstrate all of the wonderful features of your product or service, and your prospect becomes very enthusiastic and says, "How much does it cost?" to which you reply, "$100,000." Your prospect may push back because you haven't been able to calculate what it costs them to do business today without your solution. However, if during your discovery process you were able to identify $250,000 worth of savings, the $100,000 price tag becomes much more palatable. Let me expand on that point further. The best time to establish value and build the cost justification is during the need-development phase of the sales cycle when the potential buyers are revealing their problems and issues. Expert salespeople spend an extensive amount of time measuring what it costs their potential buyer's organization to do business the way they do business today. By investing the time to discover the costs from the potential buyer, the perception of value will be established, thereby eliminating objections when the price is revealed.

Some of the best ways to establish value include:
- Showing how your product or service can help your prospects increase their revenue by generating more business
- Showing how your product or service helps your prospects improve their image or solidify their brand
- Showing how your product or service can help your prospects reduce their cost of doing business today. For instance:
  - Can your product or service help your prospect eliminate an existing cost completely?
  - Can your product or service help your prospect avoid paying future costs?
  - Can your product or service help your prospect redirect an existing cost to make better use of an existing resource?

I must caution you that even after you have established value with your prospect, you are still going to have to be prepared to negotiate in order to close the sale.

Key Number Eight
Standing Firm During Negotiations

Too often, salespeople, upon hearing the words "your price is too high," offer a discount without any attempt to "stand" or push back. In order to be able to push back, it is important to know what's going on in the mind of the person you will be facing in negotiations.

Our research shows that the following are "best practices" of master negotiators:
- They perceive negotiating as an ongoing part of the sales process, not as a final event needed to close the sale
- They realize that the degree of their power is directly proportional to the amount and type of information they know about the buyer's needs
- They actively listen, ask open-ended questions, and use silence as a strategic advantage
- They maintain an open, creative mindset and do not make assumptions

- Their demeanor is one of confidence and assurance (even when they are doubtful)
- They never let negotiations get down to one item, especially price
- They are fully prepared for push backs from the buyer by preparing a "stand plan"

The first bullet is that master negotiators perceive negotiating as an ongoing part of the selling process, not as a final event necessary to close. They are keenly aware that two emotional barriers need to be cleared before an agreement occurs. The emotional barrier that the buyer must clear is—am I getting the best deal, not the lowest price, but the best deal? The emotional barrier that the seller must clear is—am I willing to walk away? The toughest thing for sales professionals to do is to walk away from a huge opportunity, but the fact is that that's what the best negotiators will do. If it's not a good deal, you have to be able to walk away or at least give the appearance of walking away. That being said, if you don't have a lot of qualified prospects in your pipeline and it's February 43rd and your boss is asking, "What are you going to close this month?" it's really hard to walk away.

Another best practice that master negotiators have is that they realize that the degree of their power is directly proportional to the amount of information and type of information that they know about the buyer. The more you know about the prospect (e.g., their business issues, their vision of a solution, the competitive pressures that they are facing), the better off you are in handling negotiations.

The third bullet is that salespeople listen actively, ask open-ended questions, observe, and use silence as a strategic advantage. Sales professionals, even the best in the world, sometimes get nervous when it comes down to final negotiations. What do people have a tendency to do when they get nervous? They have a tendency to talk more, and normally talk louder. It's best to talk in your normal tone, and it is very wise to use silence as a strategic advantage. If you use silence effectively, it lets the person to whom you're speaking absorb what you just said. If you said to them, "From our discussions, it looks like you're spending $100,000 a year doing things the way you're doing them today, and you indicated that you need to bring your costs down to less than $20,000. You indicated that you thought we could help you achieve your goal, but the fact is that your problem doesn't go away unless you take action." At that point, just be quiet and let your prospect absorb the full impact of your previous statement.

The next bullet is that master negotiators maintain an open, creative mindset, and they don't make assumptions. Please note that once the buyer admits a need, all assumptions stop. Once the buyer admits a need, you should start asking specific questions about the need and the costs associated with that need, not to mention what they're currently trying to do to address it. Remember, the best negotiators don't make assumptions; they deal in facts.

The next bullet indicates that master negotiators are confident and assured even if they are doubtful. Our research shows that top-performing salespeople have dollar thresholds that make them nervous. Do you remember your first $10,000 sale? How about your first $50,000 sale or your first $100,000, $500,000, or million-dollar sale? If you've never sold at that level before, it can be pretty nerve-racking.

The last bullet is that master negotiators never let negotiations get down to one item. It doesn't matter what the one item is, whether it's price, delivery, or terms; it doesn't matter. If you let negotiations get down to one item, somebody has to win, and somebody has to lose. The best negotiators are always looking for a win/win solution. We recommend that the best way to create a win/win solution is to create a "stand plan" in advance of the final negotiations.

Preparing a "stand plan" BEFORE entering into negotiations can prove extremely valuable when the heat is on! A well prepared "stand plan" should have at least three "push backs" against the pressure to drop price.

"Stand One" against "your price is too high" should be your somewhat puzzled observation that the buyer had previously approved the price and payback at the time when the value justification was revealed. For instance, you could say, "I'm confused; when we calculated the original ROI, the payback was less than six-months, which you said was more than acceptable. Why are you asking me to lower my price?" If your buyer validates your comments but pushes back with, "Things have drastically changed and you need to drop your price," proceed to "Stand Two."

"Stand Two" should reinforce the successes the buyer will gain by purchasing your product or service. For example, if your product or service enables your prospect to gain market share, increase revenue, shorten their time to market, ensure a successful product rollout, and so on, now is the time to reiterate those facts. If the buyer is still adamant about the need to reduce price, continue to "Stand Three."

"Stand Three" should reinforce the consequences of delaying the purchase of your product or service. For example, costs continue to escalate, sales targets could be missed, market share may be lost, employee turnover may increase, and so on.

The first three stands can be executed in any order that makes sense based upon the buyer's behavior. If, after three stands your buyer still refuses to budge, it's time for the "quid pro quo," or the "give and get" approach. At this point, say to your buyer, "The only way that I can do something for you is if you can do something for me," and then stop and wait for a reaction. Almost always the buyer will respond with something like, "What do you have in mind" or "Like what"? Your "stand plan" preparation should include at least three "gets" and three "gives" to bring the negotiations to a successful conclusion. "Gets" may include a longer-term contract, exclusivity, joint press release, referrals, and so on. Examples of "gives" may include free shipping, special terms, use of additional products at a discounted rate, and so on.

Once the buyer asks, "What do you have in mind?" ask, "Is it possible...?" For example, say, "Is it possible to discuss a longer-term contract? We have been discussing a one-year contract. Is it possible to extend it to a two-year agreement?" Wait for the buyer to respond. If you get a positive response from the buyer, then offer up one of the "gives." "If you agree to a two-year agreement, then I am prepared to offer you 40 hours of free consulting time during the two-year term." Please note, top salespeople never offer up a "give" until they get the prospect to commit to one of their "gets."

As we conclude this chapter, let's review the eight ways we have identified to "outsmart" your competition:

1. Creating a competitive advantage in your marketplace: Remember to use BLC's three "W" strategy. Identify **who** you are targeting, **what** product or service you are targeting, and **why** your prospect would use your product or service.

2. Establishing and implementing a consistent account planning process: One essential step in gathering account information is to have an IDEA of whom you are selling to. In other words, what is the role or responsibility of the person to whom are speaking at the account? Is your point of contact the influencer (I), the decision maker (D), the end user (E), or the approver (A)? I realize that in most businesses people may wear multiple hats. Your job

is to discover which hat is primary so that you will be able to stay in alignment with their specific business issues and needs.

3. Developing product capability knowledge: People/companies don't buy products or services; they buy solutions! Winning salespeople have a knack for being viewed as a consultant by their clients and not as a vendor simply trying to push products. They know how their capabilities can help their clients achieve their desired business results, and they have the ability to value-justify their solutions. They are able to target their solution to the unique needs of their individual buyer.

4. Effectively targeting your prospects: The best salespeople target a minimum of three specific titles to which they want to sell in their prospect organization. They know the day-to-day responsibilities of each job title, and they know what challenges they may face by not buying his or her solution. In addition, these salespeople target specific solutions that they want to introduce to the prospect and how that solution would make their jobs easier. Lastly, the master salespeople position their solutions as they relate to helping their prospect increase their revenue, decrease their costs, or improve their operating efficiencies.

5. Knowing the secrets of how organizations buy: Beware of the four warning signs that you are not the vendor-of-choice: overly-friendly buyer to unknown salesperson, compressed timeframe for a decision, a requirements list that is a mile long, and limited or no access to the decision maker.

6. Knowing how to sell to different buyer personalities: By knowing this type of information about your prospect, you will be able to adapt your selling strategy on the spot, using the approach that is most likely to pay off. You will also be able to get your prospects, of all types, to work with you during the sales process. In addition, once your prospect becomes a customer, you will be able to manage "problem" customers no matter what their problem is.

7. Selling value, not price: The primary reasons people don't buy are because they cannot justify the cost of the investment nor calculate a feasible payback. If salespeople demonstrate their product before buyers have a chance to internalize the vision of how they see themselves using it, or if the salespeople quote prices (even under pressure) before the buyer has seen value, it is al-

most guaranteed that a price war will ensue. Salespeople often mistakenly believe that they lose the deal simply because their price is too high, and that just isn't the case.

<u>8. Standing firm during negotiations</u>: Salespeople who are able to "outsmart" their competition never "wing it." They realize that value is based only on the customer's perception. They understand that negotiating takes place at the start of the sales process and continues throughout the entire sales cycle. It is not just a final event needed to close. Before entering into final negotiations, these salespeople prepare a "stand plan" that includes three "Stands," a "quid pro quo" statement and three "gets and gives." Remember, never, ever let negotiations get down to one item because, if you do, someone will have to win and someone will have to lose. Always look for a win/win solution.

By following the tips and techniques outlined in this chapter, I'm certain that you will make this your best year ever!

John Boyens

John Boyens is the President and Founder of BLC, Inc., a company that is dedicated to maximizing the productivity of the sales process. John has a proven track record with over 25 years of sales management and executive management experience with several Fortune 1000 companies. His responsibilities included leading national sales, service and marketing organizations, launching global account, national account and vertical market programs while delivering strong growth in sales, profit, productivity and revenue. Over the years, John has been invited to address thousands of business executives and salespeople in a variety of formats and venues and has delivered a number of custom-designed programs on topics such as: *Sell Value not Price/ Techniques of World Class Sellers/ Coaching for Optimal Performance/ Creating and Sustaining a Competitive Advantage/ Extraordinary Leadership.* In addition to his speaking, workshop facilitation and consulting work, John is the co-author of the book entitled, *Real World Sales Strategies that Work* as well as the co-author of the audio CD series entitled, *Techniques of World Class Sellers* with Dr. Merrylue Martin. John is a graduate of North Central College and is an active member of the National Speakers Association, the International Speakers Network, Sales and Marketing Executives International and the Brentwood Chamber of Commerce. In addition, industry experts have recognized John as a distinguished member of Who's Who Worldwide.

John Boyens
BLC, Inc.
9615 Brunswick Drive
Brentwood, TN 37027-8464
Phone: 615.776.1257
Fax: 615.776.1258
Email: john@blcinc.net
www.blcinc.net

Chapter 10

Set Yourself On Fire!

Stephen Blakesley

I began my selling career at age seventeen. The last summer before graduating from high school at Watonga High, having worked in a grain elevator the previous three summers, I wanted to do something significant. Troy Tate, an agent for Atlas Life, had an office next door to my dad's barbershop, and I noticed that he always drove a new Oldsmobile 88. I was driving my 1941 Mercury coupe that I had bought with money saved from my grain elevator days. An Oldsmobile 88 was a significant upgrade from a 1941 Mercury that I had to park with the front bumper against a tree each night, to enable me to "burn the clutch" to get moving in the morning. Every time I looked at Mr. Tate's Oldsmobile, I felt compelled to drive one, someday.

That was the first time I can recall recognizing the emotion I now know to be passion. Because of this emotion, that summer I discarded my "hi-profile job," scooping wheat from the corner of truck-beds to pursue, of all things, life insurance sales. My parents could not understand it, and my friends could not understand it, but I never considered it even the least bit strange. All I knew was that I felt driven to do something different, to pursue something with a future.

That summer and all through college, I sold life insurance and loved it. I never earned enough in that part-time effort to buy the Olds 88, but I did earn enough to be totally free from dependence upon my mother and father for support. Later I came to understand that my passion was not for an Olds 88, but for the freedom that a successful career in sales provided. That early success was the beginning of a long series of sales successes. Through the years, I observed the roll passion played in the process of sales and selling.

In the next few pages I want to share with you a few things that I have learned along the way and hope that you can find them helpful in building your sales successes. The single thread that links every successful salesperson is described by the word passion. Passion is defined as *"extreme compelling emotion"* or *"intense emotional drive."* It is my belief that all successful salespeople are, in some way, passionate about what they do, how they do it, and for whom they do it. In the next few pages, we will look at ways that you can build and use passion to **"Set Yourself on Fire."**

Okay, you say. You accept the premise that passion is a major component in moving people to act and, particularly in sales, to buy. From where does this passion come?

When I was just a teenager at Watonga High, there was this girl. Her name was Valerie Voluptuous. That was not her real name, of course, but one that very (very) adequately describes her. When I was a teenager, I used to dream of her. She had long, blond hair. She was five-foot, eleven. Her measurements were 38-25-32, or was it 48-25-32. I'm not sure, since my "buds" and I used to spend hours discussing how we would ask her to the prom and how she would actually accept. The longer we talked, the more beautiful she got. She was two years older than me and would not have been caught dead being seen with an underclassman. But, just like the Olds 88, I had my dreams of Valerie and me walking off into the sunset, holding hands, stopping occasionally to admire one another, and then walking on, all the while listening to Elvis singing "Burnin' Love."

My purpose in all this is to demonstrate that passion begins with vision. Robert Greenleaf in the Servant Leader said it best: *"Not much happens without a dream. And for something great to happen, there must be a big dream. Behind every great achievement is a dreamer of great dreams. Much more than a dreamer is required to bring it to reality; but the dream must be there first."* My vision of Valerie Voluptuous built a passion in me that still stirs me some number of years later (a big number of years). Great salespeople, great sales successes, are built upon a passion that is derived from a vision that inspires. The opening line of the prologue to the inspiring Shakespearian drama "Henry V" is a call to inspiration: *"O for a muse of fire, that would ascend the brightest heaven of invention:"* Henry went on to win a battle with the French even though he was greatly outnumbered. Great salespeople are people who first have a dream, a vision that inspires passion.

Passion alone will not produce great sales results. There must be a conduit by which the passion can be transmitted if meaningful results are to be achieved. To make this point, let me return to Valerie Voluptuous. I had a great passion for Valerie, but nothing ever came of it. Valerie went on to fulfill someone else's dream, and I was left with memories (good ones, but still memories). Such is the case with many salespeople who dream great dreams and have received that "muse of fire" but had nowhere to go with it. Salespeople, to be successful, must first "set themselves on fire," but for that fire to have any effect before is burns out, it must touch someone or something. Salespeople are the *kindling* that sets other people and things in motion. Let's take a look at a system that can best work as a conductor of passion to the customer, a passion that compels the customer to buy.

My experience has been that sales of almost every kind are composed of only four disciplines. They are: **Building Trust**, **Clarifying the Customer's Wants and Needs**, **Presenting the Solution**, and **Asking for the Decision**. If I were asked which of the four disciplines were the most important, I would say Clarifying Wants and Needs, and Building Trust. All four disciplines are essential, however, building trust and clarifying wants and needs comprise nearly eighty percent of the sale. As such, let's investigate those two tasks first.

Building Trust

I chair two groups of CEOs for TEC International in Houston, Texas. These CEOs meet monthly to work together on growing their companies. I hand pick the groups. In putting the groups together, I make sure there is diversity of industry and commitment to grow. When these two groups were first formed, the meetings were rather stiff and dealt primarily with surface issues. However, as the group members became more familiar with one another and their individual wants and needs became more apparent, they began to trust one another. As the trust grew, the depth of the issues worked on by the group deepened. As the issues became more real, the people became more real. The more real the people became, the greater became the value of their time together. I use this example to make the point that building trust is a critical part of effective communication. Unless and until I trust you, I will never listen, truly listen, to what you have to say.

The very best salespeople I have ever observed or had the pleasure of working with were excellent at building trust because they were masters at communication. Brian Tracey says that people buy from people they trust, and you don't build trust by talking, you build trust by listening. Stop a moment and think about listening. We take college courses in speech and writing, but I have never seen college credit for Listening 101. Have you? Yet masters of communication know the value of listening. Stephen Covey in his book *The 7 Habits of Highly Effective People* listed as Habit Number 5, "Seek first to understand, then to be understood." Sales trainers talk about the importance of listening 80% of the time and talking only 20%.

Let's stake our tent here for a while and explore the means of building trust. The old Zen Master quote "I don't care how much you know, until I know how much you care" is a fitting starting place. How do we as salespeople send the message to the customer that we really care? Let's start with the premise that you build trust by listening. The first thought that comes to mind is how do you do that? How do you control the dialogue (two people exchanging ideas) as opposed to monologue (one person telling)? Often the sales call ends unsuccessfully because the conversation between the seller and the buyer is not a dialogue, but, rather, a collective monologue. Have you ever observed or found yourself engaging in collective monologue? I have. A collective monologue is a conversation where the buyer and the seller are engaged in *telling* one another. While one is talking, the other is preparing to talk, and as a result hearing but not listening. Hearing is easy. You hear a train. You hear music but seldom listen to the words.

However, you listen for the baby's cry. You listen for that strange sound in the refrigerator. You listen when you ask for instruction. Listening means that you go beyond hearing and open yourself to the wants and needs of your buyer.

How do you, the seller, make sure that the conversation is a dialogue? Certainly it begins with preparation by the seller. The preparation starts with the seller's decision to remain in control of the conversation. By preparing the questions, you can commit to listening. If you know the questions, you don't have to be thinking of the question you will ask next while the buyer is answering the last question. You can truly listen. It is a funny thing about listening; when you do it, really do it, people notice. The preparation necessary to be recognized as a great listener consists of defining the features and benefits of your product clearly and designing questions that uncover the wants and needs of the buyer. This is easily said, but not so easily done. Right? Wrong! Remember that our purpose is to *structure a conversation that will enable us to listen most of the time as opposed to talking most of the time.* There are two skills a salesperson must master: probing (asking meaningful questions) and listening to the answers.

Over the years, I have developed several "I want to understand," "I care," and "I want to help" questions, and I want to share some of them with you. When you want to understand, ask these questions:

- What is important to you about _____?
- What have you already done about it?
- How did that work?
- What would be an ideal outcome?

When you want to communicate that you really care, try these questions:

- If I could show you how you could _____, would you be interested?
- Would you be interested in looking at some alternative solutions?
- Are there other options you would consider?

When you want to let them know you want to help, try these questions:

- I have found _____ to be effective; would that be something you would consider?
- If you were to _____, could that help?
- If I could _____, would that be of some assistance?

There are many more, but you get the idea. Your questions should be written down so that you don't have to think about them with a space directly below for recording the response. You can comfortably set up the fact that you will be referring to notes during the conversation by saying something like: "I have made a few notes that I will be referring to so that I will not miss anything during our conversation. Will that be alright?"

I would like to turn your attention to the second part of *building trust*: listening. As we touched on earlier, we are adept at hearing, but hearing is not listening. Listening is connecting the external sound of talking to the mind for the purpose of understanding what is being said. Nedo Qubien, in his book *How to Be a Great Sales Profes-*

sional, said that listening has three basic elements: interpretation, evaluation, and reaction. Because we think much faster than we talk, the tendency, when we listen, is to let the mind rush ahead of the speaker and anticipate what they will say. In doing so, we miss out on what the speaker, in this case the buyer, is actually saying. The first step to good listening is to put a governor on the mind. Resist the tendency to anticipate what the answer to the question will be. Pause, in the moment, to listen for the first sound from the speaker's mouth. Look them in the eye, listen, and then hear the response, and write it down or, at least, abbreviate the response. Ask a follow-up question like: "Could you tell me more about that?"

Finally, good listeners will always give feedback. Feedback can be verbally paraphrasing the speaker's response or simply body language, like occasionally shaking your head in agreement. Good listening gets the speaker/buyer involved in the sales process, but most importantly it builds trust. By asking questions and truly listening, you show that you care, and when the buyer begins to sense that you care they begin to trust. When they trust, they feel safe, and when they feel safe, they become open to you and your solutions.

Clarifying and Defining Wants and Needs

Howard Schutz became CEO of one of the most successful companies in America by paying attention to what people wanted. In his book *Put Your Heart into It: How Starbucks Built a Company One Cup at a Time*, he tells the story of how Starbucks evolved. His original idea was to sell coffee-making equipment and coffee beans, on a small scale, to coffee-lovers. One fateful day, however, he noticed that a rather small operation in Seattle was ordering more coffee makers than big volume retailers such as Macys. He flew to Seattle and was amazed at what he found: A small coffee house with a steady flow of customers who were not only buying the strongest coffee he had ever tasted but were lingering for fellowship with the "never ending" line of customers. With the vision of how society was hungering for a place, other than bars, to gather and share a drink, he began one of America's most successful sales stories. Had Schultz not taken the time to investigate the wants and needs of customers to understand what drove them, what we know as a major success today might never have come to pass.

Developing a passion for understanding the wants and needs of prospects and customers is no easy task. The natural tendency is to rush to the presentation of solutions once the first signal of need appears. Resist the temptation! It is important to "pitch you tent" on the needs area for a while. You see, people don't always buy what they need. In the trust building/discovery phase, it is important to, first, identify the prospect's needs. However, the most important discovery is not what the prospect needs, but what they want. It is here, in the "emotion of wants," that sales are made.

It is here, amidst the emotions of want, that we move beyond price and engage the prospect on an emotional level. A prospect may need reliable transportation but want a Lexus. We are first emotional beings, then rational. My observation has been that the great salespeople are people of emotion, people of passion. Most importantly, great salespeople are those who have learned how to touch their prospect in a deep way. Let's look at some tools that will deliver gigantic blocks of value to the prospect and build on the wants to the extent that "there is no close, only agreement." It is all in the skill of questioning, connecting, and listening. Example:

> **Prospect**: I am looking for good economical transportation.
>
> **Salesperson**: Great, what did you have in mind?
>
> **Prospect**: Oh, maybe something like that little car over there.
>
> **Salesperson**: Really, that Camry? What is it that appeals to you about that car?
>
> **Prospect**: I don't know, it looks like it might be in my price range.
>
> **Salesperson**: What might that be, your price range, that is?
>
> **Prospect**: Oh, about $450/month.
>
> **Salesperson**: Other than price, what else do you want in your car?
>
> **Prospect**: Well, I prefer green as an exterior color with a tan interior, and I like power windows and seats.
>
> **Salesperson**: I see. Go on, describe for me your ideal car, if price were not an issue.

Prospect: If price were not an issue? Well, I would want a much bigger car, with 4 doors, a lot of horsepower for rapid acceleration, and a moonroof.

Salesperson: What is important about the size and the number of doors?

Prospect: Well, right now we have a two-door, and it is too small to carpool, which I do twice a week. I was almost killed last week because I couldn't get up to speed fast enough as I entered the freeway.

Salesperson: So, you feel that your personal safety may be sacrificed in a small, underpowered car, is that right?

Prospect: Yes, I am scared to death to drive on the freeways.

Salesperson: I understand. Let me ask you a question. If I could show you a car that had a powerful engine, four doors, all the other amenities that you wanted, and still in your price range, would you buy it?

Prospect: Sure, but I didn't think I could afford anything like that.

Salesperson: That is my job, to get people what they want. Let's walk on around to the car that meets all of your wants, and while you are getting to know it a little better, I'll be getting the paperwork ready. If I could just have your driver's license for a minute, I can get the process started.

Time spent preparing the right questions that help to bring "wants" to the surface is what separates the good from the great. Know the questions you are going to ask to discover the wants and learn to pitch your tent there until the prospect sees so much value that the close simply becomes an agreement.

The Presentation

A water buffalo as a house pet creates a lot of problems. Few people want to live with a water buffalo. They are big and muddy, and they stink. But I loved Herby and did not want to lose him as a friend and companion. In Watonga, people are pretty much average, with not many people on either side of the bell-curve. Still, Watongans did not want a water buffalo in their town (Watonga was my home town), much less next door. I won't bore you with the story of how Herby and I became best friends and roommates. As you might imagine, my neighbors were looking for legal means to rid themselves of the stigma of living next door to a water buffalo. Sensing the pressure and the likelihood of losing Herby altogether, I developed a strategy for keeping Herby.

You will not believe the solution that kept Herby and me together...well, almost together. You see, Watonga High had as their *symbolized* mascot a bald eagle. We were the Watonga Eagles. In fact, we had been the Watonga Eagles since the beginning of time as best I know. No one, however, had ever experienced the thrill of a group of bald eagles over-flying the start of a football game, much less roosting on the backboard structure at the "home team" end of the gymnasium. You might say that Watongans were feeling unfulfilled. It did not seem likely that Watongans would ever experience the thrill of eagle poop on their shoulder, since the United States government had declared them an endangered species. There were long faces and bouts with depression until I had a flash of brilliance.

One day, while walking down Leach Street, on my way to school, I had an epiphany. Since we could not have a bald eagle as a mascot, what about a water buffalo? A water buffalo was certainly unique. It was big and powerful, yet kind of snuggly. We could parade Herby around the football field before the game and scare the "you know what" out of our opponents. Herby was a perfect solution to the deepening depression of Watongans. I proposed the idea to the Principal, then to the student body, and gained unanimous approval for Herby to be the mascot. He was given a place of prominence at the fairgrounds, was washed and groomed weekly, and was fed only the very best water buffalo foods and nutrients. The whole town was proud of Herby, and so was I.

The point that I want to make is this; Herby was unwanted when Watongans saw him as a water buffalo, but when they viewed him as their mascot, he was regarded highly. It was all in the presentation.

I have never observed a situation where a sale was made solely as a result of the presentation. On the other hand, I have observed the loss of many sales as a result of poor presentations. The real heavy lifting on the way to a successful sale is done in steps, building trust and then defining and clarifying wants and needs. If we have done our work in these first two steps, the presentation will simply cover facts discovered in these steps. How we present those facts can, however, be everything. Exactly how do we present a solution? There are, of course, many successful methods of presenting solutions, and I am not presumptuous enough to think that I have the only way. In the following example, you will observe a system that will work successfully in many different sales scenarios. Example:

> **Salesperson**: Mrs. Jones, let me see if I can recap our conversation. You both are concerned about being able to send your two children to college. Am I correct?

> **Prospect**: Yes.

> **Salesperson**: You both are concerned about having adequate retirement funds in fifteen years. Is that right?

> **Prospect**: Yes, that's right.

> **Salesperson**: You both are committed to doing something about it. Is that right?

> **Prospect**: Yes, we are.

> **Salesperson**: If I could present to you affordable solutions based on the facts we have shared earlier, you would be happy, right?

> **Prospect**: We sure would.

> **Salesperson**: Let's take a look at the solutions I have prepared, okay?

> **Prospect**: Okay!

> **Salesperson**: Most Americans are concerned about the same issues that concern the two of you, Mrs. Jones;—paying your bills, retirement, and education for your children—so you are not alone. You are wise to challenge these issues as opposed to ignoring them. Taking no action can only make these two issues more difficult to solve in the future. So, let's take a look.

At this point the Salesperson would begin to make the transition to the closing phase of the sales process. While the presentation and the close comprise only twenty percent of the sales process, there are still critical success factors that must be addressed if the process is to end in success.

The Close

As a professional sales consultant, I work with hundreds of salespeople every year. Through that experience, I have observed both good and bad, but the truly great salespeople are always masters at asking for agreement and getting the check. One of the greatest salespeople who I have ever known is a man named Gordon Kelly. Gordon is a man of average size and intellect. He has no distinguishing characteristics beyond a very pleasant Scottish accent that seems to draw a listener's ear to attention. But, the accent is not what makes him great. It is his passion for making the sale and his commitment to purpose. His closing ratio is near perfect. I have never encountered such an efficient sales professional, and his remarkable successes make for a great University of Closing. So, let's go to school!

Gordon Kelly, as all master salespeople do, has a system. It is well planned, practiced, and in a state of continuous improvement. His system begins with the "end in mind"—the end, in this case, being *The Close*. One of his very first comments in a selling interview is, "Mr. Jones, I am here today to see if there are any benefits, for you and your company, in the service my company provides. *If there are any, I will tell you*. This last statement is a remarkable tool, and we will look at it in depth just a little later.

Following that opening, he begins the trust-building process by establishing his own credibility in a very low-key fashion and beginning a probing process that brings to the surface deep background information from the prospect. He uses questions that send a message while engaging the prospect and keeping them alert and present.

After the probing process, Gordon reviews the wants and needs discovered and matches the benefits in his service with those wants and needs. He asks for agreement, and moves to the close. The close actually begins with the statement he made at the beginning of the presentation, "If there is any value in my service for you and your company, *I will tell you.*"

When I first heard Gordon make that statement, I thought, "Wait a minute, isn't the prospect supposed to identify the values?" I thought, "Isn't it arrogant for this guy to tell the customer what they will get out of this service? He has really blown this one." But, after observing him many times and finding that the prospect never once voiced an objection to his boldness, and after looking at his results compared to other talented salespeople in a similar role, I began to look for the benefit in that statement.

What I found was that this simple statement did several very important things. It established who was in control. Control is the difference between Gordon's record and the record of others. It is like going to a doctor's office. You don't go to the there for self-diagnosis. You go there to **be diagnosed**. Gordon, in that simple statement, did what most salespeople attempt but fail to do throughout their careers. He takes control, and establishes his expert status at the beginning and never relinquishes it. Here is how the conversation might go:

> **Gordon**: [He always makes the transition into the close with what seems like a long pause and a careful but determined effort to gain eye-contact.] Mr. Jones, I told you at the beginning of our conversation, if there was any value in my service for you and your company, I would tell you. This is what I see: You have no Board of Directors, and not only does my company give you access to an informal Board of Directors, but they have no hidden agendas as formal boards often do. I heard you say that you often felt isolated in your role as CEO, unable to openly discuss problems with even your closest direct report. My process gives you a coach to help you through those difficult decisions in a safe and secure environment. There are many others, but those are the major blocks of value. **Tell me, what values do you see for yourself and your company in my service?**
>
> **Prospect**: I agree with you, but I also see X, Y, or Z.
>
> **Gordon**: I agree, and it would seem to me that the next step is for us to schedule our coaching session. Do you have your calendar handy? How about next Tuesday at nine?
>
> **Prospect**: That will work.

At this point, Gordon moves from his chair, in front of the prospect's desk, walks around the prospect's desk, leans over the prospect's shoulder, lays the application in front of the prospect, and says:

Gordon: The beautiful part of our service is that there is no contract and no long-term commitment, only a pledge of confidentiality. What you see here is simply an application, not a contract. Take a look at the first five statements, which say simply that you and those in your group respect the confidential nature of the things we discuss, and anything said in the group stays in the group. [He points to the signature line.] If you agree with that, just sign and date right here.

Gordon quickly completes the application that was partially completed prior to the interview, hands the member his copy, and asks an unassuming question as he pulls out the invoice for the membership fee:

Gordon: How would you like to take care of this?

Prospect: We pay on the first and the fifteenth; I'll see that it gets out then.

Gordon: Fine, if you would just sign here and make me a copy of it, I will get your information into membership today.

The masterful part of Gordon's close is the ease with which he gets the money. I have watched him many times, and it borders on magic. Asking for the money is often awkward, but Gordon makes it a non-event. When I asked him how he makes it so easy, he pointed out his *getting up and walking around the prospect's desk* as the most powerful part of his close.

He believes that removing the barrier of the desk and standing over the prospect's shoulder are two critical actions and enhance his success significantly. He believes that removing the desk-barrier and standing in close proximity to the prospect, and looking over their shoulder, creates a sense of trust and promotes bonding. I agree. Gordon closes eight of ten of his opportunities while his peers close only three of ten. Over 300% above average, Gordon says that in closing it is the little things that make the big difference. But, certainly, *going to the close with a clear plan of action, knowing what you are going to say*, and *knowing how the prospect is likely to respond* are the things that make great salespeople.

Few salespeople enter the field to be average. Most of us dream big dreams. We are not interested in just meeting quota, but rather, blowing it away. We are all looking for that "edge," something that will give us an advantage. Passion is a major factor, but there is more required than passion.

Bruce Wilkinson, author of the *Prayer of Jabez—Breaking Through to the Blessed Life*, says that most of us live on "the cutting edge," just this side of greatness. He suggests that the real giants in this world live on the other side of the edge, but few of us have the courage to move beyond the edge. What is it, then, that compels people to move "beyond the edge?" What is it that gives people the courage to take the risk of pursuing greatness?

It certainly requires passion, but what else? We have just completed the investigation of a sales system that will work for you as it has many others, but it is of little value if it lies unused. Passion, by definition, compels action. Passion is only the fuel. Passion without action is of little value. Breakthrough sales results require persistent action—learning action, contacting action, and closing action—not just once, but over and over, persistently.

Doing one thing over and over, without a purpose, is a pretty boring task no matter what you might be doing. The sales process is a way of doing the same thing over and over. Every successful salesperson I have ever known had a purpose. They were passionate about that purpose. Their purpose might be to glorify God, to buy a new house, or to send a child to college. It is this purpose that transcends the daily "stuff." It goes beyond the surface. One might say that the formula for success is Passion + Persistence + Purpose = Success.

Become passionate about what you do, and do it often and for a reason. **"Set yourself on fire," today!**

About The Author

Stephen Blakesley

 Stephen graduated from the University of Oklahoma with a B.S. degree in Chemistry. He holds two postgraduate degrees from American College, a Masters of Science in Management and a Masters of Science in Financial Services. He was CEO and Founder of The Flagship Group from 1974 to 1997. He is currently CEO and Founder of Global Management Systems in Houston, Texas. Additionally, he serves as Chairman of several CEO groups for TEC International (The Executive Committee, an international organization of CEOs).Stephen has served as Board Chairman for Something's Happening, a youth organization in Houston. He currently serves on the State Board of Directors of Prevent Blindness Texas. Additionally, he has served on many Trade Organization Boards. He is a speaker, writer, teacher, coach, and master communicator. His passion is seeing others excel. He teaches a Bible Study class and is the husband of Lillian. They have six children and twenty grandchildren. His Life Mission is guided by the following quote; *"We all must die, but few of us ever really live."*

Stephen Blakesley
Management Systems
14550 Torrey Chase, Suite 255
Houston, TX 77014
Office Phone: 281.444.5050
Cellular: 281.687.9255
Home: 281.370.3856
Email: sjb@globalmanagementsystems.com
www.TheSpeakerMan.com

Chapter 11

The Sales Force

P. William Clarke

A Word From the Author

This chapter will focus on mental preparedness and the mental conditioning necessary to achieve greatness in sales. There will be very few sales tactics and one-liners here. Instead, I prefer to focus on the reasons that salespeople don't execute the techniques and strategies they already know. Some believe that you can't teach someone *how* to sell. This is totally not the case. In fact, it is quite easy to teach someone *how* to sell, the difficult part being actually getting them to do it. Let's face it—if you had Wayne Gretsky as your teacher, you would be able to learn what it takes to become a great hockey player. This does not mean that you could actually go out and do it. I hope you enjoy and grow from this insightful material, and I wish you all the success you truly deserve.

P. William Clarke

Introduction

At the center of George Lucas's film series *Star Wars*, there is a mystical element referred to as the Force. The Force is described as an all-powerful energy field that surrounds us, binds us together, and is the source of strength from which the Jedi Knights draw their power. Likewise, salespeople draw their power from a similar force. I call it the "Sales Force." There are many elements that make up the "Sales Force." It's no secret that the life of a salesperson can be filled with a unique set of challenges that can cause extreme highs and lows. The environment in which a salesperson performs is ever-changing, their mind is never at rest, and they are haunted by the words "what have you done for me lately?" Throughout this chapter, I will be outlining how the Sales Force elements are connected and how they can create either barriers to success or positive selling accelerants. While doing so, I will make a few references to the *Star Wars* movies and some fundamental principles of the Force. If you are already a fan of the original 3 films or have become a fan due to the release of the final 3 episodes, I think you might begin to appreciate George Lucas in an entirely different way. Either way, it makes for an interesting backdrop with which we can have some fun. For those of you among the minority who have not seen these films, you may find some new inspiration to do so.

At this point, I guess it's natural for you to be curious how I came up with this crazy concept in the first place. If you're a speed-reader or a skimmer, slow down, stop skimming, and know that this point is absolutely critical. A combination and knowledge of all the sales techniques combined is insignificant compared to the power of the Sales Force. The Sales Force is what gives a salesperson the edge; it's the unseen, unheard aura that surrounds them. In short, it is the infamous and illusive X factor. As you will find...

...Knowledge does not always correlate directly
with performance.

I have been privileged to work with thousands of salespeople across the US and with international audiences from around the globe. I have put a lot of research into what I am about to share with you. I want you to think about this while you read. There are basically four types of salespeople that I have come to recognize: Can and Will, Can and Won't, Can't and Will, and Can't and Won't. This concept, by the way, has eluded sales managers for years during the interview process. Let me share with you what I mean, by breaking each down. For the next few minutes I would like you to put yourself in the role of interviewer for an open sales position at your company.

You will be interviewing 4 individuals today, and the first one is your 8 o'clock interview, (Can and Will). This candidate walks in, and as you begin to formulate a first impression, you notice the individual is well dressed, well groomed, and perhaps even attractive. As time goes on, you notice that they are well spoken, charming, attentive, and actually quite bright. You move into the area of sales where, to your delight, the candidate's knowledge of positive sales practices, techniques, and methods is equally impressive. You think you have a tiger by the tail, but you have 3 more interviews today.

Your 10 o'clock, (Can and Won't), walks in, same as the first, looking good, sounding good, knowing everything about sales, and well connected in your industry—you couldn't ask for more. The only concern you have is how you are going to choose between the two. Just then you remember the two remaining candidates. Perhaps one of them will be even better and make your decision easier.

Your 11 o'clock, (Can't and Will), shows up. As he passes through the doorway, your candidate, a middle-aged gentleman, stumbles a bit, managing to keep his balance but in the process dropping his portfolio case and its contents all over the floor. Right off, you're thinking that this is probably not the tiebreaker you were looking for. The candidate collects his belongings from the floor, stands up, and with a big smile says, "Hi. I'm yur meetin' fur 11." You invite the candidate to take a seat, and as he wrestles with his wrinkled, full-length Columbo-like raincoat, you look out the window and notice that there is not a cloud in the sky. As the interview progresses, you find the candidate to be verbally challenged and not really articulate. His tie poor contrasts poorly with the rest of his ensemble, too short and perhaps a bit on the wide side. You ask some specific questions about the sales process and are unable to detect clearly whether this person really knows anything about sales. In the spirit of being professional, you decide to provide the candidate the allotted time remaining for the interview. Fortunately, the candidate brings up a non-business subject that you personally have some interest in that seems to pass the time. Because you feel somewhat sorry for the candidate, you decide to answer all of his questions related to your company and the position being offered. He leaves you with that same big smile that he greeted you with as you realize that you're now running late for the fourth interview.

You now have one more chance to break the tie between your first two candidates. In walks your final interview. Right off, things are not looking good. They don't look good or sound good, and you wonder how they made it to the final interview stage.

Upon completion, you walk the candidate to the front desk to see them off. The receptionist flags you that you have a call holding, and it's the President of your company. Back in your office, you pick up the phone call and are told that you must bring four candidates on board immediately. You explain about the last two interviews, but the president insists that you hire all four anyway to cover for a major marketing campaign being launched next week. Besides, the President says, when the promotion is over in six months, the company can get rid of the two worst and keep the two best.

Having no choice, you welcome all four aboard in the following weeks. Right out of the gate, the first candidate, (Can and Will), lands a terrific sale. You're not surprised due to your observations while conducting the interview. But, what happens next is unbelievable. Remember the third candidate, (Can't and Will), the one who dropped his portfolio all over the floor? He just signed a major customer who your company has been after for three years. You figure it must have been luck, and although you celebrate the victory, you really don't pay it much attention. Now, the second candidate, your other surefire salesperson, (Can and Won't), has yet to turn anything up, but they've assured you that they have some good things cooking. The fourth and final candidate, (Can't and Won't), let's just say...hasn't. You manage the promotion over the next several months, and as you predicted end up with two clear sales leaders and two who should never have been hired.

As you probably have guessed, the two top salespeople weren't the first two choices from your candidate pool. Instead, the two best salespeople ended up being candidate one, (Can and Will), and the third candidate, (Can't and Will).

Let's recap these four very different profiles. The first, (Can and Will), looked good, sounded good, said all the right things, knew everything about sales, and went in to the marketplace and actually performed. The second, (Can and Won't), was the same as the first, but, despite their positive attributes, was approaching prospects without the Sales Force as their ally, and as a result, was unknowingly plagued by forces that neutralized their apparent strengths. Let me give you an example of this. A circus elephant, when not performing, is chained to an immovable object early in life and quickly learns that when it is shackled it cannot move or run away. After years of conditioning, the elephant believes that whenever its leg is shackled it cannot move, whether or not it is secured to an immovable object. Trainers at this point can simply shackle them to a small ball and chain and keep them from moving, as the elephant believes itself to be secured and that any effort to move would be futile. Thus, the power and strength of the elephant has been neutralized by its false sense of being unable to flee. It is the same as our salesperson (Can and Won't). Our third profile (Can't and Will) didn't look good, didn't sound good, and didn't seem to know a lot about selling, but despite conventional wisdom went out and produced significant sales. Finally, the fourth (Can't and Won't) couldn't and didn't. As a sales trainer, you could imagine my frustration in dealing with people who obviously had the right stuff to make it but didn't, and also those who didn't have the right stuff but made it. It finally hit me like a brick when I figured out that I was looking at the wrong stuff altogether, and that's what prompted the research and ultimate discovery of the Sales Force.

Note:

I decided early on that the Sales Force concept would be written into a full-length book, which is currently underway. It's such a vast and important topic that it will take several hundred pages to introduce all of the elements, expose all of the barriers to success, and provide helpful solutions thereto. The nice folks at Insight Publishing, publishers of the Power Learning book series, asked me to contribute a small portion of the Sales Force to their sales collection. I was overjoyed to do it, so let me explain how we are going to move forward. In the following paragraphs, I will be outlining four essential Sales Force elements, each with its own explanation. Next, I will expose one of the sales barriers to success. At this time, we will refer back to the candidates and draw comparisons between them and things about which we were wrong when we were looking at the wrong stuff. Additionally, I will outline strategies for you to implement and begin your mastery of these four Sales Force elements immediately.

The Sale Force Elements

Desire

This element refers to the level of importance placed on obtaining any one thing. Webster's dictionary defines this as: to wish or long for, to crave, to want. It's the accelerant that feeds the motivating forces within you. These forces are in turn directly responsible for you getting what you want. Desire is specific to each task or undertaking. Some people are motivated to be successful because they have been conditioned to believe that that is what they should do. I see them as people who are motivated by external forces, and as a result, in many instances their ability to maintain desire fluctuates. Truly successful people manifest desire internally and achieve more because their internal forces are intensely focused on an objective. Salespeople who possess strong internal desire have a true sense of purpose and are more likely to maintain a high level of desire. A sense of purpose is not only essential to building desire but also to maintaining a healthy outlook, one of the crucial elements we will be discussing later.

Commitment

Commitment refers to your ability to bind yourself to a task, objective, or path without regard to the severity of obstacles placed before you on the way to accomplishment. This is an all-or-nothing state of mind. In *The Empire Strikes Back*, Luke Skywalker visits Jedi master Yoda and begins his Jedi training. At a much later point, Luke attempts to resurrect his starship from the swamp in which he crash-landed. When Luke uses Jedi mind powers, the starship begins to rise slowly, in the end only to fall deeper into the murky depths. In his failure, Luke tells Yoda that he had tried but felt the starship was too big. Yoda responds by telling Luke that the starship was too big only in his mind and further states that there is no such thing as try.

There is only do or do not!

This works the same with commitment. You either are or you are not!

Let me give you something to think about. I live in upstate New York and frequent beautiful beaches along Lake Ontario. The water temperature hovers around 67 degrees (cold). Picture yourself at a beach like this with your friends or family. It's a hot afternoon, so you all decide to go for a swim. Inevitably there are two ways to approach this situation. One is to wade in, first your feet, next your calves, and so on. The other way is the ready-set-go method, getting a good running start and diving right in. I have watched this for years. The people who make the mad dash always end up swimming, while a high percentage of the others barely make it up to their knees. The same thing happens at the pool. Some jump off the diving board right away and others try to go down the ladder. There are some subtle differences between these two groups of people. They have both verbalized their commitment to swim. The only difference between them is that one group has the desire and is committed to swim and the other has the desire to swim but has placed mental conditions on actually swimming. Very few people ever take to the ladder approach thinking they're going to just hang there, but that's what a good many do.

Commitment is a mental decision. In the preceding example, I shared with you a weakness undermining a strength. Those beachgoers and pool loungers have, in effect, created a Houdini clause, a back door to call upon if the conditions are not to their liking. In sales, a commitment filled with a host of contingencies is the same as no commitment at all. A salesperson needs to have and hold the deepest unwavering commitment. Successful salespeople are highly committed to sales, personal growth, their companies, and many other aspects of their lives. They are committed without condition. Others are committed as long as things go the way they want or expect. When a situation becomes less to their liking, they quickly exchange their commitment for an excuse. Commitment is often tied to the level of desire an individual has related to a particular undertaking. It is important to understand that desire has a direct correlation to commitment and that many people are uncommitted due to an overall lack of desire. Over time, people with a lack of desire develop a noncommittal mental condition, which undermines their efforts and leads to ultimate and inevitable defeat. When this happens within an individual, commitment becomes nearly impossible even when a strong desire of an objective is present.

Outlook

This is the most variable element, meaning that, of all the elements, this one fluctuates more on a day-to-day, week-to-week, and month-to-month basis than any other. Outlook is the lifeline of a salesperson. A salesperson often can face negative input, negative reactions, and is sometimes treated less than respectfully. This activity can create an outlook problem; in sales, this is the worst problem to have. Over time, salespeople who are susceptible to outlook problems allow prospects and customers to chip away at their self-esteem. Outlook is a culmination of views and perceptions an individual has of their own past, present, and future. Let me break these three things down, starting with the past, which is nothing more than a history lesson. We are influenced by our past as we learn life lessons. History plays a major role in who we are; after all, we are a product of our history. It's true that the things we have done have gotten us where we are, but they don't define who we are. As always, it is important to remember that the past doesn't equal the future. However, conditioning comes into play here. We are who we think we are. Our belief system determines our future. There are some folks out there who seem to have had an unlucky past. The truth is that luck had very little to do with it. I do believe in some element of luck, call it good fortune; however, my definition of luck is a place where preparation and opportunity meet. An individual who has a strong desire for success is more likely to seek it. An individual with a strong outlook is more likely to maintain their commitment to success. They are then much more likely to be "lucky" than people who do not share these characteristics. Things are what they are, and it is critically important to remember that the past doesn't have to equal the future.

The impact we have is in the here and now, which brings me to the present. Outlook is highly influenced by the present, the current, the here and now. Your outlook is a result of how you feel about your job, the company for which you work, the job you do, your family, and your friendships. And, more importantly, the present shapes our attitude. In sales, attitude encompasses self-image and mental disposition, which are influenced by how an individual perceives themselves (outlook), their company, their industry, the economic marketplace, and their role therein. A salesperson with an attitude problem is like a racecar with no engine. It's not going anywhere! My friends, there are a few types of people out there. Take the water glass theory; the glass is half empty or the glass is half full. There is a lot of each, but the ones who don't fit into these two classifications are the third type...

...Just happy to have something to drink.

If you are in a sales job that's less than perfect, get a grip. That's why you get paid more than anyone else! Just be glad that you have the ability to affect your income and financial security each day in a way that many other employees at your company could never even dream about. But, if you're working for an unethical company, get out. If you're working in a dying industry, get out. If you're selling in a marketplace in which neither you nor your competitors are selling products or services, get out. You are in the driver's seat, so take control and realize that a bad attitude is poisoning your outlook, and if allowed to run wild will spoil even the most joyous events in your life.

This brings me finally to the future, the most important and impact-full portion of your outlook. Plain and simple, it's the extent to which you believe that your dreams will actually come true. Henry Ford once said, "Whether you believe you can do a thing or not, you are right." Do you have a dream, are you on course, do you have a plan, and are you doing the things you need to do today to make your dreams come true? Are you making excuses or making things happen? Only you have the answers to these questions, but explore your answers for a moment. Be truthful with yourself. You will never fool yourself into believing that you have done your best if in fact you haven't. You have a natural call to action, and whether you like it or not, your subconscious mind is holding you accountable. It knows what needs to be done and expects you to do it! When you don't, your subconscious sends harsh messages like: "What's wrong with you?" "Are you some kind of loser?" "Are you lazy?" or "Are you ever going to amount to anything?" Over time, these messages can play heavily on how you feel about your ability to achieve results until you hear yourself saying, "Why even try?" Once this record begins to play in your mind, you begin to develop further supportive evidence to prove that you shouldn't try. Once again, you review your past for all the negativity you need to prove your point, which continues to lower your self-image, self-esteem, self-worth, and ultimately your outlook. The cycle perpetuates itself and detracts from the fundamental belief in yourself.

In the scene described above where Yoda raised the spaceship from the swamp, at one point, in disbelief, Luke whispers, "I don't believe it." Yoda quietly replies by saying, "That is why you fail." The fundamental energy that gives the salesperson their power is rooted in self-belief, the cornerstone of a healthy outlook. There are a few tips ahead in the final section for improving and maintaining your outlook.

Responsibility

The word responsibility is rooted in the word responsible. Webster defines responsible as: answerable or accountable, as for something within one's own power, control, or management. Being answerable and accountable for good results is rarely a problem; it's the negative results and our role we need to be concerned with.

Let me give you a story. A group of sixth-grade boys are playing in a park. As a condition for going to the park with the guys, one of the boys has to bring his fourth-grade sister. Over time, this boy begins to get frustrated with the tag-along sister because she is continuously in the way, trying to show off in front of the older boys. At one point, she bumps into her brother while dancing around like a loon. He reacts by shoving her to the ground, an otherwise harmless act. But, when she falls to the ground, she splits her lip, which immediately begins bleeding as she starts running home to mom. Two thoughts go through the boy's mind: is she okay?, and I'm really going to get it for this one. The boy now has a few choices: catch up to sister and convince her that she's okay and promise her anything needed to keep her from telling mom the truth; stay at the park and wait until he gets home to take his punishment; or beat her home and tell his fabricated side of the story first. I don't know about you, but in my world, staying at the park only ensured that mom would be boiling over by the time I got home, and I would get it even worse. Knowing that she has you dead to rights, there is a pretty good chance that sister is going to watch you barbecue, so the only other option is to beat her home and tell mom your side of the story first. The point this makes is that we learn pretty early on that the first story told will tend to carry the most weight.

What does this story have to do with our topic? Well, this works the same with responsibility. Both internal and external factors affect results. People use two fundamental approaches for taking responsibility for negative results. One seeks to evaluate internal factors contributing to the outcome first and then evaluates external factors. We will refer to this type as the Truth Seeker. The other, which we will refer to as the Blame Placer, reacts by first rationalizing what has happened by placing blame on external factors. In sales, it sounds like: "If I had a better territory..." "If the economy was better..." "If our pricing was more competitive..." "If customer service..." "My manager..." on and on and on. Their second reaction is to look at internal factors, which are now overshadowed by the weight placed on the external factors as being the first story told. Now we need to expose a few problems. The first problem with the Blame Placer is that they are placing the emphasis on things that they can't control. When this happens, there is a diminished call to action related to personal changes needed to affect future outcomes. The basic message: "It wasn't my fault, so why should I have to change?" The Blame Placer proceeds in hopes that future outcomes will be greater. They are of the belief that luck will prevail and that all the stars and planets will align, and future outcomes will be different. We all know the saying "If you continue to do what you have done, you'll continue to get what you've gotten." Hope is not a strategy, people. Getting back to luck, an interviewer once asked Arnold Palmer to what extent he thought luck was a factor in his golf game. Palmer smiled and said, "All I know is the more I practice, the luckier I get". The Truth Seeker believes that they have a direct or indirect effect on everything around them, even when they don't. Would you say that one golfer has an impact or effect on another tournament player? How about Tiger Woods? Without regard to how he is playing, he maintains a light-hearted yet determined demeanor. Do you think there is a psychological effect on the other player? Even if Tiger is not on top of his game, do you think the front-runner is worried about Tiger making a comeback? You bet they are, and he has direct control over creating the perception that it is possible. Like Arnold Palmer, Tiger Woods knows that he has a direct effect on his golf game, and if his game is not up to par, it is a result of his own execution. The Blame Placer would blame the weather, the course, the greens, and so on, then secondarily say, "I could have executed more effectively," again putting the emphasis on external factors. A Blame Placer would never have made it to the pinnacle of the sport. A Blame Placer will never make it to the top of any field. The ability to take full responsibility, accurately evaluating your shortcomings contributing to a negative outcome, is the only way to learn from what you have done or not done and correct it in the future.

Why are people predisposed to being a Blame Placer? I told you that I was going to tie the Sales Force elements together, so here we go. There are two manifestations for Blame Placers; one is environmental conditioning, and the other self-preservation. Some people have been brought up in an environment in which they have been allowed to make excuses, often by excuse makers, such that they have been conditioned to think like a Blame Placer. This is the reason I label this "environmental conditioning." The other reason is based largely on the preservation of an individual's outlook. People who have a fragile outlook, even Truth Seekers, are highly unwilling to take responsibility for negative results. They protect their already beat-up outlook by not allowing additional blows to strike in the area of how they feel about themselves. These people also use excuse making to validate their outlook in times when it is at its strongest. Remember, outlook is the most variable of the Sales Force elements, and as such, a fragile outlook could readily swing from positive to negative. An environmentally conditioned Blame Placer with a strong out-look will still be predisposed to making excuses, however will also have an easier time coming to terms with their shortcomings, once pointed out by others.

What's important is to understand that an excuse
will always dilute the recipe for change.

What I mean is that if there is nearly an equal balance between your fault and the external forces, it's mentally a wash, and there is no need for action or change. This is a mental deception. If there is some fault of ours, we should be diligent in our efforts to fix it if we intend to remain competitive in life. Wayne Gretsky, the greatest hockey player ever, Tiger Woods, and any other great achiever all share a common thread. They take responsibility for their actions—win, lose, or draw—and, regardless of the outcome, they work harder on it tomorrow than they did the day before.

Sales Barrier

Sales Barriers are collections of problematic conditions, which render salespeople ineffective or neutralize their strengths. In the next few paragraphs, I will be exposing one of these barriers and share some insights related to the root causes as well as some solutions for the resulting problems. Again, in addition to the four elements I am sharing with you here, there are many more that will appear in the full-length book. Likewise, there are several sales barriers related to the four elements I am sharing with you; however, I selected one of the most misunderstood barriers to success, salespeople not prospecting. Many sales managers believe that the reason their salespeople don't prospect enough is because they are lazy and don't like to work. Although work ethic is a component of this problem, it is clearly not highly influential. I've met many salespeople with strong work ethics, armed with great sales techniques, who fall short in this area. Despite these strengths, they are neutralized, unable to execute.

Problem: Not Prospecting

There is really only one reason why salespeople do not like to prospect. It stinks! We live in a society that's been conditioned for instant gratification. When we don't receive it, we receive instant disappointment. Salespeople fall into this trap, because they know up front that they are going to hear no many times more than yes. I am always astounded when salespeople return for prospecting activities surprised that they actually got the no's they knew they were going to get. The problem resides in the effect this has on outlook. Let's take our first two candidates, both with similar skill sets. Despite their similar strengths, (Can and Will) was successful and (Can and Won't) was not. A healthy outlook gives the salesperson his power, which in turn makes him rejection-proof. A salesperson with a weak outlook develops call reluctance, which is identified in people who make excuses for not prospecting. They do this in an attempt to protect their self-esteem, however this condition becomes worse when they see their lack of follow-through and poor results. This phenomenon manifests itself in salespeople who by all accounts can and should make it but don't, and I refer to them as (Can and Won't) salespeople.

Let's remember our third candidate (Can't and Will), who dropped his papers all over the floor, put it all back together, stood up with a big smile, and just kept on going. Sales is a numbers game, people. This candidate, despite his evident lack of sales savvy, went out, developed prospects, and turned those prospects into customers. I can almost imagine one of his prospecting calls.

He walks up to the front desk, where the receptionist is ditiboppin to the radio, and has the following conversation:

> **Sales Person:** "Mornin', can I see purchasin'?"
>
> **Receptionist:** "We don't like salespeople around here, so get out and don't ever come back!"
>
> **Sales Person:** "That's fine. I guess I don't like 'm much myself. Say, do you get the weather on that-there radio?"
>
> **Receptionist:** "It's coming up next."
>
> **Sales Person:** "Gee, I'm hoping this rain's gonna hold off for my little boy's first little league game tonight. Do you mind if I listen?"
>
> **Receptionist:** "Sure, no problem; just sit over there."

As he sits quietly, waiting for the weather, the receptionist asks, "What is it you are selling, anyway?" and next thing you know he is listening to the weather report from the purchasing office.

He doesn't care that she practically throws him out. He doesn't get defensive, and his feelings don't get hurt. He just keeps moving with that great big smile as if the receptionist were talking to someone else. Those comments just roll off him like water off a duck. Regardless of the outcome, he will walk right out that door and into the next with that same big smile that got him there in the first place, his strong outlook never affected.

An individual with weak or fragile outlook will tend to be really sensitive. They pick up on every negative remark and internalize it as a personal attack. Our (Can and Won't) sales profile could have potentially derailed due to an outlook problem of this sort. By internalizing inevitable rejection, outlook becomes bruised and sensitive to any and all other forms of negative feedback. Although they knew how to and were capable of selling, they would ultimately fail due to a type of paralysis. Under these circumstances, we can witness selling activities diminishing. Ironically, this is done in an attempt to protect their outlook, when in reality this lack of activity undermines one's ability to achieve positive results, which is the very thing that strengthens outlook.

How do we fix or avoid this type of outlook problem? First, understand the problem; next, identify the symptoms quickly if you manifest them; finally, get committed to work on the problem. Once we get this far, we are almost home free. There are two tools that I can give you: my Expectation Management premise and my Constructive Catalog development theory.

Expectation Management Premise

Expectation Management is based on the premise that effectively calculating probabilities for potential outcomes related to a given task or undertaking will minimize our exposure to failure. By not managing our expectations effectively, we develop false expectations, which turn into disappointment that leads to outlook-based problems and a path to the dark side of the Force.

An example from the prospecting scenario: Salespeople go into the field looking for prospects who want to buy. They know well ahead that most of them are going to say no. Yet they still make a goal of finding that one out of a hundred, hoping that the next prospect will be the one to say YES! This is a big mistake since we already know that the odds of this are terrible. It's like finding a needle in a haystack. I like to reverse this notion and actually expect a no. At the same time, I like to have fun while I work, so I made up a little game. Here's how it works. First when I was selling every day, I figured out how many no's I needed before I would get a yes normally. Then I calculated how many no's I needed to make a living each week, and I set a goal to find every one. Yes, I got disappointed every so often when someone wanted to buy, but that's the tradeoff for getting all those character building no's. The second part is that I like to earn their no, so I started making a mental note of the time it took for them to give me a no and make it stick. I found that by doing this, I was much more relaxed and less threatening, and I felt better knowing at the end of the day that I reached my daily goal and that over time I would reach my overall objective. The more I did it the better I got, and the gap between the no's and yeses closed dramatically.

Constructive Catalog Development Theory

Were you to run through a thick briar patch with shorts on, what would you look like when you got to the other side? Sure, you would have a bunch of thorn scratches, scrapes, and cuts. I would call this a negative occurrence. Similarly, if you ran through an open meadow, you might be a bit winded, but there would be no lasting mark or evidence of your activity. I would call this a positive or neutral occurrence.

Our bodies catalog evidence of negative occurrences in the form of scratches, bruises, and scars; however, our bodies retain and show no evidence for positive or neutral occurrences. Our minds work in the same way. Through an incredible computer-like filing system, our brain catalogs many of our everyday occurrences. The negative ones leave lasting traceable evidence, while the positive or neutral occurrences leave very little. This is the reason why people develop the "always-me complex." It always seems like negative things are happening to them because the positive and neutral occurrences have minimal short-term and very little long-lasting impact.

Example: John Q is making the trip in to his office for the 400th time today. Just as he is making his last turn, some guy runs a stop sign and takes out his front fender. John's initial reaction is, "If only I had left the house one minute earlier or one minute later, this would never have happened." My reply to that would be, "That's true John, but what about the other 399 times you made the trip?" Those other 399 days were positive or neutral impact occurrences, so there was not much cause to catalog them, right? That's exactly what I started to do about ten years ago, not for the drive in to the office but for other little things that could have otherwise gone unnoticed. There was the one time I was helping a friend repair his roof. He dropped his hammer while I was working below. It landed about 20 feet from me, but then again it could have landed on my head. There are many instances when negative things that could have happened to us didn't.

I made a conscious decision to look for and take note of those situations and thus have compiled a collection of positive and neutral occurrences, which highly offset the negative ones, and I refer to it as my Constructive Catalog. I hope that you will do the same. In addition, read, apply, and understand the principal of the Emotional Bank Account found in the "Paradigms of Interdependence" section of the book *The 7 Habits of Highly Effective People* by Steven R. Covey. Apply it to this theory, and if you have not read this book, make it a priority.

Fixing Desire

In sales, you really have to want it, something, anything. You must have desire. Luke Skywalker had desire. In the first film, *Star Wars*, it was clear that he wanted to be a Jedi like his father, the father he had never known. He was told as a child that his father was a great fighter pilot, a Jedi—the noblest of men in the galaxy. All of his life he had dreamed about someday being a Jedi Knight like his father before him. Perhaps in some way this would unite them. Regardless of the reason, this dream, vision, and hope intoxicated Luke. It was at the center of everything he did, stood for, and worked toward. It was his motivator.

With so much going on in our lives, it's sometimes hard to answer the age-old question, what do I want to do with my life? This is why so many motivational speakers, me included, talk about the power of goal setting. Michael Gerber, author of *The E-Myth*, makes a point that business owners need to spend more time working *on* their businesses than working *in* their businesses. I think this is a great point. More importantly, I think people need to spend more time working on their lives, when you consider the amount of hours they spend working in their lives. After all, why do we even work? Yes, yes, food, clothing, and shelter! *Review Maslow's hierarchy of needs for some additional insight on this.* What's really important to you; what do you want? Many people don't know the answer, and those who do many times see only a gap between where they are and where they want to be. Desire is critical to sales success. You really have to want something in order to go out and face the challenges and overcome your own objections to selling, as well as those of your prospects.

To build desire, you need a goal. You don't have one? That's okay. I'll give you one. Get out your pen and note pad right now! Stop reading. I am serious! Now that you have your pad and paper, write your name at the top, and under the subject line write "My Goal." In the body, write the following: My goal is to develop a goal within the next 30 days. Sounds silly doesn't it? It's a start. Next, get out your planner and schedule 4 dates with yourself. The first should be over the next few days, and weekly thereafter. They should be 2-hour time slots, done offsite, not at home, not at the office, but in a quiet place where you will concentrate exclusively on your goal. If you need some help, there are a bunch of great materials on developing goals. Seek them out. If you are unable to find what you are looking for, call my office, and my staff will assist you. I make this commitment to you because it's the single most important thing you can do in your life. Forget about your sales job—I said your life. Do it.

What's so important about writing down your goals? Nothing, and that's exactly what you should expect from them if you don't bother to write them down.

The "I have got it all up here in my mind" thing doesn't work! The terms of a signed contract are never going to change. You change your mind like you change your underwear, and you never give it a second thought. If you were stuck out on the middle of the ocean in a rowboat, would you think it wise to keep changing direction arbitrarily? Not if you expect to get to shore! Perhaps your goal of reaching shore will be filled with bad weather, high winds, and crashing waves. Still, you must set a course and remain committed to that course until you reach the shore. There are times when we don't even want to row, and it's no different in life. If you're not committed enough to write your goals down, then your goals are nothing more than an idea, and ideas change. True desire is not maintained through ideas. That would be like a castle built on a seashore firm and standing until the next storm or high tide. And, like the sand castle, your idea is swept away.

Setting goals is an important part of being successful in sales, and in addition to goals you must have well-laid plans. Your sales manager should be helping you with this. The next part is up to you. Earlier on, I had you interview 4 sales candidates. You later helped them develop individual sales activity plans. Their destiny is now in their hands. Candidate three, (Can't and Will), did because he possessed a strong desire, and was committed to executing the plan every day, day after day. This is called commitment, to do it no matter what, no matter how difficult, no matter how tough it gets. That means carrying out your individual sales plan in a consistent manner. And, consistent sales activity also will support and strengthen your outlook. The second component is responsibility, another important component for your 4 candidates. The two who didn't make it, (Can and Won't & Can't and Won't), did not possess this characteristic. Furthermore, they blamed you for their lack of sales success. You have to take responsibility for your own successes and failures. You have to take responsibility for your actions or lack thereof. Again, there are two types of people, Truth Seekers and Blame Placers. Which one are you? The key to taking responsibility is mental conditioning. If your natural tendency is to view external factors first when you cultivate poor results, then you must reprogram your thought process. Seek out what you could have, should have, or might have done differently to improve poor results. Be honest with yourself. The Expectations Management premise will help here. Poorly managing you expectations here, could otherwise have a negative effect on outlook.

Let me leave you with a story. Two mice are scurrying around in a barn, and both fall into a bucket of goat's milk. The mice try to get out, but the stainless steel bucket is too slippery to climb out. As they struggle to stay afloat, one mouse says to the other, "I don't think I can make it." "Nonsense," says the other mouse, "just keep on swimming." They churn and churn as they struggle to stay afloat, their hearts pounding as hope diminishes. Again, the first mouse says, "I can't do it; we're never going to make it," and he eventually gives up and sinks to the bottom of the bucket. Sad at the loss of his friend, the remaining mouse says aloud, "I'm going to keep on swimming until my little heart breaks." He swims and he swims, and over time the milk turns to cream, then eventually to butter, and the little mouse rises to the top of the pail, stepping off to safety.

The moral of the story: You can give out, you can give in, but you can't give up!

P. William Clarke

Paul William Clarke is a powerful speaker and is rapidly becoming a recognized authority on personal and business success. Many believe that his unorthodox high-energy approach in the presentation of success-driving topics has propelled him into the key-note speaking arena as a results generating guru. Paul was inducted into the National Speakers Association in 2001. Paul is the developer of "the Crucial Elements Of Success®" (CEO'S) concept and program, which focuses on navigating the challenges of personal and professional success. Paul is also the innovator behind the "Sales Force" and the Discovery Sales Process®, a sales training process peppered with his real world sales experience. While serving in management for an American top 10 Fortune 100 Company, Paul was recruited as a Senior Consultant within a prominent training and business-consulting firm with affiliate locations thought the U.S. and Canada. His experience there was instrumental in his launch of Discovery Systems International, Inc., (DSI) an organizational and human development company. Today, in addition to professional speaking Paul remains highly involved with the DSI operation and despite his demanding travel schedule he continues to personally conduct training for some of his long-term local clients. Paul, his wife Anna and their three children make their home in Central New York State.

P. William Clarke
Discovery Systems International, Inc.
Salina Meadows Office Park
301 Plainfield Road, Suite 195
North Syracuse, NY 13212
Phone: 315.451.5500
Fax: 315.451.5005
Email: pwc@discoverydsi.com
www.discoverydsi.com

Chapter 12

Selling To The Multicultural Market

Lenora Billings-Harris, CSP

Lee, Faheem, Tracee, Kewal, Lois, Hernando, and Dorothy are account executives for a small but rapidly growing company. Their ages range from 23 to 59; two are single, and two are married; two have domestic life partners; three are child-free, and three are parents; one is gay, and one is blind; one is caring for a parent and two children; two are single parents. There are four languages, and six religious faiths represented by this group. These are today's multicultural customers.

Have you ever lost a sales opportunity because you did not effectively connect with the potential buyer? Has a customer ever requested to speak to your manager before discussing anything with you? Have you ever passed on sales opportunities with certain customers without even attempting to greet them? Have you ever assumed you would not gel with certain people because your age, gender, ethnicity, origin, or religion was different from theirs? If the answer to any of these questions is yes, perhaps you experienced a *multicultural mishap®*.

Everyone judges and is judged by customers, clients, and prospects. In their eyes, perhaps you are too old, too young, too white, too black, or to "foreign" for them, so they decline the chance to interact with you, or visa versa. You cannot change your prospect's values or beliefs, but top sales professionals develop skills to move beyond preconceived notions, in order to develop successful relationships with all types of people.

The following suggestions will help you creatively develop a positive presence within your multicultural marketplace. Additionally, take the time to complete the Multicultural Selling Self-Assessment at the end of this chapter to determine your personal competencies.

It is important to build your knowledge and understanding of different groups, so that you do not rely on biases or stereotypes that exist due to lack of information. Additionally, you don't want to offend or confuse people simply because you were not aware of multicultural behaviors. For example, the American "bye-bye" gesture means "come here" to some people from Southeast Asia. Some Koreans can interpret smiling during business transactions as frivolous behavior. Do your homework by conducting research on the Internet, talking to people in the group you want to reach, and getting involved in organizations whose members are representative of the group with whom you wish to do business.

While it is important to be aware of cultural norms, it is equally important not to stereotype. Stay focused on the individual, and the diversity within groups. This knowledge will help you recognize and appropriately respond to norms when you encounter them and avoid alienating the many potential customers who don't reflect the cultural norms.

Diversity and multiculturalism refer to many dimensions such as height, values, communication style, age, marital status, accent, opinion, and disability, as well as ethnicity, race, and gender.

In this chapter you will have the opportunity to access your skills and discover tips, techniques, and action ideas that will enhance your ability to easily sell to all types of buyers. Other chapters in this book will help you improve your sales process. This chapter will help you improve your ability to use the sales process effectively with people different from you.

Before we explore the options available to enhance your opportunities within multicultural markets, let's take a moment to clarify the meaning of several terms that will appear throughout this chapter.

TERM DEFINITIONS

Assimilation
When the dominant group's behavior becomes the expected standard of behavior for all individuals. People who are different are expected to reject or repress their culture in order to fit in. Often rules are

made simply for the comfort of the dominant or majority group, rather than for clear business reasons. For example, some people of the dominant American culture believe that only English should be spoken in the workplace, even though there are times when two people speaking in their native non-English language would be more practical, efficient, and sometimes even safer.

Acculturation

A process used to help people interact effectively without denying their culture. Individuals across cultures respect the differences of other cultures, flex behaviors when necessary, and are allowed to show their individuality.

Culture

The integrated patterns of customs, beliefs, traits, behaviors, and social norms of various groups. Culture goes beyond race/ethnicity and sex to include age, education, tenure, values, politics, communication styles, and so on.

Multiculturalism

That which pertains to or is designed for several cultures. The effort of acknowledging and showing respect to several different cultures without judgment that one is better than or superior to the other.

Diversity Dilemma

Confusion about the appropriate action to take in various situations due to a lack of understanding or acceptance of differing cultures.

Multicultural Mishap®

A conflict or misunderstanding caused by a lack of knowledge or respect between individuals from different cultures.

Style

As used in the context of this chapter, it refers to behavioral tendencies or preferences, and personality styles.

European American

Alternative words are white, Caucasian, and Anglo; refers to people whose ancestors are descendents from Europe. In this chapter, references to American culture or behavior or mainstream culture are describing European Americans and other Americans who have been assimilated into the mainstream culture of the United States.

African American

The term preferred by most Americans whose ancestors are from one or several African countries. Individuals who immigrated to the United States from Caribbean Islands or South America do not choose this identifier. It is more appropriate to use Jamaican, Dominican, Brazilian, and so on. The term "black" is also acceptable among most people of these origins.

Hispanic

A term created by the US Census Bureau in 1970 to ascertain the number of Spanish-speaking residents. Because of the origin of "Hispanic," many individuals in this group prefer the alternative term of Latino.

Middle Eastern

When used in this chapter, it refers primarily to Arab cultures including Israel, Iraq, Iran, Saudi Arabia, Turkey, Syria, Sudan, United Arab Emirates, Egypt, Jordan, and Kuwait. There are more than 20 countries in the Middle East, each with its own cultural distinctions.

Asian

When used in this chapter, Asian refers to cultures of the Far East, India, and Pacific Islanders.

Native American

This term refers to the various nations and tribes of the indigenous people of the United States. American Indian may also be used.

Seniors

People over sixty-five years of age.

Norm

A common pattern of behaviors and attitudes that characterize a group as it relates to religion, place of birth, ethnicity, sex, age, sexuality, socioeconomics, behavior styles, and values.

Stereotype

A conventional, usually oversimplified opinion, perception, or belief about a person or group without regard to that person's individuality.

As you read this information, keep in mind that this author is not suggesting that all people in any particular group are the same. In order to understand different cultures, it is necessary to identify the most common behaviors, even though everyone does not demonstrate them. When the term "American" is used, this author is referring to anyone, regardless of ethnic group, who is demonstrating the dominant norms of the culture of the United States.

Why Are Multicultural Selling Skills Needed?

Some might assume that if their general sales skills are effective with people who are like themselves, the same skills will work across cultures. Unfortunately, this is inaccurate. People buy based on the comfort and trust they have with the salesperson. Many times sales representatives do and say things that are inappropriate or offensive to others, and they lose the sale without learning what the barrier was. A gesture as simple as crossing your legs at the knee and pointing the bottom of your shoe toward the buyer can cause you to lose the business, if the client is a Middle Easterner. If you have conscious or unconscious biases or prejudices (and all of us do) toward certain groups, your ability to communicate without showing judgment will be negatively affected. The more you know about the norms and values of cultures represented in your market, the less likely it is that you will offend by doing or saying the wrong thing.

When it comes to effective selling across cultures, the Golden Rule does not work. Every religion has some version of the Golden Rule as part of its teachings. It has become embedded in the mainstream American business etiquette. Here's the problem. The Golden Rule suggests that you should treat people the way you want to be treated. This works when you are analyzing values and ethics. For example, since I want people to tell me the truth, I tell the truth. This is a value, and it is an ethical way of doing business so it works. However, when you are trying to determine the best way to communicate and interact with others who are different from you, the Golden Rule makes an assumption that is not necessarily accurate. It presumes that the other person wants to be treated just like you do. Therein lies the possibility for a multicultural mishap®. The more effective approach is to use The Platinum Rule, made popular in Tony Alessandra's book by the same name. It professes that we *treat others the way they want to be treated.*

Effective sales professionals take the time to read their customer or prospect before launching into the sales process. Multicultural sales skills will help you to read a broader mix of customers more accurately.

Building Your Multicultural Skills

Enhancing your ability to sell across cultures includes several steps before you apply the selling process. It is not enough to know just a few facts about other cultures. A little knowledge can be dangerous if used out of context. There are four dimensions of the multicultural development process, according to Mendez-Russell, Wilderman, and Tolbert, the authors of *The Discovering Diversity Profile*. They are: *knowledge, understanding, acceptance*, and *behavior*.

The first step in this process is to learn more about the cultures of which you are a member. The more you understand yourself, the better equipped you will be to understand and interact with others different from you.

Realizing that culture is more than race/ethnicity and sex, identify the cultures of which you are a member. Each person is a culture of one. There is no one else exactly like you; even twins are different in some ways. Use the space below to identify your personal cultural footprint.

Age: _____

Sex: _____

Sexual Orientation: _____

Marital Status: _____

Parental Status: _____

Occupation: _____

Tenure: _____

Birthplace: _____

Birth Rank (e.g., first born): _____

Ethnicity: _____

Spirituality: _____

Religion: _____

Socio-Economic Level: _____

Education: _____

Appearance: _____

Size: _____

Top Value/Belief: _____

Political Preference: _____

Physical Ability or Talent: _____

Disability: _____

Other Unique Factor: _____

Other Unique Factor: _____

While each of these factors makes you unique, they also give rise to the opportunity for others to form stereotypes and biases about you. For example, what stereotypes come to your mind when you think of a fifty-year-old, female, African American born in the New York? Your biases and stereotypes about this person will depend on your own relationship to the characteristics described. For instance, if you are from the South, you might consider all Northerners as Yankees. The more you know about your own cultural groups and how others stereotype them, the less likely you will pre-judge others.

You can build your knowledge base about other cultures by reading books and magazines, watching videos, conducting Internet research, and by talking to people within the group. Remember that you are only getting the point-of-view of whoever produced the work, so it is important to use many resources. Do not expect people to be experts about their culture. When a person has been part of a group for their entire life, it is difficult to be cognizant of the norms of the group, simply because it is just a way of life. For example, many Christians, as a group, do not know the reasons behind the traditions of Christianity during the Christmas season. In fact, each denomination has its own interpretation of what is factual. So, as you study other groups and cultures, be sure to take into account that you will get different perspectives and opinions. Your job is to gather enough information to have a general understanding of the group, and then use that knowledge to enhance your ability to interact cross culturally. (A detailed listing of these resources can be found in *The Diversity Advantage: A Guide to Making Diversity Work.*)

You can develop an *understanding* of other cultures by putting yourself in a position to feel what others feel. This builds your awareness and empathy for different groups. There are several fun ways to enhance this dimension of your development. You can participate in cultural festivals, visit a new place of worship, eat various ethnic foods, and join organizations that have a large membership of people from the group you want to understand. Of course, just eating Mexican food is not going to help you understand the Mexican culture. The idea is to learn the origin or history of the particular foods of the culture. There is always a story that explains why that food became a mainstay for the culture. Join organizations like the Hispanic Chamber of Commerce, the Asian Chamber of Commerce, and various women's groups even if you are not a member of the culture. Most groups welcome others to join. By doing so, you will learn why cultures are the way they are. This broadens your understanding and enables you to relate to others at a deeper level.

Enhancing your acceptance of others requires a real commitment to get involved. Practicing this dimension of multicultural development will help you become more open-minded when dealing with people with whom you have had little experience in the past. You can develop this dimension by volunteering to support community organizations that have a cultural focus or user population that you want to learn more about. In this case, your commitment of time and service will build your *acceptance* dimension.

The last dimension of *behavior* requires that you develop a plan that supports your behavior change toward cultures different from your own. This is the dimension that will have an effect on your sales results. Asking others to observe you and then provide feedback on your comments, body language, listening skills, and so on, when you are selling cross-culturally is very beneficial, although impossible to obtain in most selling situations. If you sell in a one-on-one environment, it may be difficult or inappropriate to ask a third-party observer to be present. The next option is to role-play with colleagues to provide an opportunity for skill practice.

A Word of Caution

It is very easy to stereotype groups when studying them. As you learn the norms of various groups, acknowledge that a person in the group MIGHT possess these characteristics or beliefs, but that person also MIGHT NOT fit the norm. When considering different ethnic groups, the individual's behavior will be affected based upon how much he has assimilated into the American mainstream culture. As you people-read, use this information as a starting point to test your assumptions. Always allow yourself the opportunity to see if this person is more or less like their group's norm. There are so many factors that determine an individual's behavior in a sales situation; you need to be very careful not to jump to the wrong conclusion. Refrain from judging the person based on the group that she is in, and take steps to understand and build a relationship with her.

The Sales Process

As you progress through each step of the sales process, this author will assume that you already have understanding of each sales step based on your experience and the information you learned from other authors featured in this book. We will explore the steps specifically as they relate to multicultural selling.

The Greeting

The sale starts before you say hello. Begin your approach by people-reading the communication style of your client. Because it is impossible to know every nuance about every culture, one way to build your knowledge base is to identify the general style of the customer or client. There are many assessments and profiles available such as Myers-Briggs and the Personal Profile System (DISC) that will help you learn the strengths of your own style and teach you how to *people-read* other styles. Each uses its own names to identify the styles. I will discuss the four broadest categories of styles using names that are similar to the most popular profiles and assessments. They are the Dominant Driver, the Expressive Socializer, the Steady Relater, and the Cautious Thinker. Because communication styles are cross-cultural, people-reading styles is an easy way to determine how to interact with most cultures. Once you have isolated the customer's primary style, flex your own style to match theirs. By doing this, you are complimenting the person, making it easier for her to listen and trust you.

As you observe the client, even before you greet him ask yourself the following questions:

1. Is this person action-oriented and fast paced, or reserved and slower paced?
2. Is he more focused on getting the task completed, or more focused on interacting with people?

Based on your answers, you can determine which one of the following styles is probably the primary style of your buyer.

Basic Style Characteristics

Dominant Driver—This style is direct, fast paced, confident, controlling, impatient, task-oriented, fears being taken advantage of, and likes to win. As a customer, this style responds favorably to choices and expediency.

Expressive Socializer—This style is people-oriented, fast paced, optimistic, enthusiastic, disorganized, emotional, fears rejection, and likes to talk. As a buyer, this style responds favorably to testimonials, and a low level of detail.

Steady Relater—This style is reserved, dependable, a good listener, easy-going, family-oriented, stubborn, fears change, and likes sincere personal attention. As a customer this style responds favorably to an assurance of stability, and an easy-going atmosphere.

Cautious Thinker—This style is reserved, accurate, analytical, organized, indecisive, unemotional, fears criticism, and likes logical approaches. This prospect responds favorably to high quality and detail.

As you communicate, create the environment that compliments their style. Avoid doing anything that will cause them to become defensive. For example, Cautious Thinkers want to avoid criticism, so don't try to prove your data is right and theirs is wrong. Instead compliment their attention to detail and share your additional data.

Regardless of your buyer's sex, ethnicity, or religion, understanding styles will enable you to lay the foundation for a positive relationship.

The greeting can be a sensitive encounter when you are approaching a male/female couple, especially if the couple appears to be other than European American. Do not assume the couple is married. If they are co-workers and you immediately make the wrong assumption, you will have to work hard to regain their respect. Take clues from them to determine whether or not to shake hands. Hasidic Jews and some Muslims do not touch any member of the opposite sex except their parents or spouse. In this case, an acknowledging nod of the head is acceptable from you. American women expect professionals in the business setting to treat them the same as men would be treated, so do offer a handshake in this case. Although on rare occasion, an older woman (over 65) may not expect a handshake, it is better to err on the side of formal business practice, offering your hand.

Female sales representatives may encounter initial rejection from some customers because of cultural norms. It is best to have a pre-planned strategy ready when the buyer requests a male sales professional. Some Middle Eastern and some Asian as well as some other males may prefer to interact with a man. Although it is insulting to most female sales professionals, this is not the time to try to teach the customer a lesson, or to attempt to change his values. There will be a loser, and it will not be the customer. Because an acceptable response differs depending on your product or service, and the environment in which you sell, the most effective approach is to brainstorm several replies with people you know who are in the group with which you are trying to develop rapport. Think of a few responses and test them with colleagues and friends, and ask for their opinions. Ask for help with this.

In some situations, it is appropriate to exchange business cards at the beginning of the meeting. When this is the case, be sure to show respect. Many Asian cultures, especially the Japanese, view the exchange of business cards as a ceremony. They call it *meishi*. Hold the card with both hands, print facing up, and then bow slightly. Accept the card with your right hand and give your card with your right hand. The left hand is considered unclean in many Asian and Middle Eastern cultures. Stop to read it in detail, and ask which is the family name. Often the family name is listed first within many Asian cultures, and some Latinos use more than one surname. If necessary, ask how to pronounce the name correctly. Write it phonetically to help you remember, but do not write on the card!

When in doubt, follow the lead of your client. Americans tend to be more informal than several other cultures, so err on the side of formality.

When interacting with blind customers, the best way to accommodate their needs is to remember this: If you treat each person as an individual, whether blind or not, most of the barriers will disappear.

When you want to shake hands, introduce yourself audibly. This will give the blind person an opportunity to determine where you are standing. She will probably extend her hand to you. Do not make her judge where your hand is; grab her hand and shake. Follow your normal rules when exchanging business cards. I hear your wheels turning, and you're thinking, "But this person is not going to be able to read my card." That's not your problem! The sight impaired individual will either "read" your card by having someone else transfer the data into a format that can be handled, or will read it himself with technology that enables him to do this independently. When you exchange business cards, let him know what you are doing and place the card in his hand. Again, he should not have to guess where you are or where you are holding the card.

Establishing Rapport

It is during this step of the sales process that many opportunities are lost, and the sales professional is unaware of the reason. When you are engaged in small talk with your client, it is at the moment you think you have connected, that you are most likely to encounter a multicultural mishap®. It is then that you are most likely to make statements or use terms that you think nothing of, but that raise a red flag for your prospect. Although it is impossible to avoid all off-putting terms, because you cannot know which are offensive to whom, the following list of suggestions can help you incorporate words into your conversational language that are more respectful. Although these terms have nothing to do with sales specifically, they are the types of words that come up during relaxed conversations.

Alternative Choices

The following list highlights words and phrases that can be substituted for the less respectful terms. If you think this is too much work, ask yourself, "If I were in the group being referred to, would I still feel this is too much work?" Remember most people who decline to buy from you do not tell you the real reason.

Insensitive Words & Phrases	Possible Alternatives
Black sheep	Outcast
"Guys" (when referring to a mixed group)	Friends; folks; group
Oriental (when referring to people)	Asian (using the specific nationality, e.g., Korean, is even better, when possible)
Acting like wild Indians	Out of control
Girls (when referring to co-workers)	Women
Policemen/postman	Police officer/mail carrier
Yankee	Northerner
Chairman	Chair
Handicapped	People with special needs; people who are physically/mentally challenged; people with disabilities
Retarded	Developmentally challenged
Gifted children	Advanced learners
Uneducated (when referring to adults)	Lacking a formal education
No culture (when referring to parts of the U.S. where the opera and the theater are scarce or nonexistent)	Lacking European culture
The little woman; the wife	Your wife; his wife

Insensitive Words & Phrases	Possible Alternatives
"Don't go postal on me!"	No alternative; someone in your audience may have relatives who are postal workers
Acting blonde	No alternative
Old people	Seniors; "Chronologically Advantaged"
Bitchy or "PMSing"	Assertive
"White" lie	Lie (calling it white does not make it okay)
Wheel-chair bound	A person who uses a wheel-chair
Jew down	Negotiate
Half-breed	Multi-ethnic
Blacklisted	Banned
"Manning" the project	Staffing the project

It is during this step in the sales process that diversity dilemmas® arise due to a lack of knowledge and understanding of various ethnic cultures. Follow the lead of your client to determine whether to discuss non-business related topics such as family and hobbies. Most cultures want to know about whom you really are before they decide to do business with you. Don't be offended if the customer wants to know about your family. Be careful not to launch into the sales presentation when the client still wants to discuss non-business issues. This is actually part of the process from their point-of-view.

If your normal process is to discuss your product or service over a meal with your client, it is time to do a little research to be sure you do not inadvertently offend him. Muslims, Hindus, Mormons, and some Protestant sects do not drink alcoholic beverages. Some Native Americans don't eat fish. Hindus don't eat beef. Muslims and Jews don't eat pork. Seventh Day Adventists do not eat meat. If you are invited to a meal and the eating style is to use your hands, it would be an insult not to follow suit. This is a common practice for many cultures. Regardless of the culture, they all have one thing in common. Always touch food only with your right hand. The left hand is considered to be unclean, as it is the hand used in the bathroom. Even if your client has acculturated to American customs, the beliefs about the left and right hand often remain. Your demonstration of this sensitivity will enhance your rapport.

Since non-verbals can make or break a sale, it is important to know some of the gestures that affect the sales relationship. The following quiz can help you test your multicultural sensitivity regarding gestures behaviors and norms. Have fun with it! Let it pique your interest to learn more about the cultures in your marketplace. Share it with colleagues as a way to generate conversation about cultural behaviors. Ask them about the norms of their culture that are misunderstood, and share any norms within your culture as well. The correct answers are at the end of this chapter.

Multicultural Interactions Quiz

Directions: Write the letter (a-m) that corresponds to the culture(s) that have the following customs and behavioral norms. More than one answer is sometimes appropriate. The same answer may be used more than once.

Did you know that sometimes...?

1. When they hold their hands together, it is a sign of death: _____

2. The American "bye-bye" gesture means "come here" to people from _____.

3. Thumbs up is an obscene gesture in _____, _____, and _____.

4. Smiling is equated to frivolous or thoughtless behavior among the _____ and _____ cultures.

5. Avoidance of eye contact is a sign of respect in the _____ culture.

6. The Gathering of Nations occurs each year in _____.

7. Body contact among strangers of any kind, especially among the opposite sex, is taboo with the _____ culture.

8. Same-sex hand holding between _____, _____, and _____ is just a sign of friendship.

a. Latino/Hispanic	h. American Indian
b. African American	i. Southeast Asia
c. Nigeria	j. Australia
d. Korean	k. Middle-East
e. Japanese	l. Guatemala
f. Asian	m. New Mexico
g. Orthodox Jews	

Interviewing to Identify Customer Needs

As a sales professional, you already know the importance of asking questions at this stage of the process. When interacting in the multicultural environment, asking questions becomes even more important. Chris Clarke-Epstein, the author of *78 Important Questions Every Leader Should Ask and Answer*, says, "Asking questions and absorbing the answers those questions elicit will take time, and time is often in short supply." Your task is to identify what questions to ask, and how to ask them to obtain the information you need, and to deepen your rapport with the client at the same time. As you people-read your client's style, you will discover that this is the time when the Expressive Socializer customer will really want to chat. He may talk far more than you want or need him to. Be careful not to cut him off. Your job is to guide the conversation here, not try to show impatience or any other judgments about the client's style.

Depending on your own communication style, you may need to practice external listening skills to improve your ability to engage the client, and not interrupt her or take a mental vacation to plan your response. Be sensitive to the cultural norms of your client and then apply appropriate body language to indicate that you are fully attentive to his comments.

If English is not the client's primary language, ask permission to take notes and be willing to admit you did not understand something said. They want you to understand, so don't proceed in the sales process if you are confused. Comments such as "I am sorry, please say that again," "I did not understand," "please repeat that slowly," or "please help me understand" usually will help you and the client.

If you are selling to domestic partners, be sure to give appropriate attention to both individuals. In the Latin cultures, chivalry is not dead, so if you are a male, opening doors for females and holding their chair to be seated will not go unnoticed. On the other hand, be aware of your eye contact behavior. Most women expect to be included in the discussion. Depending on the religious or ethnic culture of your customers, how to show respect and inclusion of women will differ.

Presentation of the Product/Services and Its Benefits

Use as many communication aids as needed to communicate your message clearly, if English is a challenge. The use of pictures and brochures that explain the features and benefits of your product or service are helpful. Speak clearly and slowly, but refrain from talking louder. Volume does not aid the interpretation of languages. On the other hand, if your customer seems to have a hearing problem, be sure to face him directly so he can see your mouth fully as you speak.

You will gain faster acceptance among clients who speak other languages if you learn how to say a few words in their language. Learn a greeting as well as a few phrases describing your product or service in Spanish, Japanese, Vietnamese, or whatever language is prominent in your marketplace. Even if your pronunciation is not perfect, they will appreciate your effort. It is a great way to put the customer at ease.

Colors carry significance in most cultures. Learn which colors represent luck, death, wealth, and so on, among the cultures in your marketplace. To some Chinese, a yellow sticker denotes a defective product, so make sure your inspection stickers are not yellow. Green usually connotes harmony, prosperity, and good health in most cultures. Purple is a positive color in most cultures except among some Chinese, Mexicans, and Brazilians. It can connote death or fast-fading relationships. White means death to many Asians, while yellow means the same thing to some Iranians and Mexicans. Consider these factors when giving gifts and sending flowers to clients and prospects.

Handling Objections and Giving Feedback

Silence is an important component of communication for many Asians, Native Americans, and East Indians. This can cause significant stress for Americans, who tend to be more uncomfortable with silence. Refrain from assuming that the customer has an objection to your proposal if they are silent. Allow them time to think. Perhaps they have a question they are trying to formulate. If you interrupt the silence, you may be perceived as weak or untrustworthy.

To avoid a multicultural mishap®, note that among many Asians, nodding the head does not mean yes. The nonverbal nodding only means the client heard what you said. She may not necessarily agree with what you said. Depending on how acculturated the Asian client is to American customs, you may have difficulty reading any nonverbal buying signs. Do not assume that the absence of body language means rejection of your proposal. It's just cultural behavior. Fine-tune your questioning skills to discern what this type customer is thinking.

When English is not the primary language of a client couple, expect that they may talk to each other in their language. Although it may feel uncomfortable for you, it is the most efficient way for them to move the sales process forward. *Choose* not to be offended; instead encourage them to do it. Even leave the room if possible to allow them to chat.

African American males and females and Northerners are stereotyped as aggressive by some people who are not in these groups. Instead of making inaccurate assumptions, rely on your people-reading skills, using the styles information previously discussed, to determine the best approach for the individual who is a member of these groups. Remember that the questions and objections the customer raises are buying signals. They would not waste their own time otherwise. Your ability to respond without judgment will strengthen your chance to close the sale.

Gaining Commitment

Within some Middle Eastern and some Asian cultures, the female is reasonably silent during the sales presentation when she is accompanied by her domestic partner, but has a great deal of influence in the decision making in private. In these situations, do not expect your clients to make a final decision with you present. Allow the couple some privacy to discuss the proposal.

As people approach the final buying decision, there may be several factors that contribute to that decision. Some customers may say they need to pray on it, or consult their astrologer, or apply numerology to determine the right day and time to decide. (If you just laughed or cringed when you read the last sentence, you have just identified an area of cultural development for yourself ☺.) What is a superstition to you may be a strong belief for someone else. For example, the number 13 is not unlucky in many other cultures, so when Asians, as an example, visit the USA they are fascinated that hotels rarely have a 13th floor, or airplanes don't have a 13th row. Whatever your client's beliefs, just honor them; don't comment on them.

Within the mainstream American culture, the signed contract is final and binding. Among many other cultures the agreement is perceived as the beginning of the real relationship, not the end. Many Latin and Middle Eastern customers may want to further negotiate after the "deal is made" or the contract is signed. Each culture has its own predominant negotiation style. Some are *dominant drivers* while others are more like the *steady relater*. Apply your cultural people-reading skills during this step to determine the best way to respond, rather than accidentally stereotyping all people from various cultures.

Maintaining the Relationship and Follow Up

Many Americans consider delivery of the product or service to be the end of the transaction. Some Asian cultures, especially the Japanese, are continually concerned about the quality of the overall relationship, and don't expect it to end at the end of the sale. Your ability to maintain a relationship effectively will depend on how well you navigated the multicultural waters of selling. Just as with any customer, the more you connected with the individual the more likely you will be able to sell to him again in the future, and obtain referrals in the meantime.

Conclusion

Does this seem like a great deal of work? Well, it is. However, the multicultural marketplace is only going to grow. These emerging markets contribute billions of dollars of discretionary income to the US economy. The more time you take to know, understand, appreciate, and respect the many cultures of your market, the better your sales results will be.

Quiz Answers:
1. L, 2. I, 3. C,J,K, 4. D,E, 5. F,A, 6. M 7. E,G 8. F,K,A 9. R
10. Q 11. T 12. T 13. P,S

Multicultural Selling Self-Assessment©

How do you feel about your current knowledge and ability around issues of diversity and multiculturalism? Complete the following assessment as honestly as possible. Respond based on how you actually behave, not how you wish to behave. Use the results to develop your own multicultural awareness action plan.

	Almost Always	Generally	Sometimes	Almost Never
I avoid stereotyping others, by searching for the facts regarding individuals.				
I am completely comfortable with cultural differences in my environment.				
I work well with diverse clients.				
I listen actively to the verbal and non-verbal cues when communicating with others.				
I communicate effectively with people from different backgrounds and cultures.				
I am familiar with my customers' cultural backgrounds and traditions.				
I speak up when inappropriate comments or behavior occur in my workplace among co-workers.				
I mentor individuals whose backgrounds are different from my own.				

My decisions about others are based on objective behavioral criteria, not my own biases.				
I seek and give honest constructive feedback.				
I seek to understand different points of view.				
My words and actions are consistent.				
My actions show respect and dignity toward others whose beliefs differ from my own.				
I involve others in helping to create and sustain an environment that supports differences while building camaraderie.				

©2003 Excel Development Systems. Inc. ALL RIGHTS RESERVED. Call 336-282-4443, or email Lenora@LenoraSpeaks.com for a reprintable version.

Alessandra, Tony, O'Connor, Michael, *PeopleSmart-Powerful Techniques for Turning Every Encounter into a Mutual Win*, 1990, Keynote Publishing Company, ISBN: 0-9625161-0-4

Billings-Harris, Lenora, *The Diversity Advantage: A Guide to Making Diversity Work*, 1998 Oakhill Press, ISBN: 1-886939-25-X.

Carr-Ruffino, Norma, *Managing Diversity; People Skills for a Multicultural Workplace*, 1996, Thomson Executive Press, ISBN: 0-538-84456-6.

Clarke-Epstein, Chris, *78 Questions Every Leader Should Ask and Answer*, McGraw Hill, 2002.

Dresser, Norine, *Multicultural Manners—New Rules of Etiquette for a Changing Society*, 1996, John Wiley and Sons, Inc., ISBN: 0-471-11819-2.

Esty, Katharine, Griffin, Schorr Hirsch, *Workplace Diversity: A Manager's Guide to Solving Problems and Turning Diversity into a Competitive Advantage*, 1995, Adams Media Corporation, ISBN: 1-55850-482-6.

Lee, Michael D., *Opening Doors—Selling to Multicultural Real Estate Clients*, 1999, Oakhill Press, ISBN: 1-886939-32-2.

Lenora Billings-Harris, CSP

Lenora Billings-Harris, a Certified Speaking Professional, is a multicultural diversity consultant, coach and author of *The Diversity Advantage: A Guide to Making Diversity Work*, and is a contributing columnist of Performance Magazine. She helps organizations and individuals maximize results by minimizing multicultural mishaps, thus enhancing productivity and sales results within their diverse environments. Billings-Harris has the unique ability to deliver thought-provoking presentations that address sensitive issues in a results-oriented, non-judgmental, energetic and positive way. Her topics include selling and marketing to emerging markets, gender communications, and building a respectful workplace. A few of Lenora's recent clients include Ford Motor Company, the US Army, Ritz Carlton, the City of Winston-Salem, former Vice President Gore's Special Task Force for Diversity, AT&T, Hewlett-Packard, and Cornell University. Her expertise is sought after worldwide, most recently in Russia, Mexico, Canada, Spain, Germany, South Africa, the Caribbean and across the South Pacific, as well as the USA. She serves on the Board of Directors of the National Speakers Association, and is on the adjunct faculty at the University of North Carolina-Greensboro. Before starting her business in 1986, she held management positions with The University of Michigan, CIGNA Corporation and General Motors.

Lenora Billings-Harris, CSP
Excel Development Systems, Inc.
PO Box 1628
Greensboro NC 27402-1628
Phone: 336.282.4443
Fax: 336.282.4487
Email: Lenora@LenoraSpeaks.com
www.LenoraSpeaks.com